THE BASICS
ENGLISH

Michele Goulet Miller
Milwaukee Area Technical Colleges
Milwaukee, Wisconsin

Clarice Pennebaker Brantley
Escambia County School System
Pensacola, Florida

Australia · Brazil · Canada · Mexico · Singapore · Spain · United Kingdom · United States

The Basics: English, 3e
Michele Goulet Miller and Clarice Pennebaker Brantley

VP/Editorial Director:
Jack W. Calhoun

VP/Editor-in-Chief:
Karen Schmohe

Acquisitions Editor:
Jane Phelan

Developmental Editor:
Penny Shank

Production Editor:
Darrell E. Frye

Marketing Manager:
Valerie A. Lauer

Manufacturing Coordinator:
Kevin Kluck

Compositor:
Cadmus Inc.

Production Manager:
Graphic World Inc.

Consulting Editor:
Elaine Langlois

Printer:
Edwards Brothers

Art Director:
Stacy Jenkins Shirley

Cover and Internal Designer:
Lou Ann Thesing

Cover Images:
© Getty Images

Printed in the United States of America
1 2 3 4 5 08 07 06 05

Student Edition ISBN: 0-538-97461-3
Student Edition with CD ISBN: 0-538-72882-5
Student Edition with CD and iLrn access ISBN: 0-538-72974-0

For more information about our products, contact us at:

Thomson Higher Education
5191 Natorp Boulevard
Mason, Ohio 45040
USA

Asia (including India)
Thomson Learning
5 Shenton Way
#01-01 UIC Building
Singapore 068808

Canada
Thomson Nelson
1120 Birchmount Road
Toronto, Ontario
M1K 5G4
Canada

UK/Europe/Middle East/Africa
Thomson Learning
High Holborn House
50/51 Bedford Row
London WC1R 4LR
United Kingdom

Australia/New Zealand
Thomson Learning Australia
102 Dodds Street
Southbank, Victoria 3006
Australia

Latin America
Thomson Learning
Seneca, 53
Colonia Polanco
11560 Mexico
D. F. Mexico

Spain (including Portugal)
Thomson Paraninfo
Calle Magallanes, 25
28015 Madrid, Spain

CONTENTS

PREFACE

The Basics: English, 3e, presents the essential rules of English usage. This text-workbook also provides many opportunities for review and practice so that you will express yourself effectively when you write and when you speak.

Organization

The text presents fundamental English grammar, punctuation, capitalization, and number usage guidelines in the following order:

Print and electronic references: Chapter 1
Parts of speech: Chapters 2 through 8
Phrases, clauses, and sentences: Chapter 9
Punctuation: Chapters 10 and 11
Capitalization and numbers: Chapter 12

Special Features

The following special features will help you achieve fundamental English competencies:

- **Learning Objectives** describe expected outcomes after you complete the chapter.
- **Checkpoints** "check" your understanding of important chapter concepts. **Checkpoint Solutions** appear on pages 219–242.
- **Examples** follow each principle to illustrate correct usage.
- **Margin notes** provide helpful usage tips and reinforce key points.
- **Workplace Connections** relate language skills to job and school success.
- **Chapter Summaries** recap the essential points of the chapter.
- **Chapter Applications** encourage practice and application of chapter principles.
- **Chapter Reviews** assess your overall understanding of chapter content and readiness for the chapter test.
- **The Frequently Confused/Misused Words Appendix,** an easy-to-use reference, offers definitions of frequently misused and confused words to help you make correct word choices.
- **NEW! Student CD Exercises** provide additional opportunities to check your understanding of important chapter concepts.
- **NEW! Web-based Resources**
    - *The Basics: English* **website** at **http://miller.swlearning.com** offers additional activities, crossword puzzles, links to useful sites, and other helpful materials for each chapter.
    - **iLrn Activities,** correlating with each chapter, evaluate your understanding of chapter concepts and give you immediate feedback.
    - **Web Exercises** reinforce correct English usage and sharpen your Internet search skills.

Icons

Icons help you identify certain special features of *The Basics: English*.

Chart of Icons

Icon	Explanation
[Web Exercise icon]	The Web Exercise icon alerts you to Internet-based exercises that complement chapter content.
ILrn	The iLrn icon signals a variety of interactive, Web-based applications designed to reinforce your understanding of chapter content.

The Series

The Basics: English may be used as a stand-alone resource or in conjunction with **The Basics Series**, a series of text-workbooks that helps you master the communication skills needed in the workplace. The other books in the series are *The Basics: Business Communication*, *The Basics: Writing*, *The Basics: Employment Communication*, *The Basics: Speech Communication*, and *The Basics: Proofreading*.

Acknowledgments

The contributions of these individuals are greatly appreciated.

Timothy Allen Brantley, Freelance Writer
Miami, FL

Jerrie Sue Cleaver, Coordinator, Office Technology Department
Central Texas College
Killeen, TX

Denise M. Cosper, Adjunct Instructor
Management and Information Systems
Mississippi State University
Starkville, MS

Charmaine E. Kuczmarski, English Instructor Adult High School
Milwaukee Area Technical College
Milwaukee, WI

Marguerite E. Lara, Teacher, Business Department
Wright Business School
Oklahoma City, OK

Alton O. Rice, Jr., Instructor, Drafting & Design Technology
Northwest-Shoals Community College
Muscle Shoals, AL

Michele Goulet Miller
Clarice Pennebaker Brantley

http://miller.swlearning.com

Print and Electronic References

CHAPTER 1

Are you *eager*, or are you *anxious*? *To* careful or *too* careful? Is the correct spelling *illiterate* or *iliterate*? Do you give someone *advice* or *advise*? The words you choose make a difference! A wrong word not only can change the meaning of your message but also can affect what others think of you. Dictionaries help you spell, define, use, and pronounce words correctly. Thesauruses help you choose the best word for the situation. Other references help you present information in grammatically correct form. Together, these tools aid you in communicating your thoughts and ideas clearly so that others will understand what you say.

Learning Objectives

- Locate words in the dictionary efficiently.
- Identify and explain the basic parts of a dictionary entry.
- Use a thesaurus to find appropriate word options.
- Identify types of electronic references.
- Discuss advantages and disadvantages of electronic references.

THE DICTIONARY

Most people use a dictionary to confirm spelling and to learn what a word means. In addition to spelling and definitions, dictionaries show word origins, parts of speech, syllables, grammatical forms, and pronunciations. They may show brief examples of how to use the word. Depending on size and purpose, dictionaries may contain historical and geographical entries, abbreviations, punctuation and style rules, illustrations, common foreign words and phrases, and other helpful information.

Buying a Dictionary

What kind of dictionary fits your needs?

Dictionaries are divided into two broad categories: general and specialized. A **general dictionary** contains everyday words as well as some technical words; a **specialized dictionary** is specific to one field, language, or topic. Dictionaries are either **abridged** (a shortened version) or **unabridged** (the most complete of its kind). Collegiate dictionaries and pocket dictionaries are abridged. The collegiate dictionary is a good reference for students or employees. The pocket dictionary is an easy-to-carry reference that has limited features because of its size.

Look at several dictionaries before making a purchase. Ask yourself the following questions to help you decide which size and type of dictionary is best for you:

- *How* am I most likely to use the dictionary? Is my main purpose to confirm spelling? To develop language skill?
- *Where* will I store my dictionary? Will I keep the dictionary at home? In my office? In my backpack?

Using a Dictionary

To use a dictionary efficiently, read the introductory pages, which contain information about the format and symbols used in that particular dictionary. Although dictionary formats vary, the following labeled selection from *Merriam-Webster's Collegiate® Dictionary* will help you identify typical parts of a dictionary entry.

① guide words ② main entry ③ syllabication ④ pronunciation ⑤ part of speech ⑥ inflected forms ⑦ word origins ⑧ definitions

confide . conformal **261**

con·fide\kən-'fīd\ *vb* **con·fid·ed; con·fid·ing** [ME (Sc), fr. L *confidere*, fr. *com-* + *fidere* to trust — more at BIDE] *vi* (15c) **1 :** to have confidence : TRUST **2 :** to show confidence by imparting secrets <~in a friend> ~ *vt* **1 :** to tell confidentially **2 :** to give to the care or protection of another: ENTRUST *syn* see COMMIT — **con·fid·er** *n*

con·fi·dence\'kän-fə-dən(t)s,'-',den(t)s\ *n* (14c) **1a :** a feeling or consciousness of one's powers or of reliance on one's circumstances <had perfect ~ in her ability to succeed> <met the risk with brash ~> **b :** faith or belief that one will act in a right, proper, or effective way <have ~ in a leader> **2 :** the quality or state of being certain : CERTITUDE <they had every ~ of success> **3a :** a relation of trust or intimacy <took his friend into his ~> **b :** reliance on another's discretion <their story was told in strictest ~> **c :** support esp. in a legislative body <vote of ~> **4 :** a communication made in confidence : SECRET <accused him of betraying a ~> *syn* CONFIDENCE. ASSURANCE, SELF-POSSESSION, APLOMB mean a state of mind or a manner marked by easy coolness and freedom from uncertainty, diffidence, or embarrassment. CONFIDENCE stresses faith in oneself and one's powers without any suggestion of conceit or arrogance <the *confidence* that comes from long experience>. ASSURANCE carries a stronger implication of certainty and may suggest arrogance or lack of objectivity in assessing one's own powers <handled the cross-examination with complete *assurance*>. SELF-POSSESSION implies an ease or coolness under stress that reflects perfect self-control and command of one's powers <answered the insolent question with complete *self-possession*>. APLOMB implies a manifest self-possession in trying or challenging situations <handled the reporters with great *aplomb*>.

Spirit and among Protestants full church membership (2) : a ceremony esp. of Reform Judaism confirming youths in their faith **b :** the ratification of an executive act by a legislative body **2a :** confirming proof : CORROBORATION **b :** the process of supporting a statement by evidence — **con·fir·ma·tion·al** \-shnəl, -shə-n'l\ *adj*

con·fir·ma·to·ry\kən-'fər-mə-,tȯr-ē\ *adj* (1636) : serving to confirm : CORROBORATIVE <a ~ test>

con·firmed \kən-'fərmd\ *adj* (14c) **1a :** marked by long continuance and likely to persist <a ~ habit> **b :** fixed in habit and unlikely to change <a ~ do-gooder> **2 :** having received the rite of confirmation *syn* see INVETERATE — **con·firm·ed·ly**\-'fər-məd-lē\ *adv* — **con·firmed·ness**\-'fər-məd-nəs, -'fərm(d)-nəs\ *n*

con·fis·ca·ble\kən-'fis-kə-bəl\ *adj* (ca. 1736) : liable to confiscation

con·fis·cat·able\'kän-fə-'skā-tə-bəl\ *adj* (1863) : CONFISCABLE

[1]**con·fis·cate**\'kän-fə-'skāt, kən-'fis-kət\ *adj* [L *confiscatus*, pp. of *confiscare* to confiscate, fr. *com-* + *fiscus* treasury] (ca. 1533) **1 :** appropriated by the government : FORFEITED **2 :** deprived of property by confiscation

[2]**con·fis·cate**\'kän-fə-'skāt\ *vt* **-cat·ed; -cat·ing** (1552) **1 :** to seize as forfeited to the public treasury **2 :** to seize by or as if by authority — **con·fis·ca·tion**\'kän-fə-'skā-shən*n* — **con·fis·ca·tor**\'kän-fə-'skā-tər*n* — **con·fis·ca·to·ry**\ kən-'fis-kə-'tȯr-ē\ *adj*

con·fit\kōn-'fē, kȯn-'n-*n* [F, fr. OF, preparation, preserves, fr. pp. of *confire* to prepare — more at COMFIT] (1951) **1 :** meat (as goose, duck, or pork) that has been cooked and preserved in its own fat **2 :** a garnish made usu. from fruit or vegetables that are cooked until tender in a seasoned liquid

The dictionary may show that a word has more than one acceptable spelling. The most common spelling is generally listed first.

1. **Guide words: Guide words** appear at the top of each page of entries to help you decide whether the word you are seeking is on that page. The left guide word tells which word, or main entry, appears first on the page, and the right guide word tells which main entry appears last on that page.
2. **Main entry: Main entries** are the words included and defined in the dictionary. Each main entry is flush with the left margin of the column and is printed in bold.
3. **Syllabication:** The main entry is usually divided into **syllables** (parts of the word) by means of centered dots. (Some dictionaries use the dots to show where a word may be divided at the end of a keyed line.) The phonetic spelling, between backward slash marks (\) or in parentheses, shows syllables separated with hyphens. An accent mark (') shows which syllable to emphasize during pronunciation.

Phonetic *means that each sound of speech is represented by a specific symbol.*

4. **Pronunciation:** The phonetic spelling of a word appears between backward slash marks (\) or in parentheses to aid in pronouncing the word. If you have difficulty finding a word in the dictionary because the spelling differs from the way the word sounds, you will find the following "sound" guide helpful.

Sounds Like	Possible Spelling
f	f, pf, ph
k	k, c, ch
n	n, gn, kn, pn
r	r, rh, wr
s	s, c, cy, psy
t	t, ct, pt
z	z, x, xa, xe, xi, xy

Mini Pronunciation Guide

ā as in āte
ă as in ăpple
ē as in ēven
ĕ as in ĕvery
ī as in īce
ĭ as in ĭnterest
ō as in ōpen
ŏ as in nŏt
ū as in ūnit
ŭ as in ŭncle

5. **Part of speech:** The **part of speech** of a main entry is abbreviated and placed before the definition(s) of the word. Labels indicate the part of speech and the classification of verbs:

Label	Term	Label	Term	Label	Term
adj.	adjective	*n.*	noun	*tr. v.* or *v.t.*	transitive verb
adv.	adverb	*prep.*	preposition		
conj.	conjunction	*pron.*	pronoun	*intr. v.* or *v.i.*	intransitive verb
interj.	interjection	*v.* or *vb.*	verb		

6. **Inflected forms: Inflected forms** show suffixes or other changes to the stem form, including principal parts of regular and irregular verbs, degrees of adjectives and adverbs, and plurals of irregular nouns.

7. **Word origin: Word origin,** also called **etymology**, appears in brackets. The etymology tells what language(s) the word comes from and, sometimes, how the original word has changed over the years.

8. **Definition:** When a word has more than one **definition** (meaning), each definition is numbered. An example may follow a definition to show how the word is used with that particular meaning. Carefully reading definitions and examples helps you find the meaning that makes the most sense.

9. **Synonyms and antonyms:** Sometimes **synonyms** (words that are similar in meaning) and **antonyms** (words that are opposite in meaning) follow a definition.

[CHECKPOINT 1-1]

Use the Dictionary

The words below are spelled phonetically. Review the pronunciation guide on page 3 or in your dictionary. Then locate each word in the dictionary, and provide this information: (1) the correctly spelled word, (2) its part of speech (page 3 contains part-of-speech abbreviations), (3) any inflected forms, and (4) the first definition listed in the dictionary.

Phonetic Spelling	Correct Spelling	Part of Speech	Inflected Forms
1. ĭn-vād'			
Definition:			
2. tō'mān'			
Definition:			
3. mē'dē-ō-kər			
Definition:			
4. ăk-nŏl'-ĭj-mənt			
Definition:			
5. ī-nĭsh'ē-āt'			
Definition:			
6. grēv'vəs			
Definition:			
7. prĭ-sĭp'ĭ-tāt			
Definition:			
8. so͞od'n-ĭm'			
Definition:			
9. pər-tĭk'yə-lər-lē			
Definition:			
10. nĭ-mŏn'ĭks			
Definition:			

THE THESAURUS

When a word you are using is not quite the right fit, a thesaurus provides synonyms. Although a thesaurus contains some of the same information as a dictionary, the main purpose of a thesaurus is to help you find words that best represent your ideas. Use a thesaurus to:

- *Avoid* repeating words.
- *Add* interest to your message by varying the vocabulary.
- *Choose* words that best convey your meaning.

Read the introductory pages of your thesaurus so that you will know how to use this reference quickly and correctly. A typical arrangement for a thesaurus is as follows: At the top of each page is a guide word or a pair of guide words. Entries follow in alphabetical order. Main entries appear in bold and are followed by the part of speech, a brief definition, and synonyms. A thesaurus may also include examples of how a word is used as well as antonyms for that word.

Words that may be used as more than one part of speech and words that have significantly different meanings are listed separately. For example, the word *light* has many variations; a few are shown below.

Word	Thesaurus Definition with Example	Synonyms
light *n.*	Electromagnetic radiation. *Turn on the light.*	illumination, luminosity
light *v.*	To cause to burn. *Light the candle.*	ignite, torch
light *adj.*	Free from worry. *Tina's mood was light.*	carefree

Not many words are exactly interchangeable. You may want to use both a dictionary and a thesaurus to confirm that you have chosen the best words to represent your ideas. Always use these references to confirm your word choice whenever you use unfamiliar words. Otherwise, you might say something that you did not intend to say!

Complete Applications 1-1 and 1-2.

"Knowledge is of two kinds. We know a subject ourselves, or we know where we can find information upon it."

-Samuel Johnson, British writer and lexicographer (1709–1784)

A thesaurus is a collection of synonyms.

WORKPLACE CONNECTION

We live in a knowledge-based society. No one expects you to know everything; but if you know *where* to find information, you possess a highly desirable job skill.

Use the Thesaurus

Use a thesaurus to find each of the main entries listed below. Choose one definition for the main entry, list at least two synonyms for the definition you chose, and list antonyms, if provided.

1. promote (*v.*) ____________________

   Definition: ____________________

   Synonyms: ____________________

   Antonyms: ____________________

2. insipid (*adj.*) ____________________

   Definition: ____________________

   Synonyms: ____________________

   Antonyms: ____________________

3. huff (*n.*) ____________________

   Definition: ____________________

   Synonyms: ____________________

   Antonyms: ____________________

4. hot (*adj.*) ____________________

   Definition: ____________________

   Synonyms: ____________________

   Antonyms: ____________________

5. defeat (*v.*) ____________________

   Definition: ____________________

   Synonyms: ____________________

   Antonyms: ____________________

ELECTRONIC REFERENCES

Electronic references are computerized versions of standard reference material, such as dictionaries, thesauruses, and encyclopedias. Electronic references are available on the Internet, on CD-ROM, as handheld devices, and in various software programs. Word processing and other software programs include common electronic reference tools such as spell checkers, thesauruses, and grammar checkers.

Many electronic references are enhanced with capabilities such as audio. With some electronic dictionaries, for example, you can click an icon and hear the pronunciation of a word. Handheld electronic translators are especially popular. These pocket-sized devices can translate thousands of words and phrases into other languages.

Complete Application 1-3.

Electronic references are usually "spelling tolerant." You can key a reasonably close phonetic spelling, and the word you seek or words similar to your entry will be displayed.

Spell Checker

The most popular electronic reference is the **spell checker**. The spell checker compares the words in your document to a dictionary in the spell-checker software. When a word in your document is misspelled or not included in the dictionary, the word is **flagged**, or marked, usually by highlighting. The spell checker may offer a list of alternative words from which you can choose. You can also key the correct spelling in the spell-checker dialog box or directly in the text.

A spell checker is a helpful but limited tool. Word choices are offered, but you must make the correct choice. When the spell checker presents no options, you must decide whether or not the word is spelled correctly. Spell checkers usually *do not* flag words that are spelled correctly but used incorrectly. None of the errors in the following examples would be flagged by a spell checker.

Incorrect:	Did June *ad* the cost of the *add* to her budget?
Correct:	Did June *add* the cost of the *ad* to her budget?
Incorrect:	*Wear* will you *where* that jacket?
Correct:	*Where* will you *wear* that jacket?

Also, spell checkers do not include most proper names, specialized terms (unless you are using a spell checker for a specialized vocabulary), abbreviations, or acronyms. Most spell checkers can be customized so that you can add names, acronyms, and other words (including any words that you frequently misspell) as well as abbreviations.

Do not rely solely on a spell checker to find errors. When in doubt, use a dictionary or spelling reference to confirm that you have spelled a word correctly.

Acronyms are shortened forms of names or expressions typically formed from the first letter of each word. For example, AARP *stands for* American Association of Retired Persons.

Most spell checkers have an autocorrect feature that corrects common spelling errors as you key. If you frequently misspell a word, you can add the troublesome word to autocorrect.

[CHECKPOINT 1-3]

Conduct a Spell Check

The following paragraph contains five errors that a spell checker would not flag. Underline each error, and write the correction above the error.

Did you no that the word *ballot* (related to the English words *ball* and *balloon*) is of Germanic origin? Small, individually marked or colored balls have been use over the centuries fore secret voting. For example, jurors in ancient Athens voted to free ore to condemn a person using balls. Even today, some clubs except or reject candidates for membership using white balls and black balls (thus the word *blackball*).

Complete Application 1-4.

"It looks like your blog was hacked into by someone with really terrible spelling and grammar skills. Oh, guess not. Nevermind."

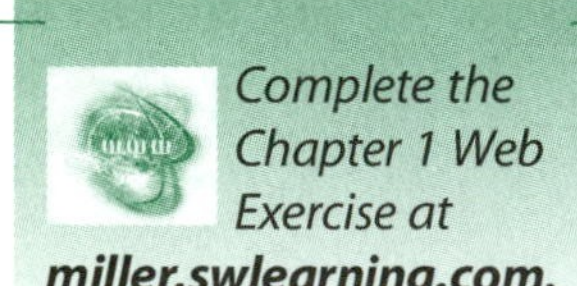

Complete the Chapter 1 Web Exercise at ***miller.swlearning.com.***

Thesaurus

An **electronic thesaurus** presents a word, its part(s) of speech, its meanings, and its associated synonyms. Each synonym you select typically will cause the electronic thesaurus to offer a new selection of words to consider—synonyms for the synonym!

Grammar Checker

A **grammar checker** evaluates the grammar and style of a message and suggests corrections and improvements. Grammar checkers identify typical grammar errors. They also suggest improvements in style, such as changing from the passive to the active voice, varying sentence structure, and reducing wordiness.

The grammar checker compares your message with the rules for grammar and style contained in the software program. As shown in the following example, a grammar checker does not catch all errors, nor is the checker able to evaluate the intent of your message. Sometimes, the grammar checker makes suggestions that are incorrect or inappropriate for the situation.

> *You may be able to set the grammar checker to reflect different writing styles, such as casual or business.*

Original Sentence: Once your credit application have been approved you will receive a 15 percent discount on your 1st purchase.

Grammar Checker Review: The grammar checker flagged the words *application have* because the singular subject *application* does not agree with the plural helping verb *have*. The grammar checker suggested these options to correct the subject-verb error: *application has* (singular) or *applications have* (plural).

Analysis: The grammar checker did identify the subject-verb problem but did not recognize that the sentence begins with an introductory clause that should be followed by a comma. Also, the grammar checker did not flag the ordinal figure *1st*, which should be the ordinal word *first* in this situation.

Corrected Sentence: Once your credit application has been approved, you will receive a 15 percent discount on your first purchase.

Electronic spell checkers, thesauruses, and grammar checkers help make writing and editing easier, but they *are not* substitutes for careful proofreading and good language skills. A grammar handbook, style manual, or other writing reference (printed or online) provides you with adequate information to make the correct choices for your message.

> *Run the spelling and grammar checkers just before you proofread (check your document for errors). When you proofread, be alert to errors that the software missed.*

Chapter Summary

- To use print and electronic references efficiently, first study the explanatory notes for each reference.
- Familiarize yourself with the kind of information contained in each reference.
- Use a dictionary to confirm the correct spelling, meaning, and usage of your word choices.
- Use a thesaurus to avoid repeating words, add interest, and choose words that best convey your meaning.
- Use electronic references as "helpers," not as substitutes for manual proofreading and editing.

Complete the Chapter 1 Review.

iLrn

Complete the Chapter 1 iLrn Activities at **miller.swlearning.com.**

Application 1-1

Using a Dictionary

In the space provided, write the letter of the correct answer. Use a dictionary if necessary.

0. A *beneficiary* is likely to receive a(n) ____a____

   a. inheritance
   b. court summons
   c. speeding ticket
   d. recommendation letter

1. To *placate* means to ________

   a. weave in a particular pattern
   b. provide supervision
   c. lessen someone's anger
   d. turn sharply

2. *Censure* refers to a(n) ________

   a. population count
   b. agreement
   c. edited story
   d. act of blaming

3. If you are *meticulous*, you ________

   a. act impulsively
   b. pay attention to detail
   c. do not eat meat
   d. move slowly

4. Someone who is *gregarious* ________

   a. enjoys the company of others
   b. is very curious
   c. is unsocial
   d. is irritable

5. Someone who is *fastidious* might be called ________

   a. fashionable
   b. feeble
   c. felicitous
   d. fussy

6. Insignificant details may be referred to as ________

   a. mintage
   b. transference
   c. minutia
   d. pulmonic

7. If you live in a cold, rainy climate, you may wear a ________

   a. madrigal
   b. shank
   c. mackintosh
   d. gambit

8. A classification according to rank is called a(n) ________

   a. hierarchy
   b. aggregation
   c. integument
   d. coalition

9. Someone who collects garbage may be called a(n) ________

   a. systole
   b. scavenger
   c. philanthropist
   d. laggard

10. When you act kindly, you are ________

    a. malevolent
    b. parietal
    c. obtuse
    d. benevolent

Application 1-2

Using a Dictionary

Part A. In the space provided, write the word from the Choices column that best matches the word in the Definition column. Use a dictionary if necessary.

Definition		Choices	Best Choice
0.	praise	complement // compliment	compliment
1.	to make a suggestion	imply // infer	
2.	distinct, unconnected	discreet // discrete	
3.	to go forward	precede // proceed	
4.	free of favoritism	fair // fare	
5.	a bird	foul // fowl	
6.	to destroy or damage	ravage // ravish	
7.	string, rope	chord // cord	
8.	adjust	adapt // adept	
9.	roof of the mouth	palate // pallet	
10.	one instead of the other	alternate // alternative	

Part B. Identify the incorrectly spelled word in each group. Write the correction in the space provided. Use a dictionary if necessary.

0.	uneasy	unerve	unacceptable	unnerve
1.	interrogate	innate	ining	
2.	irresponsible	irritable	irresistable	
3.	accomodate	accumulate	access	
4.	accredidation	accurate	excessive	
5.	disservice	disspell	dissolve	
6.	dissent	disociation	dissuade	
7.	illicet	illegal	illiterate	
8.	misfortune	misstate	missuse	
9.	illegible	illadvised	illegitimate	
10.	innovate	innoculate	innate	

Application 1-3

Using a Thesaurus

Part A. Underline the synonym that best matches the original word. Use a thesaurus if necessary.

Original Word	Synonyms		
0. implicate (*v.*)	recommend	involve	destroy
1. fatal (*adj.*)	false	ruinous	touching
2. botch (*v.*)	fumble	direct	fix
3. diligent (*adj.*)	industrious	modest	helpful
4. monition (*n.*)	resistance	warning	motion
5. reconcile (*v.*)	return	reply	restore
6. harangue (*v.*)	work out	rant	administer
7. illusion (*n.*)	fantasy	ignorance	movie
8. assert (*v.*)	attack	declare	gather
9. fathom (*v.*)	doom	portion	understand
10. provoke (*v.*)	smother	excite	refuse
11. erudite (*adj.*)	wandering	learned	argumentative
12. deplorable (*adj.*)	decisive	clear-cut	shameful
13. moor (*v.*)	fasten	cut	release
14. revel (*v.*)	frolic	restore	revise
15. mute (*adj.*)	angry	speechless	thoughtful

Part B. Underline the antonym for the original word. Use a dictionary or thesaurus if necessary.

Original Word	Antonyms		
0. negligent (adj.)	lax	petty	attentive
1. monotony (*v.*)	humor	tedium	diversity
2. impudent (*adj.*)	bold	respectful	impromptu
3. melancholy (*adj.*)	unscrupulous	sad	happy
4. impoverished (*adj.*)	wealthy	helpful	depressed
5. embark (*v.*)	start	complete	review

APPLICATION 1-4

Using a Dictionary and a Thesaurus

Part A. Underline the misused and misspelled words in the following paragraph. Write the correction above the error. Use a dictionary if necessary. Then key the paragraph exactly as is using word processing software. Run the spell checker and grammar checker. Compare your findings to the findings of the spell checker.

Most readers due not want to take the time to reed at a vocabulary level that requires extra effort, and they do not want two read wordy messages. When you prepare messages, therefore, choose the rite words—words with meanings that are readily excepted buy most readers. (Sometimes an "old" word develops a knew meaning, but not everyone may understand the new meaning.) In edition, write efficiently by deleting unecessary words; but confirm that you're message is complete so that you do knot confuse readers. Also, write in a courteous tone because readers truely appreciate courtesy. Visit a library, a bookstore, or online sources too find more helpful tips for writting effective messages.

Part B. Above the italicized words, write an appropriate synonym. Use a thesaurus or dictionary if necessary.

Spyware and adware are *nasty* programs that threaten the security and privacy of certain computer users. These programs try to steal a user's personal information and track the websites the user visits. They *pass on* the information to others, who arrange for ads to be displayed on the user's browser based on user preferences. *On occasion*, unscrupulous people steal a user's identity, using the personal information gathered by the software to make fraudulent transactions in the user's name. Spyware is often installed on PCs without user permission because some *squalid* businesses believe that this is a *permissible* form of advertising.

Print and Electronic References

Part A. Using a Dictionary

Underline the correct word of those given in parentheses. Use a dictionary. Each correct answer is worth two points.

1. Being able to distinguish between right and wrong refers to having a (conscience // conscious).
2. When ink is (indelible // illegible), the ink cannot be removed by washing.
3. (Alleys // Allies) are narrow streets or passageways.
4. An (insolent // insolvent) person has an insulting manner.
5. When a substance cannot be dissolved, the substance is (insoluble // insolvent).
6. (Imperceptible // Impervious) means "incapable of being penetrated."
7. An outer part or edge is referred to as a (boarder // border).
8. One definition of (impassioned // impassive) is "emotionless."
9. The word (moral // morale) refers to principles of right and wrong.
10. (Moron // Maroon) is a color.
11. If you are nearsighted, you may suffer from (anoxia // myopia).
12. To put forth strenuous effort is to (exert // exhilarate) oneself.
13. To remove a body from a grave is to (exhort // exhume) the body.
14. (Cache // Cachet) refers not only to a secure place to store supplies but also to the high-speed storage buffer in a computer.
15. When discussing a gem, you would use the word (cabochon // cabotage).

Part B. Using a Thesaurus

Use a thesaurus to choose the word from the Synonym column that best matches the term in the Original Word column. Write the synonym in the space provided. Each correct answer is worth two points.

Original Word	Synonym	Best Match
1. prevalent (*adj.*)	agreement	______________
2. nuisance (*n.*)	annoyance	______________
3. liability (*n.*)	bowl-shaped	______________
4. impede (*v.*)	common	______________
5. incumbent (*n.*)	debt	______________
6. facilitate (*v.*)	gloomy	______________

7. implement (*n.*)	help	______
8. implausible (*adj.*)	incompatible	______
9. incongruous (*adj.*)	mean-spirited	______
10. morose (*adj.*)	obstruct	______
11. inconsequential (*adj.*)	office holder	______
12. dastardly (*adj.*)	petty	______
13. concord (*n.*)	temperate	______
14. concave (*adj.*)	tool	______
15. balmy (*adj.*)	unlikely	______

Part C. Using a Dictionary

Use a dictionary to help you find the word error(s) in each sentence. Underline each error; then write the correction above the error. Each correct answer is worth four points.

1. Hordes of people gather in New Orleans for the annul Mardi Gras celebration, which is famous for it's spectacular custom balls.
2. Gramercy Park, a hysteric district of New York City, offers a look into the city's passed.
3. Some famous residence of Key West, Florida, were Ernest Hemingway, John Hersey, and Tennessee Williams.
4. Charleston, South Carolina, was formally known as Charlestown or Charles Town. The city adapted the name *Charleston* in 1783.
5. Drayton Hall is the oldest persevered plantation house in America that is open to the public. Drayton Hall, completed in 1742, stands on a 630-acre sight in Charleston, South Carolina.

Nouns

CHAPTER 2

If language is intimately related to being human, then when we study language we are, to a remarkable degree, studying human nature.

Charlton Laird
The Miracle of Language (1953)

The main form of communication in English is the **sentence**—words grouped together to express a complete thought. Words are classified into eight parts of speech, and each part of speech plays a different role in expressing a complete thought. Also, a word may act as more than one part of speech and may play different roles in a sentence.

LEARNING OBJECTIVES

- Distinguish between common and proper nouns.
- Identify collective nouns and determine their use in a sentence.
- Distinguish between nouns used as subjects and nouns used as objects.
- Form plural nouns correctly.
- Form singular and plural possessive nouns correctly.

NOUN CLASSIFICATION

Studying English begins with learning the eight parts of speech: nouns, pronouns, verbs, adjectives, adverbs, prepositions, conjunctions, and interjections.

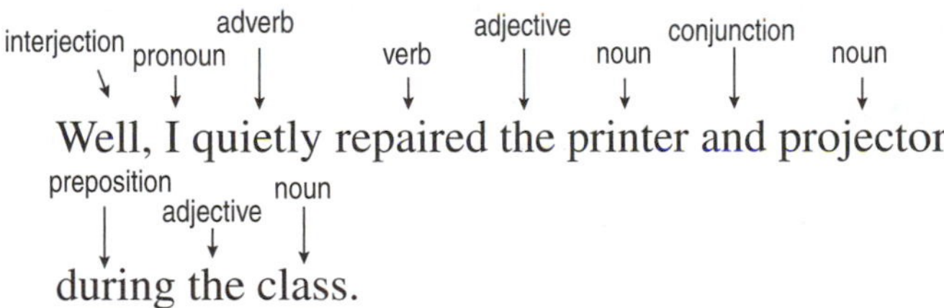

In the following chapters, you will learn about the parts of speech; and you will begin by studying nouns.

Nouns are important because they name *people*, *places*, *things*, *concepts*, *qualities*, and *events*. Because nouns are "namers," they are everywhere. Nouns are categorized in different ways.

Person:	teacher	Maria Olemedo	doctor
Place:	Chicago	restaurant	island
Thing:	necklace	tree	cereal
Concept:	democracy	fear	trust
Quality:	kindness	reliability	dependability
Event:	fiesta	recital	orientation

How a word is used in a sentence determines its part of speech.

Capitalization rules are presented in Chapter 12.

Titles such as Mr., Mrs., Ms., and Dr. are part of proper nouns.

Complete the Chapter 2 Web Exercise at **miller.swlearning.com**.

Common Nouns and Proper Nouns

Nouns are classified as common or proper. **Common nouns** are general names for people, places, things, concepts, qualities, or events. Common nouns are capitalized only when they begin a sentence.

Proper nouns are formal names for *specific* people, places, things, concepts, qualities, or events. Proper nouns are always capitalized.

Common Nouns	Proper Nouns	Common Nouns	Proper Nouns
woman	Ms. Jane Smith	country	Canada
city	Portland	lake	Lake Winnebago
state	Wisconsin	math	Math 101

To help you decide whether or not a word is a noun, place *is* or *are* after the word. If the combination makes sense, the word is a noun.

buildings *are*   silence *is*   Porcupine Mountains *are*

To help you distinguish between a common noun and a proper noun, place *a*, *an*, or *the* before the word. If the combination makes sense, the word is a common noun.

a dog   an instructor   an idea   the book

[CHECKPOINT 2-1]

Identify Common Nouns and Proper Nouns

Underline the common nouns and circle the proper nouns in each of the following sentences.

1. Utah is their favorite place to ski.
2. When the judge asked the question, Aaron answered.
3. Bungalows surround the Lake of Seven Colors in Mexico.
4. Elise raised more money than Lupe.
5. TrimArt Inc. shapes bushes into interesting sculptures.

Collective Nouns

Collective nouns name a collection or group of people or things.

family	class	pair
company	flock	committee

Collective nouns are usually singular in form, which means that everyone or everything in the group is acting as one unit. However, the collective noun is considered plural if the members of the group are acting separately.

The jury is deliberating today. (Jury members are acting as one unit.)

The jury were assigned rooms on the sixth floor. (Jury members are acting individually.)

[CHECKPOINT 2-2]

List Collective Nouns

List six collective nouns other than those shown in the example.

______________ ______________ ______________

______________ ______________ ______________

NOUNS AS SUBJECTS AND OBJECTS

Every sentence has a subject. The **subject** of a sentence is who or what is being talked about, and nouns serve as subjects. Sentences also have **verbs.** Verbs either tell what the subject is doing or link the subject to words that describe the subject. Every subject is paired with at least one verb.

You will find more details about subjects in Chapters 5 and 9 and more details about verbs in Chapters 4 and 5.

Melinda sings.	*Melinda* is the subject; *sings* is the verb that tells what the subject is doing.
My *sister* was a musician.	*Sister* is the subject and *was* is the verb. *Musician* describes the subject, and *was* links *musician* to *sister.*

In the above example, Melinda sings. Sometimes the combination of a subject and an action verb (a verb that tells what the subject is doing) expresses a complete thought.

Other times a direct object is needed to make the thought complete. A **direct object** follows an action verb and tells who or what receives the action of the verb. Nouns also serve as direct objects.

Incomplete Thought	Complete Thought
Ms. Marino opened. (Ms. Marino opened *what*?)	Ms. Marino opened the account. (The direct object *account* completes the action of the verb *opened*.)

[CHECKPOINT 2-3]

Identify Nouns as Subjects or Objects

In the space above each italicized noun, identify the noun as a SUB (subject) or a DO (direct object).

1. The *Kramms* repainted their *house.*
2. *Saran* ordered a *computer* yesterday.
3. *Amy* accepted her *award* with pride.
4. Two *employees* passed the *examination.*
5. The new shipping *containers* hold *vegetables.*

Complete Application 2-1.

SINGULAR AND PLURAL NOUNS

When a noun names *one* person, place, thing, concept, quality, or event, the noun is considered **singular.** When a noun names *more than one*, the noun is considered **plural.**

Rules for Most Nouns

The following rules will help you form the plurals of most nouns. When in doubt, though, consult a dictionary.

MOST NOUNS. Add *s* to form the plural of most nouns.

Singular	Plural	Singular	Plural
cookie	cookies	laser	lasers
piece	pieces	tablet	tablets
swing	swings	Clark	Clarks

Nouns Ending in *CH, S, SH, X, Z*. Add *es* to form the plural of nouns that end in *ch*, *s*, *sh*, and *x* and some nouns ending in *z*.

Singular	Plural	Singular	Plural
sandwich	sandwiches	box	boxes
glass	glasses	waltz	waltzes
bush	bushes	Nitz	Nitzes

Make proper nouns (formal names) plural by adding es *to words ending in* ch, s, sh, x, *or* z *and by adding only* s *to most other proper nouns.*

[Checkpoint 2-4]

Add *S* or *ES*

Add *s* or *es* to make the following nouns plural. Use a dictionary if necessary.

1. song ____________________
2. bunch ____________________
3. mass ____________________
4. drape ____________________
5. career ____________________
6. crutch ____________________
7. fox ____________________
8. match ____________________
9. crash ____________________
10. tire ____________________

Nouns Ending in Vowel + *Y*. Add *s* to form the plural of nouns that end in *y* when a vowel comes before the *y*.

Singular	Plural	Singular	Plural
chimney	chimneys	attorney	attorneys
convoy	convoys	survey	surveys

Vowels are a, e, i, o, *and* u. *Consonants are letters other than vowels.*

Nouns Ending in Consonant + *Y*. Drop the *y* and add *ies* to form the plural of common nouns that end in *y* when a consonant comes before the *y*.

Singular	Plural	Singular	Plural
daisy	daisies	company	companies
activity	activities	quality	qualities

Proper Names With *Y* Endings. Add only *s* to proper names that end in *y* to maintain the correct spelling of the proper name.

Singular	Plural	Singular	Plural
Farley	Farleys	Rajady	Rajadys

[CHECKPOINT 2-5]

Add *S* or *IES*

Add *s* or drop the *y* and add *ies* to make the following nouns plural. Use a dictionary if necessary.

1. patty __________
2. agency __________
3. sky __________
4. birthday __________
5. mystery __________
6. McEly __________
7. valley __________
8. fly __________
9. tray __________
10. McCraney __________

Complete Application 2-2.

NOUNS ENDING IN VOWEL +*O*. Add *s* to form the plural of nouns that end in *o* when a vowel comes before the *o*.

Singular	Plural	Singular	Plural
radio	radios	studios	studios
ratio	ratios	rodeo	rodeos

You will find more than one way to form plurals of words ending in o when a consonant comes before the o. Use a dictionary to help you choose the correct plural form.

NOUNS ENDING IN CONSONANT +*O*. When a consonant comes before the *o*, check a dictionary to be sure of the correct spelling.

Singular	Plural	Singular	Plural
potato	potatoes	zero	zeroes
ego	egos	mosquito	mosquitoes

MUSICAL TERMS. Musical terms form plurals in a consistent manner by adding *s*.

Singular	Plural	Singular	Plural
banjo	banjos	alto	altos
solo	solos	piano	pianos

Remember, a dictionary is a valuable tool to help you determine plural forms.

NOUNS ENDING IN *F* OR *FE*. To form the plural of most nouns that end in *f* or *fe*, drop the *f* or *fe* and add *ves*.

Singular	Plural	Singular	Plural
half	halves	knife	knives
self	selves	wife	wives

For some nouns that end in *f* or *fe*, however, simply add *s* to form the plural. For a few others, both forms are correct.

Singular	Plural	Singular	Plural
belief	beliefs	sheriff	sheriffs
safe	safes	wharf	wharfs or wharves

[CHECKPOINT 2-6]

Add *S, ES,* or *VES*

Choose the appropriate ending, *s, es,* or *ves,* to make the following words plural. Use a dictionary if necessary.

1. zoo ______________
2. contralto ______________
3. life ______________
4. tomato ______________
5. piano ______________
6. video ______________
7. logo ______________
8. roof ______________
9. tariff ______________
10. hero ______________

Rules for Compound Nouns

A **compound noun** consists of two or more words acting as a single unit.

COMPOUND AS A SOLID WORD. When compound nouns are written as a solid word, the last "word" is made plural as if the word stood alone. Follow the appropriate rule for making that word plural.

Singular	Plural	Singular	Plural
chairwoman	chairwomen	rattlesnake	rattlesnakes
strawberry	strawberries	housewife	housewives

NOUN AS MAIN ELEMENT. When compound nouns are spaced or hyphenated words and include a noun, make the main element, which is usually the noun, plural. Follow the appropriate rule for that word.

Singular	Plural	Singular	Plural
vice president	vice presidents	mother-in-law	mothers-in-law
mail carrier	mail carriers	rule of thumb	rules of thumb

No Noun Element. If a hyphenated compound does not contain a noun, make the last "word" in the compound plural.

Singular	Plural	Singular	Plural
go-between	go-betweens	trade-in	trade-ins

Rules for Numbers, Letters, and Abbreviations

Typically an *s* is added to make numbers, capitalized alphabetic letters, and capitalized abbreviations plural. An *'s* is added to lowercase alphabetic letters and abbreviations, and is sometimes added to uppercase letters and abbreviations, to prevent misreadings.

We spent most of the *1990s* in Europe.

Caroline had all *Bs* and *Cs* on her grade report.

That institution graduates more *R.N.s* than any other school in the state.

Did you notice that all the *a's* in the letter are blurred?

How many *c.o.d.'s* did you receive today?

ILLINOIS was printed with too many *I's* on the concert program.

Rules for Unusual Noun Plurals

Some singular nouns change form to become plural, some nouns do not change form, and other nouns always look plural but may be singular.

Nouns That Change Form. Use a dictionary to determine the plural of those nouns that change form to become plural.

Singular	Plural	Singular	Plural
child	children	man	men
foot	feet	ox	oxen

Nouns That Stay the Same. Use a dictionary to confirm that some words have the same spelling for both the singular and the plural form. How the noun is used in the sentence will tell you whether the noun is singular or plural.

Singular	Plural
We saw a *deer* in our backyard.	Seven *deer* were drinking from the lake.
Caleb drew a *sheep*.	*Sheep* live in flocks for protection.

NOUNS THAT LOOK PLURAL. Some nouns look plural yet are always considered singular. Others look plural and are always considered plural. Check these nouns in a dictionary.

Singular Only	Plural Only
Our *headquarters* is located in Omaha.	My *earrings* are in the drawer.
Mathematics is my favorite subject.	Calla's *pants* are too short.
The *news* is on at 10 p.m.	The *scissors* are dull.

[CHECKPOINT 2-7]

Form Plurals

Write the plural form of the following nouns. Use a dictionary if necessary.

1. mouse ____________________
2. caboose ____________________
3. goose ____________________
4. clerk ____________________
5. bookshelf ____________________
6. tooth ____________________
7. runner-up ____________________
8. city ____________________
9. account payable ____________________
10. printout ____________________

POSSESSIVE NOUNS

Complete Application 2-3.

Possessive nouns show ownership. To show **possession** (belonging to someone or something), two nouns generally appear together, and the first noun is written in possessive form.

Make a noun possessive by adding either an *'s* or only an apostrophe (').

Their *daughter's* recital is tonight.
(possessive—the recital of one daughter)

Their *daughters'* recital is tonight.
(possessive—the recital of more than one daughter)

Their *daughters* are in the recital.
(plural—more than one daughter is in the recital)

Do not confuse plural nouns with possessive nouns.

For words ending with an s, x, or z sound, the way you pronounce the word often determines whether you will add an 's or only an apostrophe. If adding an 's results in awkward pronunciation, add only an apostrophe to form the possessive, or reword to use an of phrase.

To check whether a noun should be possessive, substitute an *of* phrase for the possessive form. If the substitution sounds appropriate, the noun should be possessive.

Question: **Should the italicized nouns be plural or possessive?**
The *student's* textbook cost $75.95.
My *neighbor's* son received a scholarship.

Test: **Substitute an *of* phrase to test for ownership.**
The textbook *of the student* cost $75.95.
(The possessive form is correct.)
The son *of my neighbor* received a scholarship.
(The possessive form is correct.)

Singular Possessive Nouns

The following rules will help you form the possessive of singular nouns.

MOST SINGULAR NOUNS. Add *'s* to form the possessive of most singular nouns, including abbreviations.

Singular Noun	Singular Possessive	Singular Noun	Singular Possessive
senator-elect	senator-elect's view	CFO	CFO's opinion
salesperson	salesperson's commission	witness	witness's testimony
man	man's hat	genius	genius's theory
dog	dog's bone	Max	Max's plan
doctor	doctor's patients	wife	wife's career

WORKPLACE CONNECTION

CFO, an organizational title, means *chief financial officer.*

AWKWARD CONSTRUCTION. Avoid awkward possessive construction. Reword the sentence or use an *of* phrase.

Awkward Possessive Construction	Improved Construction
My sister's friend's house overlooks Pelican Lake.	My sister's friend has a house that overlooks Pelican Lake. OR A friend of my sister has a house that overlooks Pelican Lake.

SEPARATE OR JOINT OWNERSHIP. When each person "owns" a separate item, make each noun possessive. When more than one person "owns" the same item, make only the last noun possessive.

Separate Ownership	**Joint Ownership**
Lea's and Anna's bedrooms are small. (Lea and Anna each have a small bedroom.)	Lea and Anna's bedroom is small. (Lea and Anna share a small bedroom.)
The coach's and the team's seats are in first class. (The coach and members of the team have individual seats in first class.)	The coach and the team's victory was well deserved. (One victory was shared by all.)

Complete Application 2-4.

[CHECKPOINT 2-8]

Form Singular Possessives

Write each italicized noun as a singular possessive.

1. *press* reaction ________________
2. *firefighter* uniform ________________
3. *hero* welcome ________________
4. *Ross* story ________________
5. *secretary-treasurer* report ________________
6. *coworker* illness ________________
7. *Christie Company* dividend ________________
8. *Tim* and *Kristen* computer ________________ (joint ownership)
9. *Isabel* and *Rick* condo ________________ (separate ownership)
10. *CBS* schedule ________________

Plural Possessive Nouns

Use the following rules to help you form the possessive of plural nouns. Remember to place the *'s* or only the apostrophe at the end of the plural form of the original word.

Proper names that are already plural are made possessive by adding only the apostrophe.

PLURAL NOUNS ENDING WITH AN *S* OR *Z*. Add only an apostrophe to form the possessive of most plural nouns. A helpful approach is to make the noun plural first; then make the plural noun possessive.

Singular	Plural	Plural Possessive
senator-elect	senators-elect	senators-elect's views
CFO	CFOs	CFOs' opinions
salesperson	salespersons	salespersons' commissions
witness	witnesses	witnesses' testimonies
genius	geniuses	geniuses' theories
dog	dogs	dogs' bones
Cox	Coxes	Coxes' plans
doctor	doctors	doctors' patients
wife	wives	wives' careers

OTHER PLURAL NOUNS. Add *'s* to form the possessive of nouns that have changed form to become plural.

Singular	Plural	Plural Possessive
child	children	children's clothes
woman	women	women's locker room

Inanimate Object Possessives

Avoid making the names of most *inanimate objects* possessive. ***Inanimate*** means "not having qualities of living organisms." Instead, use an *of* phrase.

Possessive Construction	Improved Construction
The computer's keyboard broke.	The keyboard of the computer broke.
The saw's chain needs to be oiled.	The chain of the saw needs to be oiled.

The exceptions to this guideline are possessives representing a collection of people or animals or the possessive of expressions of time and measurement.

association's handbook (collection of people)
herd's grazing land (collection of animals)
one *year's* probation (expression of time)
a *dollar's* worth (expression of measurement)

[Checkpoint 2-9]

Form Plurals and Plural Possessives

Write the plural for each italicized noun; then write the plural possessive.

	Plural	Plural Possessive
1. *chef* kitchens	____________	____________
2. *child* games	____________	____________
3. *vice president* offices	____________	____________
4. *brother-in-law* homes	____________	____________
5. *niece* and *nephew* camping gear (joint ownership)	____________	____________
6. *author* names	____________	____________
7. the *Lynch* and the *Navarro* pets (individual ownership)	____________	____________
8. *Army* gains	____________	____________
9. *teacher* degrees	____________	____________
10. *community* leaders	____________	____________

Complete Application 2-5.

Chapter Summary

- Use common nouns for general names (*author*) and proper nouns for specific names (*Jane Austen*).
- Use collective nouns to name a collection or group of people or things.
- Use nouns as subjects to name who or what the sentence is about; also, use nouns as direct objects to name who or what is receiving the action of the verb.
- Make most nouns plural by adding *s* (*desk/desks*) or *es* (*glass/glasses*) or dropping the ending and adding *ies* (*company/companies*) or *ves* (*knife/knives*).
- Make the last "word" plural as if the word stood alone when compound nouns are written as a solid word (*chairwoman/chairwomen*) or when they are hyphenated and do not include a noun (*go-between/go-betweens; trade-in/trade-ins*).
- Make the main element plural when compound nouns that include a noun are spaced or hyphenated (*vice president/vice presidents; mother-in-law/mothers-in-law*).
- Add *s* to make numbers and most capitalized alphabetic letters and capitalized abbreviations plural; use *'s* to make lowercase alphabetic letters and abbreviations plural.
- Consult a dictionary to determine the plural form of nouns that end in a consonant plus *o*, nouns that change form to become plural, nouns that keep the same form, and nouns that look plural but may be singular.
- Add *'s* to form the possessive of most singular nouns.
- Avoid making inanimate objects possessive except for collections of people or animals or expressions of time and measurement.
- Make each noun possessive to show separate ownership; make the last "owner" possessive to show joint ownership.
- Add only an apostrophe to form the possessive of plural nouns that end with an *s* or *z* sound; add *'s* to form the possessive of other plural nouns.

ILrn

Complete the Chapter 2 Review.

Complete the Chapter 2 iLrn Activities at **miller.swlearning.com.**

Application 2-1

Noun Identification

Part A. Underline the nouns in the following sentences.

0. Benjamin Franklin shared his talents with the world.
1. Benjamin Franklin, a complex man, was born in Boston.
2. The titles of statesman, scientist, author, and inventor are appropriate for Mr. Franklin.
3. He printed paper money.
4. Our economy was shaped by his ideas.
5. He also organized a fire department, raised money to build a hospital, and founded a school.
6. A man of wisdom and integrity, Benjamin Franklin helped draft the Declaration of Independence.
7. Since his vision was poor, he needed reading glasses.
8. To compensate for his visual problems, he invented bifocals.
9. Mr. Franklin wrote an almanac.
10. As a representative from the United States, he traveled to Europe and talked about democracy.

Part B. Identify each italicized noun as a **SUB** (subject) or a **DO** (direct object).

SUB **DO**

0. *Kristen* kicked the soccer *ball.*
1. *Julia* scored the first *goal.*
2. Our *society* emphasizes personal *freedom*.
3. The *players* identified the *positions* they wanted to play.
4. *Perseverance* brought great *rewards*.
5. The *brides* selected *crystal* and *tableware*.
6. *Hector* broke two *vases*.
7. The *visitor* requested a *bulletin*.
8. *Ms. Trotter* collects *coins* and *fossils*.
9. *Renee* presented the *proposal* to the board.
10. *Jacob* keyed the *reports*.

Application 2-2

Plural Nouns Using *S*, *ES*, or *IES*

Part A. Write the plural form for each of the following nouns.

Singular	Plural	Singular	Plural
0. canoe	canoes		
1. marsh	______	11. crunch	______
2. immigrant	______	12. ferry	______
3. purchase	______	13. class	______
4. saint	______	14. attorney	______
5. survey	______	15. century	______
6. tuba	______	16. mouth	______
7. comedy	______	17. church	______
8. tragedy	______	18. tax	______
9. guide	______	19. Delaney	______
10. huckleberry	______	20. holiday	______

Part B. In the space provided, write the plural form of the singular noun given in parentheses.

0. (Tuesday) Tuesdays seem to be the best time to meet.
1. The (boundary) ______ were clearly marked.
2. The (inspector) ______ found no evidence of tampering.
3. E-mail attachments are the source of most (virus) ______.
4. A series of three (flash) ______ is the signal used when the team is ready to descend.
5. Professor Ramirez donated five (box) ______ of books to the library.
6. Kyra bought three (watch) ______ to give as (gift) ______.
7. Several college (student) ______ visited African (family) ______ in the exchange program.
8. Gina and Allison obtained parts in the (play) ______.
9. The restaurant offered three (menu) ______ from which to choose a variety of (dish) ______.
10. Humidity will affect the plaster (mold) ______.

APPLICATION 2-3

Plural Nouns Using *S*, *ES*, or *VES*, Changing Form, or Staying the Same

Part A. Write the plural form for each of the following nouns.

Singular	Plural	Singular	Plural
0. echo	echoes		
1. website	______________	11. courthouse	______________
2. plaintiff	______________	12. piano	______________
3. gross	______________	13. life	______________
4. knife	______________	14. shampoo	______________
5. sister-in-law	______________	15. grandchild	______________
6. shoelace	______________	16. chief	______________
7. 1400	______________	17. trio	______________
8. belief	______________	18. CEO	______________
9. sheaf	______________	19. sheriff	______________
10. leaf	______________	20. half	______________

Part B. In the space provided, write the plural form of the singular noun given in parentheses.

0. Shawna purchased (photo) photos from three (studio) studios.
1. The (head of state) ______________ did not expect the (veto) ______________.
2. The lake has a healthy population of (perch) ______________.
3. Sid picked two buckets of (blueberry) ______________.
4. Matt participated in six (rodeo) ______________ last June.
5. We surveyed six (stockbroker) ______________ and six (VP) ______________ for investment advice.
6. Thirty-five men and women were awarded (Ph.D.) ______________.
7. The (congresswoman) ______________ voted for the proposal.
8. The (soprano) ______________ typically sing the (solo) ______________ at our concerts.
9. Warships called (man-of-war) ______________ wreaked havoc on the high seas.
10. As a result of the (tornado) ______________ last summer, our company replaced several (roof) ______________.

Application 2-4

Singular Possessive Nouns

Part A. For each italicized noun, write the correct singular possessive noun.

0. *firefighter hose* firefighter's
1. *tailor* shop ____________
2. assistant *director* phone ____________
3. *baby* diaper ____________
4. *Video Time* outlet ____________
5. *Dr. Manz* clinic ____________
6. *pollster* response ____________
7. *choir* repertoire ____________
8. *bailiff* position ____________
9. *brother-in-law* voice ____________
10. *R. A.* pictures ____________
11. *Grisham* novels ____________
12. *umpire* decision ____________
13. *historian* research ____________
14. *worker* leave ____________
15. *citizen* arrest ____________
16. *child* toy ____________
17. *girl* shirt ____________
18. *boss* report ____________
19. *Mario* job ____________
20. *Felix* truck ____________

Part B. Replace the *of* phrase with the correct singular possessive noun.

0. The *work of my accountant* is guaranteed. accountant's work
1. The *selections of the buyer* are quality items. ____________
2. Marlee was happy with the *ruling of the* judge. ____________
3. The *uncle of Mrs. Cottle* works for my company. ____________
4. The *report of the officer* is due today. ____________
5. The *aunt of Ms. White* is an engineer. ____________
6. Would you say that the *commitment of Virginia* is firm? ____________
7. The *schedule of the manager* was posted. ____________
8. The *house of Tomas and Joyce* sold for $250,000. (joint ownership) ____________
9. I stamped each letter with the *date of today.* ____________
10. During the festival, the *voice of Daniel* could be heard everywhere. ____________

Application 2-5

Plural Possessive Nouns

Part A. Write the plural and the plural possessive of each of the following words.

	Plural	Plural Possessive
0. lady	ladies	ladies'
1. raccoon		
2. ambassador		
3. grandfather		
4. PDA		
5. Wentz		
6. gentleman		
7. family		
8. member		
9. deer		
10. mouse		

Part B. In the space provided, write the plural possessive form of the singular noun given in parentheses.

0. My (neighbor) ____neighbors'____ houses were damaged by the hurricane.
1. Five (inductee) ________________ ceremonies were held this year.
2. The Nova (gallery) ________________ openings will occur on the same night.
3. The (stockbroker) ________________ advice was considered carefully.
4. Their (executive) ________________ suites are on the fourth floor.
5. Ten area (doctor) ________________ offices use Medistaff software.
6. The (Karpinski) ________________ mowers are for sale.
7. Our (investor) ________________ monthly newsletters have been mailed.
8. We read the (committee) ________________ reports.
9. The (Mitchell) ________________ trailers need new tires.
10. (Bookseller) ________________ permits are available from 9 a.m. until 3 p.m.

Nouns

Part A. Form Possessive and Plural Nouns

Provide the required form for each noun. Each correct answer is worth two points.

	Singular Possessive	Plural	Plural Possessive
1. foreman	______	______	______
2. incumbent	______	______	______
3. manufacturer	______	______	______
4. spokeswoman	______	______	______
5. classmate	______	______	______
6. editor in chief	______	______	______
7. aunt and uncle (individual ownership)	______	______	______
8. secretary	______	______	______
9. guide	______	______	______
10. employee	______	______	______

Part B. Use Plural and Possessive Nouns Correctly

Read the following selection carefully. Find and correct the **singular possessive**, **plural possessive**, or **plural noun** errors; write the correction in the space above the error. Each correct answer is worth four points.

Americans cell phone use has increased dramatically in the last few year's. Apply common sense and etiquette when using a cell phone.

Keep other peoples' needs in mind. Avoid phone conversations when you are with others. Check caller ID to confirm that incoming calls are prioritys. Otherwise, let them go to voice mail. Respond to caller's messages promptly.

Save private conversations for private place's. Make or answer calls away from a public's area. Use a landline phone or personal meeting for serious issues to avoid the frustration that can result from a dropped connection and eavesdroppers, including electronic eavesdropper's. Sending text messages at concerts, plays, or speechs distracts the performers and interferes with fellow patrons enjoyment.

Employees need to understand the overall intent and purpose of technology so that they use technology thoughtfully and wisely.

Pronouns

CHAPTER 3

Do you write or talk like this?

> Mr. Tai arranged for Laura, Viktor, and Tishanda to attend the voice recognition seminar because Mr. Tai knows that Laura, Viktor, and Tishanda are especially interested in voice recognition technology.

Typically, you do not always refer to someone or something by repeating the same name again and again. Instead, you are more likely to replace the name with a substitute:

> Mr. Tai arranged for Laura, Viktor, and Tishanda to attend the voice recognition seminar because *he* knows that *they* are especially interested in *this* technology.

The part of speech that replaces nouns is called a **pronoun.** Using different pronouns correctly makes your messages more interesting because you eliminate unnecessary repetition.

Learning Objectives

- Explain how pronouns function in sentences.
- Use subjective, objective, and possessive case personal pronouns correctly.
- Use compound personal pronouns and indefinite pronouns correctly.
- Use relative, interrogative, and demonstrative pronouns correctly.
- Identify antecedents and use pronouns that agree with their antecedents in person, number, and gender.

PERSONAL PRONOUNS

Personal pronouns are substitutes for nouns, so personal pronouns represent persons, places, things, concepts, qualities, or events. The person, place, thing, concept, quality, or event the pronoun refers to is called its **antecedent.** Personal pronouns are identified by *person* (first, second, third), *number* (singular or plural), *gender* (masculine, feminine, neuter, or common), and *case* (subjective, objective, or possessive).

Table 3-1 shows the correct forms of personal pronouns.

Person

Person tells whether the subject is speaking, is spoken to, or is spoken about. Person is represented by first, second, or third.

First person refers to the person speaking. First-person personal pronouns are *I*, *me*, *my*, *mine*, *we*, *us*, *our*, and *ours.*

> *I* exercised until 4:30 p.m.
> *We* drove to Nashville.
> Can you explain the procedure to *us*?
> The red car is *ours.*

Table 3-1: The Forms and Functions of Personal Pronouns

	Subjective Case (subject: doer of the action)		Objective Case (object: receiver of the action)		Possessive Case (ownership without a noun)		Possessive Case (ownership of a noun)		Compound Personal Pronouns	
	Singular	Plural	Singular	Plural	Singular	Plural	Singular	Plural	Singular	Plural
First Person (person speaking)	I	we	me	us	mine	ours	my	our	myself	ourselves
Second Person (person spoken to)	you	you	you	you	yours	yours	your	your	yourself	yourselves
Third Person (person or thing spoken of)										
Masculine gender	he	they	him	them	his	theirs	his	their	himself	themselves
Feminine gender	she	they	her	them	hers	theirs	her	their	herself	themselves
Neuter gender	it	they	it	them	its	their	its	their	itself	themselves

Second person refers to the person being spoken to. Second-person personal pronouns are *you*, *your*, and *yours*.

You may use a calculator. Is the CD player *yours?*

Third person refers to the person, place, thing, concept, quality, or event being discussed. Third-person personal pronouns are *she*, *he*, *it*, *her*, *him*, *hers*, *his*, *its*, *they*, *them*, *their*, and *theirs*.

She owns two computers.
They repaired 20 roofs.

The teacher gave *her* an award.
Theirs is the winning team.

Personal pronouns change form based on how they function in a sentence. They also change form for person, gender, number, and case.

Number

Pronouns are singular or plural in **number.** Singular refers to one; plural refers to more than one.

She bought the ticket. (singular)
They called *their* families from the airport. (plural)

"*Grammar is the analysis of language.*"

-Edgar Allan Poe
"The Rationale of Verse"
The Pioneer
March 1843

Gender

Gender identifies whether the pronoun is *feminine* (female), *masculine* (male), *neuter* (neither female nor male), or *common* (either male or female).

Masculine:	he, him, his
Feminine:	she, her, hers
Neuter:	it, its
Common:	I, we, you, they, our, their

Case

Case tells how the personal pronoun is used in a sentence. Personal pronouns have three cases: *subjective*, *objective*, and *possessive*.

Pronouns in the Subjective Case.

Singular subjective case pronouns are *I*, *you*, *she*, *he*, and *it*. Plural subjective case pronouns are *we*, *you*, and *they*.

Subject of the Verb. Use the subjective case when the pronoun is the subject of the verb.

They flew to Orlando. (*They* is the subject of the sentence.)

Li-ming and *I* ordered new laptops yesterday. (*Li-ming* and *I* are subjects of the verb *ordered*.)

When a sentence has two subjects (as in the preceding example), check your choice of pronouns by dropping the extra words and reading the sentence.

The word subject *may help you remember that the subject of a sentence is in the subjective case. Subjective case pronouns also are called* nominative case pronouns.

A verb expresses action or state of being. Chapters 4 and 5 discuss verbs in detail.

I ordered new laptops yesterday. (The subjective pronoun *I* is the correct choice.)

Linking verbs express a state of being or a condition. Common linking verbs are am, are, is, was, were, been, *and* being.

Subject Complement. Use the subjective case when the pronoun is a subject complement. A **subject complement** *renames* the subject and follows a verb (linking verb) that links a description to the subject.

The director is *she*. (*Director* and *she* are the same person. The verb *is* links the description *she* to the subject.)

The cab driver is *he*. (*Cab driver* and *he* are the same person. The verb *is* links the description *he* to the subject.)

When the pronoun is used as a subject complement, you can quickly check your pronoun choice by turning the sentence around.

She is the director. (The subjective pronoun *she* is the correct choice.)

He is the cab driver. (The subjective pronoun *he* is the correct choice.)

Understood Comparison. Use the subjective case when the pronoun follows *than* or *as* because these words often introduce an *understood* comparison. Only the subject of the comparison is stated in the sentence. The rest of the comparison is *understood.*

Britta is taller than *she*. (Britta is taller than *she is tall.*)

Sharese is as relieved as *he*. (Sharese is as relieved as *he is relieved.*)

PRONOUNS IN THE OBJECTIVE CASE. Singular objective case pronouns are *me*, *you*, *her*, *him*, and *it*. Plural objective case pronouns are *us*, *you*, and *them*.

The word object may help you remember that objects are in the objective case.

Direct Object. Use the objective case when the pronoun is the direct object of a verb. A **direct object** tells *who* or *what* receives the action of the verb.

To decide whether a subjective case pronoun or an objective case pronoun is correct, drop the extra words and read the sentence: Mr. Allen thanked me.

Mr. Whibbs chose *him*. (*Him* is a direct object because *him* receives the action of the verb *chose.*)

Mr. Allen thanked Oday and *me*. (*Oday* and *me* are direct objects because they receive the action of the verb *thanked.*)

Indirect Object. Use the objective case when the pronoun is the indirect object of a verb. An **indirect object** tells *to whom* or *for whom* or *to what* or *for what* something was done. The indirect object usually follows the verb and comes before the direct object.

Shelley sent *me* the money. (*Me* is an indirect object because *me* tells to whom the money was sent.)

Randy told *them* the news. (*Them* is an indirect object because *them* tells to whom the news was told.)

Object of a Preposition. Use the objective case when the pronoun is the object of a preposition. The combination of a preposition, one or more nouns or pronouns, and words like *the* that fall between them is called a **prepositional phrase.** A noun or pronoun that follows a preposition is called an **object of the preposition.** A few common prepositions are *among, between, for, from, to,* and *with.*

Kate identified the flowers *for them.* (*Them* is the object of the preposition *for.*)

Emily received a gift *from him.* (*Him* is the object of the preposition *from.*)

To test whether a pronoun is a direct object or an indirect object, reword using a to *phrase:* Kristin sent the report to me. *An indirect object can be used with a* to *phrase; a direct object cannot.*

Prepositions *show how a noun or pronoun is connected to some other part of a sentence. Chapter 8 discusses prepositions.*

Complete Application 3-1.

[Checkpoint 3-1]

Choose the Correct Case Pronoun

In the space above each sentence, replace the word(s) in parentheses by writing an appropriate subjective case pronoun or objective case pronoun.

1. (Vianne and Carrie) should arrive within an hour.

2. David and (Miss Rocher) opened a new shop across the street.

3. The club recommended a new style of hiking boots for (Craig and Joanne).

4. "The furniture was divided between Radji and (myself)," said Tanya.

5. The letter from (Sam) says nothing about (you and me).

6. The manager complimented Chris and (Larry).

7. When I asked for Roberto, he answered, "This is (Roberto)."

8. Bradley's mother sent money to (Bradley).

Possessive pronouns do not use apostrophes to indicate possession.

A possessive pronoun should precede a gerund (a verbal noun ending in ing): The board members appreciated your donating time and money.

To check the accuracy of your choice, read the sentence using the two-word combination, such as it is: It is coat is wet is incorrect. If your choice doesn't fit, use the possessive form: Its coat is wet.

Complete Application 3-2.

PRONOUNS IN THE POSSESSIVE CASE. Singular possessive case pronouns are *my*, *mine*, *your*, *yours*, *her*, *hers*, *his*, and *its*. Plural possessive case pronouns are *our*, *ours*, *you*, *yours*, *their*, and *theirs*.

Ownership of an Adjacent Noun. Use these possessive case pronouns to show ownership of an adjacent noun: *my*, *your*, *his*, *her*, *its*, *our*, and *their*.

> Nan sold her DVD to Ellen. (*Her* shows ownership of the noun *DVD*.)
>
> *Their* offer was too late. (*Their* shows ownership of the noun *offer*.)

Ownership Without an Adjacent Noun. Use these possessive case pronouns to show ownership when the pronoun is not adjacent to a noun: *mine*, *yours*, *his*, *hers*, *its*, *ours*, and *theirs*.

> The boat is *mine*. His is the *slowest* of all the cars.

Possessives and Contractions

Some possessive case pronouns and some contractions sound alike. Because they are not the same, you must know the difference between a possessive pronoun and a contraction. A **contraction** is a shortened form, usually of two words.

Possessive Pronoun	Contraction
its	it's (it is)
theirs	there's (there is)
their	they're (they are)
your	you're (you are)

[CHECKPOINT 3-2]

Choose the Correct Form

Underline the correct choice of those given in parentheses.

1. Please take (you're/your) seats before the presentation begins.
2. (Their/They're) home page is excellent; (their/they're) scheduled to update the site next week.
3. The patent is (our's/ours).
4. The choice is (mine/mine's) to make.
5. The bird lost (it's its) tail feathers during the tropical storm.

Compound Personal Pronouns

Compound personal pronouns direct attention to an antecedent, the word or words to which a pronoun refers. An antecedent is usually a single noun or pronoun. **Compound personal pronouns** are formed by adding *-self* (singular) or *-selves* (plural) to certain personal pronouns.

Singular	**Plural**
myself	ourselves
yourself	yourselves
himself, herself, itself	themselves

Compound personal pronouns are also intensive or reflexive. An **intensive** pronoun immediately follows its antecedent and thus emphasizes the antecedent. A **reflexive** pronoun refers to a noun or pronoun that appeared earlier in the sentence.

> The chef *himself* cooked the dinner. (*Himself* is an intensive pronoun that emphasizes the antecedent *chef*.)
>
> If the students miss the exit, they will find *themselves* on snow-covered back roads. (*Themselves* is a reflexive pronoun that refers to the antecedent *they*.)

Do not use hisself, ourselves, theirself(s), theirselves, *and* themself(s); *these are not words.*

[CHECKPOINT 3-3]

Choose the Correct Compound Personal Pronoun

Write the correct compound personal pronoun for each of the following sentences.

1. Gerald, please do not place ____________________ in danger by exceeding the speed limit.
2. The Turners taught ____________________ how to ski.
3. Tarah ____________________ signed the documents.
4. You ____________________ said that the vote was surprising.
5. We must lower the bid, or we will find ____________________ without a contract.
6. I ____________________ will never encounter that kind of issue.
7. Must we wait for approval, or may we proceed with the changes ____________________?
8. The Kleins ____________________ offered a sizable reward.

RELATIVE PRONOUNS AND INTERROGATIVE PRONOUNS

Relative pronouns and interrogative pronouns share similar forms but function differently in sentences.

Who and whom may be either singular or plural in meaning.

Relative Pronouns

Relative pronouns connect a dependent clause to its antecedent. A **dependent clause** is a group of words that has a subject and a verb but is not a sentence. A relative pronoun begins the dependent clause, so the clause is often called a **relative clause.** *Who, whoever, whom, whomever, whose, which,* and *that* are relative pronouns. *Who, whoever, whom,* and *whomever* refer to people. *Which* refers to places, things, concepts, qualities, or events. *That* refers to people, places, things, concepts, qualities, or events.

Subjective Case: who, whoever (used as the subject in a clause)
Objective Case: whom, whomever (used as an object in a clause)
Possessive Case: whose (used to show ownership in a clause)

WHO/WHOEVER. Use *who* or *whoever* if you can substitute the subjective case personal pronouns *I, he, she, we,* or *they. Who* and *whoever* function as subjects or subject complements of a clause. (A subject complement renames the subject.)

Kayla Jones, *who is a skilled driver,* won the national race.

(*She* can appropriately replace *who* in this clause. *Who* connects the clause to its antecedent, *Kayla Jones.*)

WHOM/WHOMEVER. Use *whom* or *whomever* if you can substitute the objective case personal pronouns *me, him, her, us,* or *them. Whom* and *whomever* function as objects.

Rearranging (inverting) the sentence order and substituting an objective case pronoun help you determine which pronoun is correct.

Annmarie is the soloist *whom I hired.* (Invert the order of the clause and replace *whom* with *her.* The clause now reads *I hired her. Whom* relates the clause to the antecedent, *soloist.*)

WHOSE. Do not confuse *whose* with *who's. Whose* is in the possessive case; *who's* is the contraction of *who is.*

Susan, *whose* grammar is excellent, cannot help me.
(*Whose* shows possession of the noun *grammar.*)

Who's going to the dance? (*Who's* is the contraction of *who is.*)

THAT. Use *that* to introduce clauses that are necessary to the meaning of the sentence. Without these clauses, the meaning of a sentence would change.

> Heather wrote the report *that recommended a four-day schedule.* (*That* connects the clause to its antecedent, *report.*)

WHICH. Use *which* to introduce clauses that are helpful but not necessary to the meaning of a sentence. The main idea of the sentence remains even without these clauses.

> The Allis Art Museum, *which is located on Vine and Conrad,* opens at 9 a.m. (*Which* relates the clause to its antecedent, *Allis Art Museum.*)

Interrogative Pronouns

Interrogative pronouns are used to ask questions. Common interrogative pronouns are *who, whom, whose, which,* and *what.* To help you decide which is correct—the subjective *who* or the objective *whom*—appropriately reword the question into a statement and substitute a different subjective or objective case pronoun.

> Do you know *who* your new doctor is? (Reword this sentence: *You do know she is your new doctor.*)
>
> *Whom* do I call? (Reword this sentence: *I do call him.*)
>
> *Whose* is this? (Use *whose* to show ownership.)
>
> *Which* is correct? (Use *which* when referring to places, things, concepts, qualities, or events and when distinguishing one of them from another.
>
> *What* is the number? (Use *what* when referring to places, things, concepts, qualities, or events.)

Complete Application 3-3.

[CHECKPOINT 3-4]

Choose the Correct Relative Pronoun or Interrogative Pronoun

Underline the correct relative or interrogative pronoun from those given in parentheses.

1. (Who's/Whose) briefcase was left in the foyer?
2. Elena is on the committee (which/that) drafted the retirement plan.
3. The computer, (that/which) was assembled in Canada, is mine.
4. For (who/whom) was the report prepared?
5. (Which/What) is better—the first suggestion or the second?

Do not confuse demonstrative pronouns with demonstrative adjectives. When this, that, these, *and* those *are placed immediately before a noun, they are demonstrative adjectives. Adjectives are discussed in Chapter 6.*

DEMONSTRATIVE PRONOUNS

Demonstrative pronouns point out specific persons, places, things, concepts, qualities, or events. Demonstrative pronouns stand alone; they do not come immediately before a noun. The demonstrative pronouns are *this*, *that*, *these*, and *those*.

Singular:	*This* is her desk.	*That* is mine.
Plural:	*These* are my pliers.	*Those* are yours.

Chapter 5 discusses subject-verb agreement, including indefinite pronouns as subjects.

When appropriate, singular indefinite pronouns are made possessive by adding 's: Somebody's papers are on the floor.

INDEFINITE PRONOUNS

Indefinite pronouns make a general reference to someone or something—they do not refer to any specific person, place, thing, concept, quality, or event. Indefinite pronouns stand alone; they do not come immediately before a noun. Most indefinite pronouns are singular, some are plural, and some are singular or plural.

Common Singular Indefinite Pronouns

anybody (anyone)	everybody (everyone)	no one
anything	everything	somebody (someone)
each	neither	something
either	nobody	

Everybody in our family likes chocolate. (*Everybody* is the singular subject of the sentence.)

Each of the restaurants is donating canned goods to the local food pantry. (*Each* is the singular subject of the sentence.)

Plural Indefinite Pronouns

both few many others several

Several were unable to attend the festival. (*Several* is the plural subject of the sentence.)

Many have applied for citizenship. (*Many* is the plural subject of the sentence.)

Singular or Plural Indefinite Pronouns

all any more most none some

Most attend regularly. (*Most* in this sentence assumes more than one person; thus, *most* is the plural subject of the sentence.)

Most of the pie is gone. (The reference is to the whole pie; thus, *most* is the singular subject of the sentence.)

[CHECKPOINT 3-5]

Identify Demonstrative Pronouns and Indefinite Pronouns

Underline indefinite pronouns and circle demonstrative pronouns in the following sentences.

1. Is anyone available to help us?
2. Someone needs to explain that to the audience.
3. Some of the font styles do not transmit clearly; those should be changed.
4. Neither of your proposals is appropriate because both have disadvantages.
5. I noticed that everybody has chosen something from the catalog.

PRONOUN–ANTECEDENT AGREEMENT

Since a pronoun and its antecedent refer to the same person, place thing, concept, quality, or event, the pronoun and its antecedent must agree in number and gender. Use the following rules to determine correct pronoun-antecedent agreement.

WORKPLACE CONNECTION

In order to communicate effectively, employees must present information clearly and accurately.

Number

Use a singular pronoun when the antecedent is singular; use a plural pronoun when the antecedent is plural.

Everyone has *his or her* own ideas about fundraising. (*His or her* agrees with the singular antecedent *everyone.*)

The company released *its* sales figures yesterday. (*Its* agrees with the singular antecedent *company*, which is a collective noun acting as a single unit.)

I will schedule the members so that *they* can begin *their* training modules. (*They* and *their* agree with the plural antecedent *members.*)

When the antecedent is a collective noun (such as committee*) whose members are acting individually, use a plural pronoun.*

ANTECEDENTS JOINED BY *AND*. Use a plural pronoun when referring to two or more antecedents joined by *and.*

Jill and Alice asked for *their* rewards. (*Their* is plural and agrees with the two antecedents joined by *and.*)

The Nordinas and the Chous already bought *theirs.* (*Theirs* is plural and agrees with the two antecedents joined by *and.*)

Or and *either . . . or* mean "one or the other." *Neither . . . nor* means "none."

Antecedents Joined by *Or*, *Either . . . Or*, or *Neither . . . Nor*.

Use a singular pronoun to refer to singular antecedents joined by *or*, *either . . . or*, or *neither . . . nor*.

Zach or Ryan will transmit *his* material. (Singular antecedents joined by *or* require a singular pronoun.)

Neither Elyse nor Valerie knows *her* account number. (Singular antecedents joined by *neither . . . nor* require a singular pronoun.)

When the antecedents are plural, use a plural pronoun.

Either the doctors or the nurses will submit *their* reports. (Plural antecedents joined by *either . . . or* require a plural pronoun.)

When referring to both a singular and a plural antecedent joined by *or*, *either . . . or*, or *neither . . . nor*, use a pronoun that agrees with the nearest antecedent. Typically, place the plural antecedent closest to the verb and use a plural pronoun for ease of reading.

Either the teacher or the students will give *their* recommendations.
Neither the principal nor the teachers want *their* names listed.

Gender

Match the gender of the pronoun to the gender of the antecedent.

Ralph represented *his* manager at the meeting. (The masculine antecedent *Ralph* requires the masculine pronoun *his*.)

The team lost *its* lead in the ninth inning. (The neuter antecedent *team* requires the neuter pronoun *its*.)

Mayella completed *her* report. (The feminine antecedent *Mayella* requires the feminine pronoun *her*.)

The True Antecedent. To determine the true antecedent, ignore phrases that come between the noun and its antecedent. Then choose the pronoun that agrees with the antecedent.

Gina, along with the others, left *her* car in the lower circle. (The singular antecedent *Gina* requires the singular pronoun *her*.)

The students, as well as their professor, lost *their* luggage. (The plural antecedent *students* requires the plural pronoun *their*.)

Antecedent Gender Unknown. Unless you are sure of the gender of an antecedent, select alternatives that do not reflect gender bias. One option is to use *his or her* with a singular indefinite pronoun when the gender of the antecedent is unknown or when the antecedent includes both males and females. Other options include omitting the pronoun or making the pronoun and its antecedent plural.

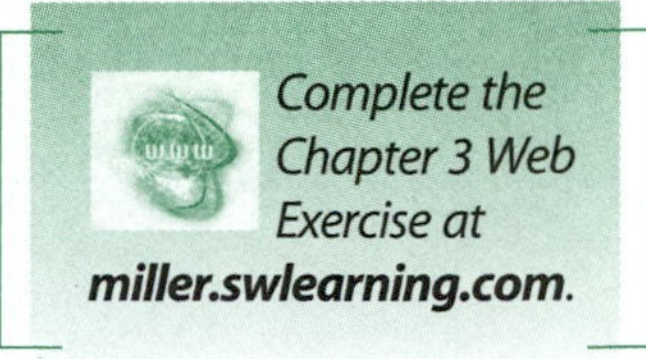

Complete the Chapter 3 Web Exercise at ***miller.swlearning.com****.*

Everyone has *his* or *her* personal interests. (Use *his or her*.)

Everyone has personal interests. (Omit the pronoun.)

Employees must sign *their* payroll sheets on the first of every month. (Make the pronoun and its antecedent plural.)

Complete Application 3-4.

[Checkpoint 3-6]

Make Pronouns and Antecedents Agree

Circle the antecedent(s) in each sentence. In the space provided, write the correct pronoun(s).

1. Neither Heather nor Lisa has received ________________ check.
2. The employees requested new computers, but ________________ are not likely to have ________________ requests approved.
3. Abelardo takes good care of ________________ ghost costume.
4. The company has closed ________________ doors after 30 years in business.
5. Several agreed to have ________________ cell-phone numbers published.
6. Few of the beach residents have returned to ________________ property.
7. Mrs. Delgado, as well as the others, thinks that ________________ visa will be approved.
8. Both have ________________ reports ready.
9. Larry and Karen donated to ________________ favorite charity.
10. Everyone wants ________________ grades today.

CHAPTER SUMMARY

- Create interest and avoid repetition by using personal pronouns as substitutes for nouns.
- Remember that personal pronouns change form for person, number, gender, and case, depending on their role in a sentence.
- Use the subjective case when a pronoun is a subject or a subject complement.
- Choose the objective case when a pronoun is a direct object, an indirect object, or the object of a preposition.
- Use the possessive case when a pronoun shows ownership; do not use apostrophes with possessive pronouns.
- Use compound personal pronouns to add emphasis to the word or words to which the pronoun refers (intensive) or to refer to a noun or pronoun that was used earlier in the sentence (reflexive).
- Select a relative pronoun to connect a dependent clause to its antecedent.
- Form questions using interrogative pronouns.
- Call attention to specific people, places, things, concepts, qualities, or events with demonstrative pronouns.
- Use indefinite pronouns to make a general reference to someone or something.
- Choose pronouns that agree with their antecedents in person, number, and gender.

Complete the Chapter 3 Review.

iLrn Complete the Chapter 3 iLrn Activities at **miller.swlearning.com**.

APPLICATION 3-1

Subjective and Objective Case Pronouns

Part A. In the space provided, replace the word(s) in parentheses with an appropriate **subjective case pronoun.**

0. Did you ask Lola if (Lola) ____she____ has an e-mail address?
1. Did you find out if (you and I) __________ have the same schedule?
2. Deanna said that (Deanna) __________ will return tomorrow morning.
3. Victoria did not realize that Cici, Alberto, and (Victoria) __________ would be transferred.
4. The temperature dropped so low that (Yao and I) __________ could not start our car.
5. Dulce is taller than (David) __________.
6. Does Teresa know if (Teresa) __________ can jump higher than the other players?
7. I ran the mile faster than (Lisa) __________.
8. His manager and (Daniel) __________ signed the contract.
9. Did Sheldon ask Mario if (Mario) __________ printed the boarding passes?
10. The instructor asked if (Quang, Oti, and I) __________ could meet at 7 a.m.

Part B. In the space provided, replace the word(s) in parentheses with an appropriate **objective case pronoun.**

0. I hired (my neighbors) ____them____ to paint the building.
1. The new sales strategy applies to everyone, including (Josh, Sandy, and me) __________.
2. Please deliver a copy of the outline to (Jeffrey) __________.
3. When you pay (Fred) __________, he can repay (Vicki) __________.
4. Carrying cases will protect (the components) __________.
5. If you give the package to (Martin and me) __________, we can send (the package) __________ to (Carlos and Raymond) __________.
6. Lillie quoted the price to (Diam and Kimsan) __________.
7. The director asked (Janice) __________ to attend the meeting with us.
8. The committee invited (students) __________ to host discussion sessions.
9. The color wheel uses light blue with (that paint and tile) __________.
10. If the decision had to be made by (Minna and me) __________, we would say, "Complete the project."

APPLICATION 3-2

Possessive, Subjective, and Objective Case Pronouns

Part A. In the space provided, write the appropriate **possessive pronoun** to replace the word(s) in parentheses.

0. Have you read (belonging to Marsha) ___her___ book?
1. How many of (Mr. Clayton's) ______________ classes have you completed?
2. (Phillip's) ______________ portfolio includes three recommendation letters; (belonging to me)______________ includes two.
3. (Belonging to you and me) ______________ accomplishments speak for themselves.
4. Anthropology is (Greta's) ______________ main interest.
5. Kelly bought (Kelly's) ______________ brother lunch at (belonging to me) ______________ café.

Part B. In the following sentences, underline the correct pronoun from each pair given in parentheses. Then identify the case of each pronoun by writing **S** (subjective), **O** (objective), or **P** (possessive) above the pronoun.

0. (We [S]/Us) may be late for the reception because (it [S] / they) begins at noon.
1. (They're/Their) travel guides include more than 200 photos.
2. When (we/us) won, our team congratulated (their/them) team.
3. (We/Us) haul the timber on large trucks.
4. Dana asked Tony and (them/they) to call.
5. The treasurer is (her/she).
6. During the hunt, the fox runs for (its/it's) life.
7. The manager told Crystal and (I/me) to mark the sale items.
8. The thin slices will appear more attractive to (they/them).
9. A sharp knife makes cutting easier for (she/her).
10. (Her/She) and her friends visited Petri in Pensacola.
11. Jagruti and (I/me) will prepare the slides.
12. You are just as clever as (him/he).
13. You and (I/me) will write the report; (your/you're) background makes you the better choice.
14. The discounted items were tagged by (I/me).
15. The right to question the decision is (there's/theirs), after they get advice from (their/they're) attorney.

APPLICATION 3-3

Compound, Relative, and Interrogative Pronouns

Part A. Underline the correct compound pronoun from those given in parentheses. Then identify the pronoun as **INT** (intensive) or **REF** (reflexive) in the space provided.

0. The manager (herself/hisself) wrote the policy. INT
1. The special solution allows the plants (themselves/theirselves) to grow without soil. ____________
2. Did Mr. Rosso see the construction site (himself/hisself)? ____________
3. You (yourselfs/yourselves) witnessed the accident. ____________
4. Callie said, "I want to plan the trip (herself/myself)." ____________
5. The members (theirselves/themselves) admitted that the last auction was unsuccessful. ____________

Part B. The relative clause in each of the following sentences is italicized. Underline the relative pronoun and circle the antecedent of the relative pronoun.

0. The (fee), *which is due Friday*, is not refundable.
1. The spectacle *that takes place every July 4* always pleases the crowd.
2. Their fireworks, *which are among the best I have seen*, illuminate the entire sky.
3. Your cousin, *who makes me laugh*, plans to attend.
4. The sales associates *who work on Labor Day* will receive a holiday bonus.
5. Her voice mail, *which was cleared on Friday*, is again full.

Part C. In the following sentences, underline the correct **relative** or **interrogative** pronoun from the pair given in parentheses.

0. Do you know (who/whom) wants the job?
1. (Who/Whom) phoned you yesterday with the big news?
2. (Who's/Whose) turn is next?
3. (Who/Whom) will you choose?
4. Have you read *For (Who/Whom) the Bell Tolls?*
5. The Treaty of Vienna contains (who's/whose) signatures?
6. (Who's/Whose) participation was denied when the Treaty of Vienna was written?
7. Everyone (which/who) provided input will be able to vote.
8. Did you ask (who/whom) can work tomorrow?
9. She is the physician (who/whom) treated your sister.
10. Carlos, for (who/whom) this appointment was made, canceled at the last minute.

APPLICATION 3-4

Pronouns and Pronoun-Antecedent Agreement

Part A. If the relative or interrogative pronoun in each of the following sentences is used correctly, write **C** (correct). Otherwise, write the correct pronoun above the error.

0. Who will repair the door? **C**
1. Rudy wants to know whom locked the spring.
2. Whomever wrote that memo deserves credit.
3. With whom did you speak regarding your credit report?
4. Do you know whom is responsible?
5. Whoever finishes first will go on to the next round.

Part B. In the following sentences, underline the pronoun that agrees with its antecedent.

0. The doctor or the nurses will explain (his/<u>their</u>) decision at the board meeting.
1. Neither Jacob nor Henry can find (his/their) shoes.
2. The winner and the loser took (his/their) bows after the match.
3. Did either Vincent or Dale make (his/their) contribution?
4. The network has increased (its/their) ratings for the fourth consecutive quarter.
5. Each of the recommendations has (its/their) advantages.
6. Either the coach or the players will accept (her/their) trophy.
7. Neither Janice nor Marjorie has returned (her/their) loan application.
8. Each of the women wants (her/their) share of the prize money.
9. Everyone in the office completed (his or her/their) evaluation by May.
10. Sam rode the train to Chicago; neither (he/him) nor his brothers like to drive in the city.
11. Both made (his/their) appointments to get (his/their) hair cut at 8 p.m.
12. The dentists, as well as the assistants, completed (they're/their) conference registration.
13. Personal trainers may request (its/their) forms at the same time.
14. If anyone fails the test, (he or she/they) will have to attend a review session.
15. Either Ms. Valerio or the agents will give (her/their) recommendations.

Chapter 3 Review

Pronouns

Part A. Identify Pronouns

Underline all pronouns in the following sentences. Each correctly identified pronoun is worth two points.

1. A speech can be a useful way to share information. However, speeches are likely to be ineffective if they are boring and disorganized.
2. People often are invited to speak because of their having expertise in a particular area. A speaker may have earned a reputation not only as someone who is knowledgeable but also as someone who gets things done.
3. Planning helps you deliver the intended message. Begin planning by asking yourself three questions: Why am I speaking? Who is the audience? What do I want to accomplish?
4. Gathering information about an audience ahead of time helps you communicate with the audience. Therefore, ask your host for information about the audience, such as occupation, educational background, and economic level. Then choose and organize the material to capture their attention.
5. As a speaker, you have the opportunity to sell yourself, your ideas, your company, and your product.

Workplace Connection

Preparing a speech or presentation involves selecting and organizing material and analyzing the makeup of the audience so that you effectively communicate your message.

Part B. Choose the Correct Pronoun

Underline the correct word from those given in parentheses. Each correct answer is worth three points.

1. Evelyn Babb, a member of the Executive Speakers Bureau, explained to (me, I) the responsibilities that listeners and speakers should assume.
2. Dr. John Kline (hisself/himself) stated, "Hearing is the reception of sound; listening is the attachment of meaning to the sound."
3. Studies reveal that students spend between 50 and 75 percent of (they're/their) classroom time listening to teachers, others students, or audio media.
4. Listening correlates positively with (our, our's) achieving personal and professional success.
5. Since abundant information is available to (us, we), both listeners and speakers should verify the information.
6. Speakers (theirselves/themselves) must attract the attention of the listeners.
7. Sometimes (its/it's) difficult to keep the attention of listeners.
8. Material should be organized logically and should include interesting stories that clarify points so that listeners, (who's/whose) attention may be easily distracted, stay focused.

9. Visual aids (that/which) accurately illustrate points add impact to a message.
10. Effective listeners (theirselves/themselves) determine the reasons for listening.
11. When listeners exhibit (their/they're) excitement or enthusiasm, speakers become more motivated.
12. Passive listeners, (who/whom) make no verbal responses, may signal nonverbal responses with facial expressions or body movement.
13. Active listening, a cyclical process, requires feedback from (they/them).
14. Speakers should strive to use correct grammar; for example, to introduce the next speaker by saying, "This is (her/she)."
15. To enhance the understanding of listeners from different cultures, speakers should avoid idioms like "the big picture" or "on the same page," (that/which) can be easily misunderstood.
16. Once a speech is prepared, most of (us/we) begin practicing the delivery.
17. As presenters, (I/we) must recognize how our vocal tones reflect attitude.
18. Attentive listeners show intercultural speakers that (there/their) contributions are valued and respected.
19. A good listener avoids asking a speaker questions when (he or she/they) has not asked for input.
20. Although listeners cannot alter a speaker's appearance, mannerisms, and delivery, (he or she/they) must look beyond distractions to the message.

Verbs

CHAPTER 4

One forgets words as one forgets names. One's vocabulary needs constant fertilisation [*sic*] or it will die.

—Evelyn Waugh, British novelist (1903–1966)

For centuries, new words made their way into common speech as people read newspapers and books and spoke to one another. Now, recorded music, movies, television, and the Internet accelerate the assimilation of words into main-stream vocabulary. New words confront you constantly. Some recent electronic-related additions are *blogging*, *flame*, *phishing*, and *spim*.

As Evelyn Waugh advised, you should nourish your vocabulary. To communicate effectively, build your vocabulary, and follow the basic rules for correct usage.

LEARNING OBJECTIVES

- Identify action verbs and linking verbs.
- Identify main verbs and helping verbs.
- Identify and form the simple tenses.
- Identify and form the perfect tenses.
- Select correct forms of irregular verbs.
- Distinguish between pairs of commonly confused verbs.
- Identify the active voice and the passive voice.

DEFINITION OF VERBS

Verbs express action (*eat*, *look*, *jump*) or state of being (*is*, *am*, *are*). A verb may be one word or a group of words. Every complete sentence must contain a verb. In certain situations, a single verb may communicate a complete thought.

Run!
Think!
Stop!

Action Verbs and Linking Verbs

Action verbs may express physical actions (*cut*, *build*, *twist*) or mental actions (*listen*, *consider*, *believe*).

Samuel *cut* the pole into four equal lengths. (physical action)
Arturo *considered* his options. (mental action)

Linking verbs connect subjects to other words or phrases to form complete thoughts. Linking verbs include forms of the **to be** verb (*is*, *are*, *was*, *were*, *be*, *am*, and *been*).

Another term for linking verbs is state-of-being verbs.

Benjamin *was* a class treasurer. (*Was* connects the subject *Benjamin* with the identification of Benjamin as the *class treasurer.*)

The new cars *were* on the loading dock. (*Were* connects the subject *cars* with the description *on the loading dock.*)

Some words may be either linking or action verbs. These words include *appear, become, feel, grow, hear, look, remain, seem, smell, sound,* and *taste.*

Complete Application 4-1.

John *felt* the edge of the board. (action verb)
The blanket *feels* warm and cozy. (linking verb)
Frank *smelled* the chemical fumes. (action verb)
The pie *smells* delicious. (linking verb)

[CHECKPOINT 4-1]

Identify Action and Linking Verbs

Underline the verbs in the following list. On the blank lines, write **A** if the verb is an action verb; write **L** if the verb is a linking verb.

trims	________	provides	________	am	________
very	________	printer	________	see	________
observed	________	was	________	sad	________
is	________	walks	________	rapidly	________
wallet	________	speak	________	draw	________

Main Verbs and Helping Verbs

Verbs that describe the primary action or state of being in a sentence and that can stand alone are called **main verbs.**

Daniel *applied* for a new position. (expresses action)
Laurie *is* in the Psychology 201 class. (expresses state of being)

In a verb phrase, the last verb is the main verb.

A **helping verb** may be used with a main verb to help complete the meaning. The combination of a main verb with one or more additional helping verbs is called a **verb phrase.**

Daniel *had applied* for a new position. (*Had* helps the action verb *applied*.)

Laurie *has been* in the Psychology 201 class for two weeks. (*Has* helps the linking verb *been*.)

Helping verbs indicate whether the action of the main verb will occur in the future or has occurred in the past.

Katrina *will deposit* her check. (future action)
Ralph *had closed* the account. (past action)

The following helping verbs are always the first verb in any verb phrase in which they are used:

will	can
would	could
shall	may
should	might
must	ought

Helping verbs sometimes are separated from related main verbs in a sentence, especially when a sentence asks a question.

Will Carlos *design* the new building? (The helping verb *will* is separated from the main verb *design*.)

Should charts and graphs *be included* in your visual aids? (The verb phrase *should be included* is separated by the complete subject *charts and graphs*.)

Helping verbs are sometimes separated from related main verbs in a sentence by adverbs, such as also.

Complete Application 4-2.

[CHECKPOINT 4-2]

Identify Main and Helping Verbs

Underline each main verb and place parentheses around each helping verb in the following sentences.

1. Colonel Hernandez had called for an appointment.
2. Will you attend the seminar?
3. Quong should have selected an alternate category.
4. You may play the second round with us.
5. The production manager has recommended more efficient techniques.

TENSES

Tenses are forms of a verb that indicate the *time* of an action or a state of being. Six verb tenses exist in the English language. These six tenses are divided into two groups: the **simple tenses** and the **perfect tenses.**

Simple Tenses

The three **simple tenses** are the *present tense*, the *past tense*, and the *future tense*.

Present tense does not require helping verbs.

PRESENT TENSE.

Present tense expresses an action occurring at the present time or an action occurring routinely.

> Terrance, please *scan* the pictures. (present time)
> Julia *commutes* to school. (present time)
> He *opens* the mail at 11:30 a.m. each day. (routine action)

Past tense does not require helping verbs.

PAST TENSE.

Past tense describes an action that has already taken place.

> Terrance *scanned* the pictures. (past time)
> Julia *commuted* to school. (past time)
> He *opened* his mail earlier today. (past time)

Regular verbs *follow a pattern for forming the different tenses.*

Form the past tense of most **regular verbs** by adding *d* or *ed* to the present form.

Present Tense	Past Tense
file	filed
mail	mailed
prepare	prepared

Rules for forming the past tense of regular verbs include the following:

1. When a one-syllable verb ends with a consonant preceded by a single short vowel, double the final consonant before adding *ed.*

Present Tense	Past Tense
ship	shipped
trim	trimmed
drop	dropped

2. When a two-syllable verb is accented on the *second* syllable and ends with a consonant, double the final consonant before adding *ed.*

Present Tense	Past Tense
occur	occurred
remit	remitted
equip	equipped

3. When a two-syllable verb is accented on the *first* syllable and ends with a consonant, do *not* double the final consonant before adding *ed.*

Present Tense	Past Tense
differ	differed
happen	happened
offer	offered

NOTE: The past tense of some words may be spelled two ways; if necessary, check the dictionary to confirm the preferred spelling.

Present Tense	Past Tense
label	labeled/labeled
total	totaled/totalled
travel	traveled/travelled

4. When verbs end with *y* preceded by a vowel, add *ed.*

Present Tense	Past Tense
obey	obeyed
employ	employed
survey	surveyed

5. When verbs end with *y* preceded by a consonant, change *y* to *i* and add *ed.*

Present Tense	Past Tense
copy	copied
cry	cried
study	studied

NOTE: The past tense of an **irregular verb** is not formed by adding *d* or *ed* to the present form. The past tense of irregular verbs may be formed in a number of ways.

Present Tense	Past Tense
do	did
choose	chose
buy	bought

Refer to page 65 for additional information on irregular verbs.

If you are in doubt about any irregular verb form, consult a dictionary. If the principal parts are not given, the verb is regular.

Use shall *instead of* will *in questions that have* I *or* we *as the subject.*

FUTURE TENSE. **Future tense** represents an action that will occur in the future. Use *will* with the main verb to form the future tense.

During the next class, Terrance *will scan* the pictures. (future time)
Julia *will commute* to school next term. (future time)
He *will open* his mail at 11:30 a.m. tomorrow. (future time)

[CHECKPOINT 4-3]

Identify the Simple Tenses

Underline the verb or verbs in each sentence. Write ***present***, ***past***, or ***future*** on the blank line to show when the action takes place.

1. Andres writes positive statements. ____________________

2. Sarah will copy the report. ____________________

3. My assistant completed the repairs. ____________________

4. The tourists climbed the hill. ____________________

5. I shall speak with Gladys and Kevin. ____________________

Complete Applications 4-3 and 4-4.

Complete Chapter 4 Web Exercise A at ***miller.swlearning.com.***

Perfect Tenses

The **perfect tenses** are the *present perfect*, the *past perfect*, and the *future perfect*. To understand how to form the perfect tenses, you must know the three principal parts of verbs.

The **three principal parts** of a verb are the *present*, *past*, and *past participle*. For regular verbs, the **past participle** is spelled the same as the past tense form.

Present Tense	Past Tense	Past Participle
forward	forwarded	forwarded
trade	traded	traded
study	studied	studied
purchase	purchased	purchased

Present Perfect Tense. The **present perfect tense** refers to an action completed recently or at some indefinite time in the past. The present perfect tense also may refer to an action that began in the past and is still continuing. Form the present perfect tense by using the helping verb *have* or *has* before the past participle of the main verb.

The perfect tenses describe in greater detail when an action is completed.

The perfect tenses require helping verbs.

PRESENT PERFECT TENSE

	Singular	Plural
1st person	I *have* walked	we *have* walked
2nd person	you *have* walked	you *have* walked
3rd person	he *has* walked she *has* walked it *has* walked	they *have* walked

Past Perfect Tense. The **past perfect tense** expresses an action that was completed at some specific time in the past or before some other event in the past. Form the past perfect tense by using the helping verb *had* before the past participle of the main verb.

PAST PERFECT TENSE

	Singular	Plural
1st person	I *had* walked	we *had* walked
2nd person	you *had* walked	you *had* walked
3rd person	he *had* walked she *had* walked it *had* walked	they *had* walked

Person *represents the viewpoint of the subject of a verb:* I/We *are first person;* you *is second person; and* he/she/it/they *are third person.*

Future Perfect Tense. The **future perfect tense** expresses action that is to be completed at some specific future time or before some other action takes place. Form the future perfect tense by using the helping verbs *will* and *have* before the past participle of the main verb.

The future perfect tense requires two helping verbs.

FUTURE PERFECT TENSE

	Singular	Plural
1st person	I *will have* walked	we *will have* walked
2nd person	you *will have* walked	you *will have* walked
3rd person	he *will have* walked she *will have* walked it *will have* walked	they *will have* walked

Identify the Perfect Tenses

Underline the main and helping verbs in each sentence. Write ***present perfect***, ***past perfect***, or ***future perfect*** on the blank line to show when the action takes place.

1. Virginia has exported the fragile items. ____________________
2. Ester will have planted the trees by March 10. ____________________
3. Ocean Blue Contractors had installed the pipes before the flood. ____________________
4. He has tested the sample many times. ____________________
5. Sonia had called before every visit. ____________________

Complete Application 4-5.

"Now, class, we will conjugate the verb 'moo.'"

Irregular Verbs

Irregular verbs form the past tense and past participle in ways other than adding *d* or *ed* to the present tense. The following list includes the present tense, past tense, and past participle of commonly used irregular verbs:

Complete Chapter 4 Web Exercise B at **miller.swlearning.com**.

Present Tense	Past Tense	Past Participle
be (am/is/are)	was/were	been
begin	began	begun
break	broke	broken
build	built	built
cost	cost	cost
do	did	done
drink	drank	drunk
give	gave	given
go	went	gone
have	had	had
know	knew	known
see	saw	seen
shine (glow)	shone	shone
swim	swam	swum

WORKPLACE CONNECTION

Since the past tense and past participle of irregular verbs do not follow a set pattern for spelling, you should memorize the spellings of irregular verbs that you frequently use.

[CHECKPOINT 4-5]

Select Correct Forms of Irregular Verbs

Underline the correct form of the irregular verb from those given in parentheses.

1. I (saw/seen) you yesterday in the bookstore.
2. Dave had never (swam/swum) in Lake Dawson.
3. Jacob has (did/done) all the baking for the reception.
4. Kelly (knew/knowed) all the answers.
5. Who has (drank/drunk) all the tea?
6. You (was/were) given two assignments.
7. Jed has (went/gone) to Columbia to visit friends.
8. Charles has (began/begun) dance lessons at Gulf Point.
9. They could not have (built/build) to code.
10. Rosa has (drawn/drawed) quilt patterns for the craft show.

Complete Application 4-6.

COMMONLY CONFUSED VERBS

Three pairs of irregular verbs are confused so frequently that they require special attention. *Lay*, *set*, and *raise* need objects to complete their meanings. *Lie*, *sit*, and *rise* do not require objects.

LIE/LAY. *To lie* means to recline or to lie down. Review the three principal parts of the verb *lie*.

Present	Past	Past Participle
lie	lay	lain

Present: The cat *lies* by the fireplace.
Past: The cat *lay* by the fireplace yesterday.
Present perfect: The cat *has lain* by the fireplace.

To lay means to put something down or to place an object in a specified position. Review the three principal parts of the verb *lay*.

Note that the present tense of lay *has the same spelling as the past tense of* lie.

Present	Past	Past Participle
lay	laid	laid

Present: Mr. Whedon, please *lay* the book on the desk.
Past: Mr. Whedon *laid* the book on the desk.
Present perfect: Mr. Whedon *has laid* the book on the desk.

To lay *or* to set *means "to place" or "to put." Both verbs take an object.*

SIT/SET. *To sit* means to sit down, to have a seat, or to remain in place. Review the principal parts of the verb *sit*.

Present	Past	Past Participle
sit	sat	sat

Present: She *sits* in the park and watches the birds.
Past: She *sat* in the park and watched the birds.
Present perfect: She *has sat* in the park and watched the birds.

To set means to place or put something in position. Review the principal parts of the verb *set*.

Present	Past	Past Participle
set	set	set

Present: You may *set* the pitcher on the counter.
Past: An hour ago, you *set* the pitcher here.
Present perfect: You *have set* the pitcher on the counter.

RISE/RAISE. *To rise* means to get up from a lying or sitting position or to ascend. Review the three principal parts of the verb *rise.*

Present	Past	Past Participle
rise	rose	risen

Present:	He *rises* from the sofa when Sara enters.
Past:	He *rose* from the sofa when Sara entered.
Present perfect:	He *has risen* from the sofa to greet Sara.

To raise means to move something to a higher position, to lift an object, or to increase the value of something. Review the three principal parts of the verb *raise.*

Present	Past	Past Participle
raise	raised	raised

Present:	Danielle, please *raise* the window.
Past:	Danielle *raised* the window.
Present perfect:	Danielle *has raised* the window.

To raise means "to move," "to lift," or "to increase value." This verb always takes an object.

Complete Chapter 4 Web Exercise C at ***miller.swlearning.com.***

Complete Application 4-7.

[CHECKPOINT 4-6]

Distinguish Between Pairs of Commonly Confused Verbs

Underline the correct commonly confused verb from those given in parentheses.

1. The workers will (lay/lie) the carpet when the shipment arrives.
2. She (set/sat) at the back of the auditorium.
3. Evelyn, please (sat/set) the vase on the second shelf.
4. The official flag has been (risen/raised).
5. Justin (sat/set) there yesterday.
6. Martha has (lain/laid) down for a few hours.
7. Aaron (rose/raised) the blinds before sunrise.

VOICE

In addition to having tenses, verbs also have voices. A verb may be in the active voice or the passive voice.

Active Voice

Active voice means that the subject performs the action. Using the active voice helps you express thoughts more directly, forcefully, and concisely.

> *Ben washes* the car. (The subject *Ben* performs the action of washing the car.)
>
> The young *pianist has played* the old piano. (The subject *pianist* has performed the action of playing the piano.)

The passive voice may sound more diplomatic or tactful than the active voice when you must write a negative message.

Passive Voice

Passive voice means that the subject receives the action. The passive voice combines the past participle of a main verb with an appropriate form of the helping verb *to be*. Using the passive voice is appropriate when you want to avoid an accusatory tone or to express sympathy. Passive voice constructions often emphasize the result of an action, place an emphasis on the receiver, or indicate that the doer is unknown or unimportant.

Complete Subject	**Helping Verb Form of *To Be***	**Past Participle of Main Verb**	**Phrase**
The keyboard	was	damaged	by humidity.
Those tests	were	written	by Dr. Adams.
I	am	entertained	by the game.
Tabatha	is	employed	by Jaco Inc.

You can change any passive voice sentence into an active voice sentence by making the subject perform the action rather than receive the action. The sentences above are changed into the active voice in the following examples:

> The humidity damaged the keyboard.
> Dr. Adams wrote those tests.
> The game entertains me.
> Jaco Inc. employs Tabatha.

[Checkpoint 4-7]

Identify Active and Passive Voice

Underline each main verb and place parentheses around each helping verb in the following sentences. On the blank line next to the sentence, write **A** if the verb is in the active voice; or write **P** if the verb is in the passive voice.

1. You have created a lovely bracelet. ____________
2. Marjorie had proofread and edited the copy by 11:30 a.m. ____________
3. The report was bound by Kimberly. ____________
4. The text was published by the new company. ____________
5. The anesthesiologist had been certified by the board. ____________
6. Luis and Gina have leased an air compressor. ____________
7. The site has listed cruises to Alaska and Mexico. ____________
8. Sympathy notes were mailed to the family members by Jessica. ____________
9. Raymond has contracted for telecommunication service from Arco. ____________
10. The stadium was cleaned by the SGA members. ____________

VERBALS

Verbals are verb forms that are used as nouns, adjectives, and adverbs.

> *Writing* the report took several hours. (verbal used as noun)
> He left *to go* home. (verbal used as adverb)
> The letter had three *misspelled* words. (verbal used as adjective)

Three kinds of verbals exist. **Gerunds** are verb forms ending in *-ing* and are used as nouns. **Infinitives** consist of *to* plus a verb form and are used as nouns, adjectives, or adverbs. **Participles** are verb forms ending in *ing*, *ed*, *en*, *d*, or *t* that are used as adjectives. Verbals can be combined with other words to form verbal phrases. You will learn about verbal phrases in Chapter 9, pages 146–147.

Complete Application 4-8.

Chapter Summary

- Prepare clear, correct messages by choosing action verbs to describe both physical and mental actions and by using linking verbs to connect subjects to other words or phrases.
- Select main verbs to describe the primary action or state of being in a sentence; select helping verbs to help complete the meaning of the main verb.
- Use simple tenses to indicate that an action is current, has occurred in the past, or will occur in the future.
- Use the present perfect tense to indicate an action that was completed recently or at some indefinite time in the past or that began in the past and is still continuing.
- Use the past perfect tense to indicate an action that was completed at some specific time in the past or before some other past event.
- Use the future perfect tense to indicate an action to be completed at some specific future time or before some other action takes place.
- Memorize the forms of irregular verbs or locate the spellings in a dictionary because the past tense and past participle of irregular verbs do not follow a set pattern.
- Give special attention to sets of verbs commonly confused in the English language.
- Choose the active voice to compose direct, forceful, and concise sentences; however, select the passive voice to avoid an accusatory tone or to express sympathy.

Complete the Chapter 4 Review.

Complete the Chapter 4 iLrn Activities at **miller.swlearning. com.**

APPLICATION 4-1

Action Verbs and Linking Verbs

Underline the verb in each of the following sentences. On the blank line next to the sentence, write **A** if the verb is an action verb or **L** if the verb is a linking verb.

0. The children's first day was September 6. L
1. Ms. Morales opened a new child care center in Memphis. ______
2. Arthur Townsend designed the facility. ______
3. The facility contains indoor and outdoor play areas. ______
4. The child care center was completed in August. ______
5. Experts polished the wooden floors. ______
6. The director of the center is Hilda Morales. ______
7. Ms. Morales interviewed ten assistants. ______
8. Eight assistants accepted employment. ______
9. Juanita Martinez is the lead teacher. ______
10. Ms. Morales purchased all the latest toys. ______
11. She bought new computers for each center. ______
12. She also ordered three digital cameras. ______
13. Nova Gourmet stocked the pantry with healthy, nutritious foods. ______
14. The mushrooms from Daley's Produce Company were fresh and white. ______
15. A professional event planner outlined the budget for the charity auction. ______
16. Twenty-six parents attended the fundraising event. ______
17. The men removed their hats inside the building. ______
18. The cookies always smell delicious. ______
19. Later, the children sang several songs. ______
20. The children were polite and attentive. ______

Application 4-2

Main Verbs and Helping Verbs

Place parentheses around each helping verb and underline each main verb in the following sentences.

0. Jeff (will) plant new trees tomorrow.
1. They have applied for a trademark.
2. The software upgrade will enable you to complete the task.
3. Canoeing has increased in popularity since July.
4. Has the kennel opened since the storms?
5. Ginger may take a taxi to the hotel.
6. Serge's salon will offer facials and manicures.
7. Could the baker make key lime cake?
8. Has Yoko shipped the package?
9. Have you removed any coral?
10. Everyone should stop at the crosswalk.
11. Yang Sheng has written an article for the current issue.
12. Speedway Delivery has always provided great service for us.
13. You could serve as an officer in the art club.
14. Have we attended either meeting?
15. The mariachis have serenaded Glenda three times this season.
16. Marcia had explained the problem before the class began.
17. With your help, Lydia may finish on time.
18. Mr. Delgado will meet you at the airport.
19. A famous artist has placed thousands of umbrellas in the building.
20. Sandy's orchids have won the competition.

APPLICATION 4-3

Simple Tenses

Underline the verb or verbs in each sentence. Write **present**, **past**, or **future** on the blank line to show when the action occurs.

0. Martha stirred the broth yesterday. ______past______
1. My company will haul the large stone blocks to the construction site. ________________
2. Petra seems happy about the results. ________________
3. Cleveland Scrap and Steel Company also will recycle scrap metal. ________________
4. Technoglass Corporation usually gives lower bids. ________________
5. Dave and Emilio caught more than 20 fish. ________________
6. The correct combination will open the locks. ________________
7. Peter found an excellent selection of pottery. ________________
8. The magic show begins at 7:30 p.m. ________________
9. Pest control services fumigated the building. ________________
10. Goro's new car looks great! ________________
11. Sheila sent the money by wire transfer yesterday. ________________
12. You agreed with me. ________________
13. What time will the home inspector arrive? ________________
14. The attorney starts work at 8:30 a.m. every day. ________________
15. Last week Heather called me about the exchange rate. ________________
16. Dr. Turnage will prescribe the required medication. ________________
17. The Milton Clinic treated my injuries after the accident. ________________
18. You parked too close to the yellow line. ________________
19. Cheryl works every Saturday. ________________
20. Advertisers in the New Horizon publications target senior citizens. ________________

APPLICATION 4-4

Simple Tenses

Write the correct verb form in each of the following sentences. The verbs are given in the first column, and the required tenses are given in the second column.

Verb	Tense	
0. wash	past	Sylvia ___washed___ her clothes at the launderette.
1. drive	present	Hugh ________________ a used car.
2. rescue	past	A neighbor ________________ the lost dog.
3. select	present	Who ________________ the next candidate?
4. repair	past	Paul ________________ the alarm system.
5. train	present	Her company ________________ people in how to cope with the media.
6. wait	past	The staff ________________ for the president to arrive.
7. listen	future	The members ________________ to the new music.
8. copy	past	Lynne ________________ the recipe from the magazine.
9. build	present	Can they ________________ a new stadium before the tournament?
10. cover	past	The production staff ________________ the exhibits with tents.
11. offer	past	You ________________ to assist me.
12. heat	future	Rosiland ________________ the chemicals in the lab.
13. replay	past	The team ________________ the game film.
14. break	present	Please do not ________________ the seals on the containers.
15. transmit	past	Did you receive the message that I ________________ yesterday?
16. request	past	Benjamin ________________ a receipt.
17. rent	future	Stephanie ________________ a car when she goes to Chicago.
18. deliver	present	Ricky ________________ packages in his truck.
19. forward	past	The postal official ________________ the mail.
20. prepare	future	Chef Lee ________________ the frosting for the chocolate cake.

APPLICATION 4-5

Perfect Tenses

Underline the main and helping verbs in each sentence. On the blank line, write **present perfect**, **past perfect**, or **future perfect** to show when the action occurs.

0. He will have finished the renovation before next year. future perfect
1. The mayor has ordered seafood for the holiday. ______
2. The studio director had developed new policies before he resigned. ______
3. The fuel tank had exploded twice before today. ______
4. Six clubs and restaurants have opened this year. ______
5. Prior to 1973, only private boats had reached the island. ______
6. The scientist had identified the gene in 1986. ______
7. The doctor will have completed the surgery by noon. ______
8. In the past decade, video frequently has replaced still photography. ______
9. The statistics will have altered the next campaign plans. ______
10. Marie had informed us of her decision on June 12. ______
11. Rosa has ordered many items from this catalog. ______
12. The desserts had disappeared before the guests arrived. ______
13. They will have reviewed all the problems before the test date. ______
14. Kim has sorted the first shipment of the season. ______
15. From June to August, gas prices had increased by seven cents. ______
16. The Parkers will have moved into their new home by January 1. ______
17. Had you driven Route 66 before your last vacation? ______
18. The board has amended the building code for the city park. ______
19. Samuel will have changed his travel plans before he leaves. ______
20. Before obtaining estimates, he had calculated the repair cost. ______

Application 4-6

Irregular Verbs

Underline the correct form of the irregular verbs in the following sentences.

0. Randy (throwed/threw) that ball through the window.
1. Has anyone (went/gone) to the new theme park in Orlando?
2. We had (driven/drove) all the way to Chicago.
3. Olivia (drank/drunk) two glasses of orange juice.
4. By the time you arrive, I will have (ate/eaten) my lunch.
5. Fort Apache, also known as Bill's workshop, had been (built/build) over many years.
6. The judge (swore/sweared) in the new president.
7. Drew boasts that he (throwed/threw) the shot put in the Olympics.
8. Nobody had (saw/seen) him walk down the stairs.
9. The most important part is that you will have (did/done) your best.
10. The balloons (bursted/burst) when the pine needles hit them.
11. The magazine had (ran/run) the ad for six months.
12. Will Celia have (forgot/forgotten) the clue by Monday?
13. Who has (selled/sold) the most raffle tickets?
14. Keiko had (grown/growed) two inches before she moved.
15. I (shook/shaked) the manager's hand.
16. Rosemary has (began/begun) the assignment.
17. They will have (came/come) to visit before June.
18. The train whistle had (blowed/blown) before the wreck.
19. Jean will have (hung/hanged) the plaque by tomorrow.
20. Sunita has (teached/taught) in Atlanta for 25 years.

Application 4-7

Commonly Confused Verbs

Underline the correct verb from the choices given in parentheses.

0. Which goose (lay/laid) this golden egg?
1. Victor, please (raise/rise) your side of the box.
2. The florist (sat/set) the arrangements on the tables.
3. Steam (rose/raised) from the hot pavement.
4. Mrs. Lopez, please (set/sit) the packages on the counter.
5. You should (lie/lay) all the boxes in rows on the floor.
6. Balloons (rise/raise) with the breeze.
7. Would you like to (sit/set) with me during the ceremony?
8. Do you know how long Pratrap has (sat/set) there?
9. Pluto (lies/lays) at the edge of the solar system.
10. During the second game, Lucia (set/sat) on the bench.
11. The nurse said, "Please (lay/lie) on the examining table."
12. The bank has (raised/risen) my credit limit.
13. You may (set/sit) the cookies on the serving cart.
14. The orchestra members (raised/rose) and bowed.
15. They have (sat/set) their luggage on the carousel.
16. Who (laid/lay) their clothes on the steps?
17. People often (sit/set) in the park and eat their noon meal.
18. At the end of the show, the façade of the house will have (raised/risen) from the stage.
19. Carolyn and I (sat/set) in the balcony area.
20. Have you (lain/laid) the boxes in the proper places?

APPLICATION 4-8

Voice

Part A. In the space provided, rewrite the following sentences and change the active voice to the passive voice.

1. Roberta painted the designs on the boats.

2. David taught the drama class.

3. Mercury Insurance Company covered the additional expenses.

4. Marshall Worley controlled the lighting.

5. The caterer provided extra plates.

Part B. In the space provided, rewrite the following sentences and change the passive voice to the active voice.

1. Our neighbor's fence was crushed by a falling tree.

2. The performances were directed by Graham.

3. The concrete was mixed by Maxwell Truck Lines.

4. The assigned project was completed by only three students.

5. Carol was given the highest rating by the critics.

Chapter 4 Review

Verbs

Part A. Identify Action vs. Linking Verbs

Underline each verb in the following sentences. On the blank line next to the sentence, write **A** if the verb is an action verb or **L** if the verb is a linking verb. Each correct sentence is worth two points.

1. Setting goals is a great way to achieve results. ________________
2. Many people go through life without a plan. ________________
3. Real goals require sacrifice. ________________
4. Commitment also is necessary. ________________
5. Goals provide a challenge. ________________
6. A wish is an unwritten goal. ________________
7. First, determine your goals. ________________
8. Write your goals on a piece of paper. ________________
9. Develop a strategy for achieving the goals. ________________
10. Regularly review your goals. ________________

Part B. Identify Helping and Main Verbs

Place parentheses around each helping verb and underline each main verb in the following sentences. Each correctly identified verb phrase is worth two points.

1. Goals have guided Ken's choices.
2. Ken has set very high goals
3. He can reach these goals.
4. He has developed a workable strategy.
5. Ken has adjusted his goals based on current statistics.
6. Have you recorded your goals?
7. You should maintain a balance between long-term and short-term goals.
8. Achieving short-term goals will reinforce your commitment to long-term goals.
9. Negative people and negative thoughts can knock you off track.
10. Have you focused on your goals for a few moments today?

Part C. Identify Tenses

Write **present**, **past**, **future**, **present perfect**, **past perfect**, or **future perfect** on the blank line to show when the action takes place. Each correctly identified tense is worth two points.

1. Nancy has worked too long for Fordyce Testing Corporation. ____________________
2. She has held the same job for five years. ____________________
3. She needs a challenge. ____________________
4. Nancy established specific goals, time lines, and strategies. ____________________
5. Nancy updates her goals according to new information. ____________________
6. Every day she checks her progress. ____________________
7. Recently, Nancy found that she had veered from her plan. ____________________
8. Goals have prepared Nancy for a different career path. ____________________
9. She will complete the final task next week. ____________________
10. She will have achieved her goal by the end of the year. ____________________

Part D. Choose the Correct Verb

Underline the correct verb from the choices given in parentheses. Each correctly underlined verb is worth four points.

1. When Tracy saw the package, she (flung/flinged) open the cover.
2. Zachary wants to (rise/raise) funds from venture capitalists.
3. For his ongoing support and loyalty, we (chose/chosed) Brian for the annual award.
4. The EMTs had (went/gone) from the emergency room.
5. Will Barbara continue (sitting/setting) in the same yoga position?
6. When I arrived, she had already (went/gone).
7. Linden (knew/knowed) better than to ask us about sharing our meals.
8. Mr. Leach will (sit/set) in the director's chair.
9. The number of items on the list has now (growed/grown) to more than ten.
10. Please (lay/lie) the list of objectives next to the file.

Subject–Verb Agreement

CHAPTER 5

Some rules of grammar shift every generation or so, but you can bet the bank that this one will never change: Subject and verb must agree.

—Patricia T. O'Conner
From *Woe Is I: The Grammarphobe's Guide to Better English in Plain English* (2003)

If I were older—or *If I was older*? *The jury is* (or *are?*) *deliberating*. Subjects and verbs must agree to communicate your ideas. This chapter explains subject-verb agreement and answers common questions like these.

Learning Objectives

- Use correct subject-verb agreement for singular and plural subjects.
- Choose the correct form of the *to have* verb.
- Choose the correct form of the *to be* verb.
- Select the correct verb for subjects joined by connecting words.
- Select the correct verb when subjects are separated from verbs.
- Select the correct verb when indefinite pronouns are subjects.
- Select the correct verb when collective nouns are subjects.

SINGULAR AND PLURAL SUBJECTS

The subject and the verb must agree in **person** (first, second, or third person) and **number** (singular or plural). A **singular subject** refers to one person, place, thing, concept, quality, or event. A **plural subject** refers to more than one person, place, thing, concept, quality, or event. A singular subject requires a singular verb. A plural subject needs a plural verb.

Pronoun Subjects

The following examples illustrate *subject–verb* agreement in both person and number when pronouns are the subjects.

> I *play* on the Stingray soccer team. (first person/singular)
>
> You *play* on the Stingray soccer team. (second person/singular)
>
> He *plays* on the Stingray soccer team. (third person/singular)
>
> We *play* on the Stingray soccer team. (first person/plural)
>
> You *play* on the Stingray soccer team. (second person/plural)
>
> They *play* on the Stingray soccer team. (third person/plural)

Plural nouns usually end in s or es, but a plural verb does not end with s.

Noun Subjects

The following examples illustrate *subject–verb* agreement when either a singular or a plural noun is the subject.

> The *train arrives* at 9 a.m. (singular subject and verb)
> The *trains arrive* at 9 a.m. (plural subject and verb)
> The *girl lives* at 1149 Oak Avenue. (singular subject and verb)
> The *girls live* at 1149 Oak Avenue. (plural subject and verb)

Note from the examples that although most singular nouns do not end in *s*, these nouns agree with singular verbs that do end in *s*. However, some singular nouns are unusual and do end with *s* (for example, *news*, *mathematics*, *electronics*, *measles*, *mumps*, *physics*, and *economics*). Keep in mind that these singular nouns still require a singular verb.

> The *news appears* on three local networks.
> *Mathematics requires* you to think logically.

Some other words that end with *s* (for example, *earnings*, *savings*, *scissors*, *pants*, *pliers*, and *tactics*) are always used as plurals, and they take a plural verb.

> Her *earnings show* a steady gain.
> The *scissors cost* $12.95.

[Checkpoint 5-1]

Choose Correct Verbs for Subjects

Underline the correct verb from those given in parentheses.

1. You (play/plays) with the city jazz band.

2. The doctor (work/works) in the clinic at 110 Langley Avenue.

3. The pants (wrinkle/wrinkles) when you sit.

4. We (perform/performs) in the 3 p.m. matinee.

5. I (approve/approves) your recommendation.

VERB FORMS

Verbs have singular and plural forms. Change most plural verbs to singular verbs by adding *s*.

Plural	Singular
set	sets
work	works
plan	plans

Change most plural verbs that end in *y* to singular verbs by dropping the *y* and adding *ies*.

Plural	Singular
fly	flies
amplify	amplifies
carry	carries

Some verbs, including *to have* and *to be*, change forms to agree with the subject in person and number.

WORKPLACE CONNECTION

If in doubt, consult a dictionary for the plural form; never rely solely on spelling or grammar checkers.

The Verb *To Have*

The chart below shows how the verb *to have* changes form. Notice *to have* has special singular forms only in the present tense.

The verb to have *may be used as a main or a helping verb.*

***TO HAVE* SINGULAR FORMS**

	Present	Past	Future
1st person	I *have*	I *had*	I *will have*
2nd person	you *have*	you *had*	you *will have*
3rd person	he *has*	he *had*	he *will have*
	she *has*	she *had*	she *will have*
	it *has*	it *had*	it *will have*

***TO HAVE* PLURAL FORMS**

	Present	Past	Future
1st person	we *have*	we *had*	we *will have*
2nd person	you *have*	you *had*	you *will have*
3rd person	they *have*	they *had*	they *will have*

Always use the plural verb form when the subject is you.

You have selected the best ingredients. (Subject *you*, singular or plural, requires plural verb *have selected*.)

Cheng has the original recipe. (Singular subject *Cheng* requires singular verb *has*.)

She has cooked for 12 years. (Singular subject *she* requires singular verb *has*.)

They have three convection ovens. (Plural subject *they* requires plural verb *have*.)

The culinary *students have* similar career goals. (Plural subject *students* requires plural verb *have*.)

[CHECKPOINT 5-2]

Choose *Have* or *Has*

Underline the correct verb from those given in parentheses.

1. You (has/have) many opportunities to advance in that career field.
2. Ramon (has/have) completed the aptitude tests.
3. (Has/Have) they made any career plans?
4. She (has/have) changed careers three times.
5. I (has/have) recommended the career DVD to my students.

The verb to be has more forms than any other verb and may be used as a main or helping verb.

The Verb *To Be*

The chart below and on the next page shows how the verb *to be* changes form. Notice *to be* has special singular forms in the present and past tenses.

***TO BE* SINGULAR FORMS**

	Present	**Past**	**Future**
1st person	I *am*	I *was*	I *will be*
2nd person	you *are*	you *were*	you *will be*
3rd person	he *is*	he *was*	he *will be*
	she *is*	she *was*	she *will be*
	it *is*	it *was*	it *will be*

TO BE PLURAL FORMS

	Present	Past	Future
1st person	we *are*	we *were*	we *will be*
2nd person	you *are*	you *were*	you *will be*
3rd person	they *are*	they *were*	they *will be*

I am excited about your receiving a promotion. (Singular subject *I* requires singular verb *am* for present tense.)

You are in the ICU at Faulkner Hospital. (Subject *you*, singular or plural, requires plural verb *are* for present tense.)

They were guests in my home last month. (Plural subject *they* requires plural verb *were* for past tense.)

She is studying at the Nobles Book Nook today. (Singular subject *she* requires singular verb *is studying* for present tense.)

Contrary-to-Fact Condition

When you want to express a condition that is not true (contrary to fact) and will probably never be true, use *were* with all subjects, singular or plural. Contrary-to-fact sentences express wishes or opinions. They usually begin with *if* or contain *as if*, *as*, or *as though*.

If *I were* our representative, I would vote for the price increase. (singular subject *I*, plural verb *were*)

If Mr. Gorbea *were* here, he would assist you. (singular subject *Mr. Gorbea*, plural verb *were*)

She behaves as if *she were* a princess. (singular subject *she*, plural verb *were*)

If *they were* present, we could vote. (plural subject *they*, plural verb *were*)

"*If the world were perfect, it wouldn't be.*"

-Yogi Berra Baseball Hall of Fame catcher (1947)

Complete Application 5-1.

[Checkpoint 5-3]

Choose the Correct Form of *To Be*

Underline the correct form of the verb from those given in parentheses.

1. I (am/is) on time for the rehearsal.
2. (Was/Were) you present for the award ceremony?
3. If Hugh (was/were) musically gifted, he would compete in the talent show.
4. They (is/are) in favor of the waste management plan.
5. The nursing program director (was/were) absent from the meeting.

SUBJECTS JOINED BY CONNECTING WORDS

Often a verb has only one subject. Sometimes, however, when two or more subjects perform the same action or share the same description, you join the subjects together as a **compound subject** (two or more subjects) to share one verb.

Ralph swims in the community pool. (one subject, *Ralph*; one verb, *swims*)

Dorothy exercises at the new fitness center. (one subject, *Dorothy*; one verb, *exercises*)

Marcus and *Carlos own* exercise equipment. (two subjects, *Marcus* and *Carlos*; one verb, *own*)

Betsy is a science teacher. (one subject, *Betsy*; one verb, *is*)

Patrick is a science teacher. (one subject, *Patrick*; one verb, *is*)

Betsy and *Patrick are* science teachers. (two subjects, *Betsy* and *Patrick*; one verb, *are*)

Subjects Joined by *And*

When a compound subject is joined by *and*, the compound subject usually requires a plural verb.

Males and females exercise at the YMCA.
Roger and Mitchell hike the mountain trails each year.
Garvin and Eryn have asked others to join them in the marathon.
Teachers, students, and parents are on the list.

When a compound subject joined by *and* means the same person, place, thing, concept, quality, or event, or when a compound subject is considered to be one unit, use a singular verb.

The *manager and director is* Mr. Snead. (one person)
Ice cream and cake was the dessert. (one unit)

When *each* or *every* precedes a compound subject joined by *and*, use a singular verb.

Each painting, photograph, and sculpture was tagged and numbered.
Every player and coach shakes hands with the opposing team.

Subjects Joined by *Or, Either . . . Or, Neither . . . Nor,* or *Not Only . . . But Also*

When a compound subject consists of singular subjects joined by *or; either . . . or; neither . . . nor,* or *not only . . . but also,* use a singular verb.

> An *aunt or* his *grandmother writes* him a letter every week.
> *Either Grace or Melissa was* the solo violinist.
> *Neither John nor Doyle buys* produce from the Richo Market.
> *Not only Raymond but also Rosiland needs* your support.

When a compound subject consists of plural subjects joined by *or; either . . . or; neither . . . nor,* or *not only . . . but also,* use a plural verb.

> Your *data or* my *reports have* errors.
> *Either* current *students or alumni receive* the monthly bulletins.
> *Neither* the *winners nor* the *losers were recognized* in the paper.
> *Not only newspapers but also journals were* on the printout.

When a compound subject includes both singular and plural subjects joined by *or; either . . . or; neither . . . nor,* or *not only . . . but also,* use the verb form that agrees with the subject nearest the verb. Typically, place the plural subject nearest the verb for ease of reading.

> The *violin or* the *flutes are* out of tune.
> *Either* the *conductor or* the *musicians select* the encore music.
> *Neither* the *drummer nor* the trumpet *players follow* the conductor.
> *Not only* the *director but also* the sound *technicians were* late.

WORKPLACE CONNECTION

Maintain a professional image by applying subject–verb agreement guidelines in both spoken and written communications.

Complete Application 5-2.

[CHECKPOINT 5-4]

Select the Correct Verb

Underline the correct verb from those given in parentheses.

1. Either a cello or a bass (play/plays) in the bass clef.
2. Either the trumpets or the flugelhorns (carries/carry) the lead brass line.
3. Neither the conductor nor the violinists (is/are) familiar with the concerto.
4. Not only the audience but also the musicians (applaud/applauds) the guest performer.
5. The violin or the flutes (is/are) out of tune.

SUBJECT–VERB SEPARATION

You will learn about phrases and clauses in Chapter 9.

Sentences sometimes include other words that come between the subject and the verb. These intervening phrases and clauses can make recognizing the subject, and choosing the verb form that agrees with the subject, difficult.

In order to find the subject in sentences like these, first locate the verb. Then ask yourself who or what is performing the action in the verb. The answer is the subject. When you have identified the verb and the subject, make certain that they agree in person and number.

> Pensacola, as well as Biloxi and Galveston, is on the Gulf of Mexico.
>
> *Verb*: is
> *What is*? Pensacola
>
> The subject is *Pensacola*; *as well as Biloxi and Galveston* is an intervening phrase. (A singular subject requires a singular verb.)
>
> The parks in the county are under a different maintenance contract.
>
> *Verb*: are
> *What are*? parks
>
> The subject is *parks*; *in the county* describes parks. (A plural subject requires a plural verb.)

In the first example above, the intervening phrase is bracketed by commas. Intervening phrases and clauses sometimes have commas and sometimes not. In either case, another way to tell the true subject of a sentence with extra words is to take them out mentally and read the sentence.

> The display ad on our website attracts many customers.
>
> Take out the prepositional phrase *on our website* and read:
>
> The display ad attracts many customers.
>
> The subject is *ad*, and the verb is *attracts*. (A singular subject requires a singular verb.)

In sentences beginning with *there* or *here*, the true subject of the sentence follows the verb. *Here* or *there* is never the subject. To find the subject, locate the verb and ask yourself who or what is performing the action in the verb.

> Here are two books on snow skiing, one of my favorite sports.
>
> *Verb*: are
> *What are*? books are
>
> The subject is *books*. (A plural subject requires a plural verb.)

[CHECKPOINT 5-5]

Match Subjects with Verbs

Place parentheses around the subject and underline the correct verb from those given in parentheses.

1. Wolves, when they run in a pack, (attack/attacks) larger animals.
2. Water from the treatment plants (spill/spills) into the bay.
3. Tires in a landfill (do/does) not stay buried.
4. The air quality index, as well as the ozone level, (is/are) important.
5. Oxygen for people with bronchitis (come/comes) in two-liter containers.

INDEFINITE PRONOUN SUBJECTS

Complete Application 5-3.

Some indefinite pronouns are always singular, some are always plural, and some may be singular or plural depending on their use. When a pronoun is the subject, remember to ignore any phrases and clauses that come between the pronoun and its verb. One exception is explained on page 90.

Always Singular

The following indefinite pronouns are always singular and require a singular verb:

another	one	anybody	anything
each	anyone	everybody	everything
either	everyone	nobody	nothing
neither	no one	somebody	something
other	someone	much	

Each of the paintings *is* worth $750. (*each is*, NOT *paintings are*)

Neither of the guides *knows* the language. (*neither knows*, NOT *guides know*)

When the train wrecked, *everything was* destroyed on the flatcars. (The singular pronoun *everything* requires the singular verb *was*.)

Everybody has received updated computer systems. (The singular pronoun *everybody* requires the singular verb *has*.)

Always Plural

The following indefinite pronouns are always plural and require plural verbs: *both*, *few*, *many*, *others*, and *several*.

Both of the trees *were uprooted* during the storm.
Several of the homeowners *attend* the storm preparedness meetings.
Many arrive early.

Singular indefinite pronouns describe part of a whole. Plural indefinite pronouns refer to many individual units.

Usage-Dependent

The indefinite pronouns *all*, *any*, *none*, *some*, *more*, and *most* may be singular or plural.

When these pronouns are singular, they describe *how much* and require singular verbs.

All of the sand *was blown* across the road. (*How much* sand? *All.*)

None of the debris *meets* the FEMA removal guidelines. (*How much* debris? *None.*)

When these pronouns are plural, they describe *how many* and require plural verbs.

All of the hotels on De Luna Drive *were* destroyed. (*How many* hotels? *All.*)

None of the power lines *were* down. (*How many* power lines? *None.*)

Complete Application 5-4.

When an *of* phrase follows one of these pronouns, the noun in that phrase determines whether the verb is singular or plural.

[Checkpoint 5-6]

Match Indefinite Pronouns with Verbs

Place parentheses around the subject and underline the correct verb from those given in parentheses.

1. Most of the students (use/uses) backpacks with wheels.
2. A few of the oranges (is/are) ready to be picked.
3. Everybody (buy/buys) snacks in the Oregon Grill.
4. All of the cherry pie (was/were) eaten at the banquet.
5. None of my prescriptions (has/have) been filled.

COLLECTIVE NOUN SUBJECTS

Collective nouns are terms that represent a group of persons, places, things, concepts, qualities, or events. Examples of collective nouns are *committee*, *company*, *faculty*, *group*, *family*, *team*, and *school*.

When the group acts as one unit, the collective noun requires a singular verb.

The *trio performs* every Saturday night. (The singular verb *performs* is used because the trio acts as a unit.)

The *company donates* large sums of money to charitable organizations. (The singular verb *donates* is used because the company acts as a unit.)

When the members of a group act as individuals, the collective noun requires a plural verb.

The *faculty are* writing their final reports. (The plural verb *are* is used because the faculty members act as individuals, writing separate reports.)

The basketball *team were* signing new endorsement contracts. (The plural verb *were* is used because the team members act as individuals, signing separate contracts.)

Organizational names, such as *Standard & Poor's*, may be singular or plural. If the organization is referred to as *they* or *who*, use a plural verb. With *it* or *which*, use a singular verb.

Complete the Chapter 5 Web Exercise at ***miller.swlearning.com.***

Complete Application 5-5.

[CHECKPOINT 5-7]

Match Collective Nouns with Verbs

Underline the correct verb from those given in parentheses.

1. The young crew (is/are) on its third mission.
2. The Harris family (travel/travels) to Washington each year.
3. After each performance, the audience (score/scores) the contestants on separate ballots.
4. The Coastal Waters Council (select/selects) grant winners.
5. The squadron (was/were) putting on camouflage suits.

CHAPTER SUMMARY

- Choose verbs that match the subject in person and number to communicate correct, clear messages.
- Follow rules for making verbs singular and plural.
- Recognize and use the correct forms for the irregular verbs *to have* and *to be*.
- Use a plural verb with most compound subjects.
- Use a singular verb for singular subjects and a plural verb for plural subjects joined by *or*, *either . . . or*, *neither . . . nor*, or *not only. . . but also*.
- When *or*, *either . . . or*, *neither . . . nor*, or *not only . . . but also* join singular and plural subjects, make the verb agree with the nearest subject. Whenever possible, put the plural subject nearest the verb for ease of reading.
- In choosing the correct verb, ignore any phrases and clauses that come between the subject and the verb, and find the true subject.
- Match singular indefinite pronouns with singular verbs and plural indefinite pronouns with plural verbs.
- When the indefinite pronouns *all*, *any*, *none*, *some*, *more*, and *most* describe *how much*, use a singular verb. If the pronoun describes *how many*, use a plural verb.
- When the group described by a collective noun acts as a unit, use a singular verb. When the members act as individuals, use a plural verb.

Complete the Chapter 5 Review.

ILrn Complete the Chapter 5 iLrn Activities at **miller.swlearning. com**.

APPLICATION 5-1

Simple Subject–Verb Agreement

Part A. Underline the verbs in the paragraphs. If a subject and verb do not agree, write the correction above the verb. Do not underline infinitives.

write
0. They writes neatly on the application.

Employment applications is like an expanded version of your resume. When you goes to apply for a job, be sure to bring all the information you will need to complete an application. Besides your resume, you should have a list of references and detailed information about any jobs you has held, including supervisors' names and phone numbers. A thesaurus is a valuable tool. Also brings two black-ink pens that you are sure do not blot when you write.

Read through the application once carefully before you begins. Determine what kind of information the application require. Employers often check information in applications, so the application reveal when you are truthful. Applications also show your education and experience.

Most often, job applications are completed by hand. Sometimes, though, you may keys your responses on a typewriter or computer. Employers accepts corrections when they is made neatly.

Mr. George Irvin talk with many students about their applications. He say that young adults makes too many errors, but I disagree. Since competition is keen, carefully proofreads your application.

Part B. Underline the correct verb from those given in parentheses.

0. Those stock earnings (is/are) inflated.
1. The scissors (need/needs) to be sharpened.
2. If I (was/were) the director, I would change the setting.
3. In developing countries, measles (cause/causes) many deaths each year.
4. Physics (deal/deals) with matter and energy.
5. He talks as if the software (was/were) not available.

APPLICATION 5-2

Subjects Joined by Connecting Words

Underline the correct verb from those given in parentheses.

0. Mr. Aguilar and Mr. Stevens (join/joins) the group on Tuesday.
1. Neither Tom nor Tim (attend/attends) the monthly meetings.
2. Renee and Jeffrey (is/are) enrolled in a French class.
3. A clerk or the receptionist (answer/answers) the telephone.
4. Red beans and rice (is/are) a popular combination in New Orleans.
5. Joshua and I (was/were) collecting newspapers from the neighbors.
6. Either Christina or Angele (was/were) the team leader.
7. Not only the temporary laborers but also the recruiters (enjoy/enjoys) the final harvest celebration.
8. The state capital and largest city (is/are) Des Moines.
9. Rowena or Vince (bake/bakes) cookies for every party.
10. Bridgette and Nicolette (take/takes) excellent care of the flower gardens.
11. Not only Michael but also Carlton (need/needs) keyboarding practice.
12. The large box and the small cartons (is/are) recycled.
13. Neither Roy nor his parents (has/have) flown.
14. Either his grandmother or his cousins (plan/plans) the summer vacation.
15. Not only Opal but also Clara (wear/wears) old clothes on trips.
16. Ellis or Clark (serve/serves) on the Building Inspection Board.
17. Food and fireworks (is/are) part of the festivities.
18. Not only adults but also children (join/joins) in the race.
19. Either the travel agent or the skiers (buy/buys) the lift tickets.
20. Abba and Pamee (is/are) going skiing during the holiday.

APPLICATION 5-3

Subject–Verb Separation

Place parentheses around the subject and underline the correct verb from those given in parentheses.

0. The antique (cars) in the mall (is/<u>are</u>) expensive.
1. The story about sports heroes (inspire/inspires) young athletes.
2. The recipes in the cookbook (is/are) easy to read.
3. The report about clearing overgrown areas (interest/interests) many citizens.
4. Four trophies from the last tournament (is/are) on display.
5. The cost of consumer goods (has/have) risen.
6. The paste, as well as the paper, (stick/sticks) to the desk.
7. Rainfall from the frequent storms (flood/floods) the rivers.
8. The cause of the fires (was/were) not determined.
9. Miss Moya and Mrs. Sanchez from the Environmental Protection Agency (is/are) certified divers.
10. The *maquiladora*, an assembly plant in Tijuana, (is/are) thriving.
11. Competition for workers (is/are) intense.
12. The reporters on television regularly (update/updates) the election results.
13. The rolls of paper, even the ones in the warehouse, (come/comes) from his factory.
14. Snowboarding, as Roberta claims, (is/are) even more fun than skiing.
15. Teak, a popular wood this season, (is/are) frequently imported from Indonesia.
16. The optometrists, as well as the dermatologists, (go/goes) to the seminars.
17. Suits for Shelley (is/are) difficult to find.
18. Hats, like the ones on this rack, (protect/protects) you from the sun's ultraviolet rays.
19. Tickets for the concert (is/are) sold at the box office.
20. Bags, either paper or plastic, (hold/holds) all your purchases.

APPLICATION 5-4

Indefinite Pronoun Subjects

Underline the correct verb from those given in parentheses.

0. None of the discount merchandise (remain/remains).
1. Each of the environmental issues (is/are) important.
2. Someone (place/places) aluminum cans in the trash bin.
3. None of the water (flow/flows) into the river.
4. Both of the stores (has/have) holiday sales.
5. Everything on the sites (was/were) brought in by helicopter.
6. Many (has/have) tried to solve the riddle.
7. Everyone (compete/competes) for the grand prize.
8. All of the DVD players (was/were) shipped to Brazil.
9. None of the beads (was/were) lost when Elizabeth's necklace broke.
10. Some of the programs (contain/contains) important information.
11. More of the interviews (is/are) airing today.
12. (Is/Are) somebody planning to remove the debris?
13. A few of the homeowners (has/have) filed insurance claims.
14. All of the fence (is/are) destroyed.
15. Neither of the cars (has/have) any dents.
16. Most of your time (was/were) spent working on the project.
17. Several of the owners (has/have) filed insurance claims.
18. Everybody (like/likes) to be recognized.
19. Nobody on the current team (jump/jumps) more than 14 feet.
20. Something (is/are) incorrect in the financial report.

Application 5-5

Collective Noun Subjects

Underline the correct verb from those given in parentheses.

0. The Arts Council (seek/<u>seeks</u>) new grant proposals.
1. The Explorers Club (publish/publishes) a quarterly magazine.
2. The cluster of molecules suddenly (change/changes) shape.
3. The Museum Foundation (support/supports) the Lexington project.
4. The squadron (check/checks) their airplanes for mechanical problems before takeoff.
5. The company (offer/offers) all employees a 401(k) plan.
6. Which way (is/are) the flock migrating this season?
7. The Mitchell Firm (employ/employs) only experienced trial attorneys.
8. My gang of friends always (band/bands) together in tough times.
9. The pack of wolves (search/searches) for food.
10. The Santa Rosa Island Authority (make/makes) an annual report to the legislature.
11. Our choir (give/gives) special performances in the mall.
12. An angry mob (gather/gathers) around the square every holiday.
13. A group of environmentalists (is/are) coming from around the world to meet here.
14. Which group (begin/begins) the competition?
15. The quartet (is/are) scheduled to entertain us at 8:30 p.m.
16. The crew (practice/practices) on the lake each morning.
17. Maurice's stamp collection (include/includes) many that I have never seen.
18. Mr. Salazar's staff always (treat/treats) clients with amazing consideration.
19. Maillot Industries (want/wants) to form a new chapter in Jackson.
20. The Environmental Protection Agency (enforce/enforces) environmental regulations.

Subject–Verb Agreement

Underline the correct verb form. Each correct answer is worth five points.

1. Everyone (has/have) responsibility for protecting the environment.
2. People often (do/does) not know what types of material may be recycled.
3. Either individuals or county groups (need/needs) to develop recycling programs.
4. Recycling (turn/turns) waste materials into valuable resources.
5. Some of the discarded metal (recycle/recycles) easily.
6. Paper and glass (is/are) the two major recyclable products.
7. Typical examples of hazardous waste (include/includes) used oil and paint.
8. Helene and Larry (identify/identifies) environmental protection tips.
9. Wax paper or aluminum foil (is/are) an alternative to plastic wrap.
10. Margaret, as well as Cristina, (collect/collects) empty printer cartridges to recycle.
11. Someone in the club (recommend/recommends) using cloth napkins or towels.
12. Many countries (introduce/introduces) legislation to protect natural resources.
13. All areas of the world (is/are) affected by pollution.
14. Not only the land but also the oceans (is/are) damaged by burning coal and oil.
15. Everyone (enjoy/enjoys) breathing clean air.
16. Many of the earth's resources (remain/remains) sustainable.
17. My team (handle/handles) the publicity for the recycling campaign.
18. The awareness committee (produce/produces) brochures.
19. Neither Mr. Foster nor Mr. Yang (has/have) submitted designs for the brochures.
20. Each of us (has/have) a responsibility to help.

Adjectives

CHAPTER 6

Adjectives clarify or add details to nouns and pronouns. Compare the following two sentences:

1. Year marks time that parks will join for celebration to observe anniversary of Disneyland.
2. This year marks the first time that all Disney theme parks will join for a global celebration to observe the fiftieth anniversary of Disneyland.

Because adjectives were removed from the first sentence, the remaining words do not provide a complete, a clear, or an interesting message. Adding just the right adjectives to your oral and written messages helps you to make accurate statements, to give your thoughts sharper focus, and to hold the attention of your audience.

LEARNING OBJECTIVES

- Identify and use different types of adjectives correctly.
- Use adjectives to make accurate comparisons.

DEFINITION OF ADJECTIVES

Adjectives modify (describe, limit, or qualify) nouns and pronouns; they provide specific information to make a message more meaningful. Adjectives usually come *before* the words they modify, and they answer questions like *what kind*? *how many*? or *which one*?

> Gary drove a *classic* car to the diner. (What kind of car? *Classic*.)
>
> *Three* members bought tickets. (How many members? *Three*.)
>
> Did you hear *that* suggestion? (Which suggestion? *That one*.)

Adjectives describe (give details about *what kind*) and limit (tell *which one* or *how many*) nouns or pronouns.

DESCRIPTIVE ADJECTIVES

Descriptive adjectives provide details about a noun or pronoun. The descriptive adjectives are italicized, and the nouns that they modify are underlined in the following sentences.

> An *office* manual is a *handy* reference.
>
> The *tired* firefighter rested before she climbed the ladder.
>
> *Peruvian* blankets are on sale.

"*The adjective is the banana peel of the parts of speech.*"
-Clifton Fadiman, editor and literary critic (1902–1999)

Most adjectives do not end in -ly. Five common exceptions are friendly, lively, lonely, lovely, and ugly.

Descriptive adjectives often have these word endings: *able*, *al*, *an*, *ar*, *ent*, *ese*, *ful*, *ial*, *ian*, *ible*, *ic*, *ical*, *ish*, *ive*, *ly*, *ous*, *ual*, and *y*.

capable	successful	foolish
informal	influential	impressive
European	Canadian	friendly
circular	possible	serious
intelligent	specific	usual
Japanese	identical	happy

PREDICATE ADJECTIVES

Not all adjectives come immediately before the nouns or pronouns they modify. Some adjectives follow linking verbs, such as *is*, *are*, *was*, *were*, *be*, *am*, and *been*. Adjectives that follow linking verbs and describe subjects are called **predicate adjectives.**

The students are *confident* that they will win. (What kind of students? *Confident*.)

Review pages 62 and 69 to refresh your understanding of participles.

NOUNS AND PARTICIPLES AS ADJECTIVES

Nouns and participles may be used as adjectives when they answer questions like *what kind*? *how many*? or *which one*?

The *Idaho* team won the tournament. (proper noun as adjective)
An *insurance* agent called today. (noun as adjective)
We walked in a *driving* rain. (participle as adjective)
The *exhausted* team boarded the bus. (participle as adjective)

PROPER ADJECTIVES

Proper adjectives are derived (made) from proper nouns; therefore, proper adjectives should be capitalized. Such adjectives are *not* capitalized, however, when they are no longer associated with the original proper noun.

> Shelby likes *Thai* food. (derived from *Thailand*)
>
> Candace has recipes for *brussels* sprouts. (derived from Brussels, Belgium)

Consult a dictionary if you are not sure whether an adjective should be capitalized.

COMPOUND ADJECTIVES

Compound adjectives consist of two or more words combined to express a single characteristic or concept. Compound adjectives usually are hyphenated.

fast-paced plot	*high-speed* Internet service
five-story building	*well-known* judge

Consult a dictionary if you are not sure whether a compound adjective should be hyphenated.

Be careful not to hyphenate such words when they do not serve as compound adjectives but play a different role in the sentence.

> My high-speed Internet service is *expensive*. (The compound adjective *high-speed* modifies the noun *service*.)
>
> I want access *at a high speed*. (*At a high speed* is a prepositional phrase.)
>
> The plot is *fast-paced*. (The compound predicate adjective *fast-paced* modifies the noun *plot*.)
>
> The plot has a *fast pace*. (The adjective *fast* modifies the noun *pace*.)

Complete Application 6-1.

[CHECKPOINT 6-1]

Identify Descriptive Adjectives

Underline each descriptive adjective (including proper and compound adjectives). Circle the word modified by each adjective.

1. A two-tiered platter of Italian pastries was at the center of the table, which was covered with a lace tablecloth.
2. Jerry Ramirez is a well-known author of mystery books.
3. Jai saw a clever comedy act at a historic theater.
4. The mysterious stranger disappeared into the deep, dark tunnel.
5. At a recent festival, Ralph purchased colorful fans, Chinese tea, and fortune cookies.

"As to the adjective, when in doubt, strike it out."

-Mark Twain, American writer (1835–1910)

LIMITING ADJECTIVES

Limiting adjectives modify nouns and pronouns by making them more precise. Limiting adjectives answer questions like *how many*? or *which one*? Typical limiting adjectives are listed below.

a	no
an	one (and other numbers)
all	possessive nouns (*Ming's, company's*)
any	
both	possessive pronouns (*my, your*)
each	some
every	such
few	that/those
many	the
more	this/these
most	which/what/whose
much	

Articles

A, *an*, and *the* are limiting adjectives called **articles.** *A* and *an* are **indefinite articles** because they make general (indefinite) references to nouns.

Alyssa visited *a* village. (no particular village)
I ate *an* orange. (no particular orange)

Use a before abbreviations that begin with a consonant sound (a B.S. degree); use an *before abbreviations that begin with a vowel sound (an M.A. degree).*

Use the limiting adjective *a* before words that begin with:

- A consonant or consonant sound, including *h* when pronounced with the *h* sound.
- The long sound of *u* (pronounced as *you*).
- The letter *o* when pronounced with the *w* sound.

a village	*a* history test (sound of *h*)
a car	*a* union issue (long sound of *u*)
a telephone	*a* one-time deal (sound of *w*)

Use the limiting adjective *an* before words beginning with a vowel sound, except for the long *u* sound (as in *you*).

an ice cream cone	*an* hour (silent *h*)
an announcement	*an* untitled manuscript (short *u*)

The refers to a specific (definite) noun and therefore is called a **definite article**.

I want *the* apple on the top of the basket. (a specific apple)

Send *the* report to Max. (a specific report)

Workplace Connection

A grammar or usage error embarrasses you and your organization and makes your message less effective.

Quantity Adjectives. Numbers (*one*, *two*, *first*, *second*, and so on) serve as limiting adjectives when they modify nouns. Words such as *all*, *few*, *many*, and *several* serve as limiting adjectives when they modify nouns, but they function as pronouns (as shown in the third example below) when they are subjects and objects.

We delivered 100 dinners. (The number *100* is an adjective that tells how many dinners.)

Several students voted. (*Several* is an adjective that tells how many students.)

Several of the faculty attended the party. (*Several* is a pronoun and is the subject of the sentence.)

Possessive Nouns and Pronouns. Possessive nouns and personal pronouns in the possessive case also serve as limiting adjectives. They show ownership (as you learned in Chapters 2 and 3).

Some texts refer to possessive nouns and possessive pronouns as possessive adjectives. *They show ownership by answering the question* whose?

Kami's picture is lovely. (The possessive noun *Kami's* explains whose picture.)

Did you read *my* book? (The possessive pronoun *my* explains whose book.)

Demonstrative Adjectives. When the words *this*, *that*, *these*, and *those* modify nouns, they are called **demonstrative adjectives**. Demonstrative adjectives point out or call attention to a particular person, place, thing, concept, quality, or event. When the words serve as subjects or objects, they function as pronouns as shown in the third example below.

Use the demonstrative adjectives this *(singular) and* those *(plural) to modify nouns that are near. Use the demonstrative adjectives* that *(singular) and* those *(plural) to modify nouns that are distant.*

This book belongs to Ali. (The demonstrative pronoun *this* tells which book belongs to Ali.)

We recently hired *those* managers. (The demonstrative pronoun *those* calls attention to specific managers.)

That is mine. (*That* is a pronoun and is the subject of the sentence.)

[CHECKPOINT 6-2]

Select and Identify Adjectives that Limit

Write *a* or *an* as appropriate in the space provided.

1. This is (a // an) unique opportunity to express (a // an) opinion. ______
2. He purchased (a // an) one-way ticket to Port Lucy during (a // an) auction. ______
3. Purchasing the swampland is (a // an) unusual tactic. ______
4. Can we meet in (a // an) hour? ______

Underline all the adjectives that limit (articles, possessive nouns and pronouns, and demonstrative adjectives).

1. These members are meeting to discuss both proposals.
2. Jonathan Cullen will receive an honorable discharge in three months.
3. Most of the letters have many errors.
4. Mario's sisters cleaned oil from the feathers of several birds.
5. Those posters were designed by our art class.
6. All the applicants should be seated either in my office or in William's office.

Complete Application 6-2.

DEGREES OF COMPARISON

Descriptive adjectives may be used to make comparisons. Most descriptive adjectives have these degrees (forms) of comparison: *positive*, *comparative*, and *superlative*.

Positive	Comparative	Superlative
short	shorter	shortest
happy	happier	happiest
favorable	more favorable	most favorable

Positive Degree

The **positive degree** is used to modify nouns without making a comparison. An adjective in the positive degree does not change.

Ms. Rosso presented a *strong* argument in favor of the bill.

Sunday was a *cold* day.

I told a *funny* joke.

She is an *enthusiastic* volunteer.

Comparative Degree

The **comparative degree** is used to compare *two* nouns or pronouns.

When a sentence contains adjectives in the comparative degree, the comparison often uses the word than.

1. Add *r* or *er* to the end of the positive form of most one-syllable and some two-syllable adjectives to form the comparative degree.

   Ms. Rosso presented a *stronger* argument than did Ms. Dodge.
   Sunday was *colder* than Saturday.

For some one-syllable adjectives such as big, *the last consonant is doubled before* er *or* est *is added.*

2. Change the *y* to *i* and add *er* (*ier*) when the positive form of the adjective ends in *y*.

   My joke is *funnier* than your joke. (funny)
   Rebecca is *friendlier* than Denise. (friendly)

3. Use the adverb *less* or *more* before most adjectives of two syllables and all adjectives of more than two syllables to form the comparative degree.

   Juan was *less* enthusiastic about the book report than he was about the spreadsheet assignment. (*Enthusiastic* has five syllables.)

   Lynne had a *more* favorable review this year than last year. (*Favorable* has four syllables.)

Superlative Degree

The **superlative degree** is used to compare *three* or more nouns or pronouns.

The superlative degree uses the word the *(the oldest house).*

1. Add *est* or *st* to the end of the positive form most one-syllable and some two-syllable adjectives to form the superlative degree.

   Of the four speakers, Ms. Rosso presented the *strongest* argument.
   Sunday was the *coldest* day of the week.

The second item in a superlative degree comparison is often introduced by of, in, *or* on.

2. Change the *y* to *i* and add *est* (*iest*) when the positive form of an adjective ends in *y*.

   My joke is the *funniest* of the three jokes that were submitted. (funny)

   Rebecca is the *friendliest* of all my coworkers. (friendly)

3. Use the adverb *least* or *most* before most adjectives of two syllables and all adjectives of more than two syllables to form the superlative degree.

   Of all the students in the class, Juan was the *most* enthusiastic about the Web design project.

   Your review of the movie was the *least* favorable of the six reviews that I received.

Sometimes the superlative degree is used for emphasis even when no comparison is being made.

Your cake is the best!

[CHECKPOINT 6-3]

Form Degrees of Comparison

Provide the comparative and superlative degree for each adjective.

Positive Degree	Comparative Degree	Superlative Degree
1. busy	____________	____________
2. cheap	____________	____________
3. high	____________	____________
4. stunning	____________	____________
5. incredible	____________	____________

Well is an adjective when it refers to health but an adverb when it refers to how something is done. *Good* is only an adjective.

Less and *least* are often used to refer to quantity. *Farther* and *farthest* refer to actual distance; *further* and *furthest* mean "to a greater degree or extent."

Irregular Forms

Some adjectives are considered **irregular** because they completely change form to make the comparative and superlative degrees:

Positive	Comparative	Superlative
bad	worse	worst
good or well	better	best
little	less	least
many or much	more	most

He has had *bad* investment experiences.
He had a *worse* experience this year than he had last year.
Of all the years, this year was the *worst*.

Double Comparisons

Do not use double comparisons. Use only *one* of these methods to form a comparison:

Add an appropriate ending to the adjective.
Change the form of the adjective (irregular adjectives).
Place more/less or *most/least* before the adjective.

Correct	Incorrect
Regina is *stronger* than Kyle.	Regina is more stronger than Kyle.
You made the *best* choice.	You made the most best choice.
Shoa is the *most* qualified candidate.	Shoa is the mostest qualified candidate.

Some adjectives cannot be used in comparisons; for example, an exam cannot be "more final." Other words that cannot be compared are dead, empty, single, unique, square, *and* round.

Complete Application 6-3.

[CHECKPOINT 6-4]

Form Comparisons

Write the appropriate degree (positive, comparative, or superlative) of the adjective given in parentheses.

1. Her claim is the (outrageous) ____________________ claim that I have ever heard.
2. Your cake is (good) ____________________ than the cake that I bought at the bakery.
3. Of all the offices in the building, Anna's office is the (relaxing) ____________________.
4. Which of the three sofas is the (good) ____________________ choice for my apartment?
5. Evan bought the (expensive) ____________________ camera in the store.
6. This salsa is (spicy) ____________________ than the salsa that I make.
7. My dog is (smart) ____________________ than my neighbor's dog; in fact, my dog is the (smart) ____________________ dog on the block.
8. Jackson was (hungry) ____________________ than Miriam.
9. My husband is the (young) ____________________ of four children.
10. I feel (well)____________________ today than I did yesterday.

Chapter Summary

- Use adjectives to describe nouns and pronouns and to make their meaning more specific.
- Use descriptive adjectives to provide interesting details about nouns or pronouns.
- Capitalize most proper adjectives.
- Use the indefinite articles *a* and *an* to make general references to nouns; use the indefinite article *the* to make specific references to nouns.
- Use quantity adjectives to tell how many nouns or pronouns are being discussed.
- Use possessive nouns and pronouns and demonstrative adjectives to show precisely which nouns or pronouns are being discussed.
- Use the positive degree of adjectives (the adjective itself) when not making comparisons.
- Use the comparative degree of adjectives when comparing two nouns or pronouns.
- Use the superlative degree of adjectives when comparing three or more nouns or pronouns.

Complete the Chapter 6 Review.

ILrn Complete the Chapter 6 iLrn Activities at **miller.swlearning.com**.

Complete the Chapter 6 Web Exercise at ***miller.swlearning.com.***

Descriptive Adjectives

Part A. Underline each descriptive adjective (including proper and compound adjectives). Circle the word modified by each adjective.

0. Henrik Ibsen was born in a tiny coastal town.
1. Ibsen was a Norwegian playwright.
2. When Ibsen lived abroad, he wrote many of his best-known works.
3. Ibsen wrote realistic dramas about psychological conflict.
4. *Peer Gynt* is a story about the legendary Peer Gynt, a boastful peasant farmer of Norwegian folklore.
5. *Pillars of Society* tells how the actions of a wealthy and hypocritical businessman almost lead to the death of his son.
6. *Hedda Gabler* is the study of a woman torn by internal conflict, who feels trapped by the circumstances of her life.
7. Many people outside Norway considered Ibsen a progressive writer; but in his home country, he was seen as a moral preacher.
8. Toward the end of his life, Ibsen suffered from mental illness.

Part B. Write the correct adjective form for each word in parentheses.

0. (China) Chinese lanterns were hung in the courtyard.
1. Andrea prepares the (week) ____________________ payroll for the employees.
2. I ordered (Germany) ____________________ dinnerware and (Japan) ____________________ silverware.
3. His (courtesy) ____________________ manner and (depend) ____________________ employment record impressed the interviewers.
4. Avoid (fool) ____________________ mistakes; think before you act.
5. The officer has an (admire) ____________________ military record.
6. His (comic) ____________________ (face) ____________________ expressions made us laugh.
7. Jack gave an (impress) ____________________ presentation on increasing the (hour) ____________________ wage.
8. To enhance your networking opportunities, join a (profession) ____________________ organization.

APPLICATION 6-2

Adjectives that Limit

Part A. Underline the correct article or demonstrative adjective of those given in parentheses.

0. McKenzie is wearing (a // an) knee brace.
1. Did you make (a // an) appointment with (a // an) insurance agent?
2. (A // The) report that we have before us is excellent.
3. Loretta received (a // an) honorable mention at the horse show.
4. (These // Those) clients in the reception area are waiting to see you.
5. (A // An) heavy load may cause the tires to lose pressure.
6. Please have (those // these) coats in the warehouse delivered to the showroom.
7. The bedroom furniture, which is (a // an) unique blend of old and new pieces, looks wonderful.
8. Miss Scott made (a // an) hasty judgment because she did not have all the facts.
9. Mr. Zhou held (a // an) one-man show at (a // an) theater in the Third Ward.
10. (A // An) EMT is an emergency medical technician; (a // an) R.N. is a registered nurse.

Part B. Underline articles, quantity adjectives, possessive nouns and pronouns, and demonstrative adjectives in the following sentences.

0. Eight drivers requested the third shift.
1. Few people attended the open house.
2. Three supervisors invited Michael for a second interview.
3. Peter's expenses exceeded the travel budget.
4. The parts for this aircraft are imported from four countries.
5. For several months, a panel of six people will discuss every recommendation.
6. A Creole artist has many pictures displayed in the window of this gallery.
7. Both members questioned the fifth item on the agenda.
8. Alberto's manager recommended Alberto for a promotion.
9. All students must complete their projects by the first week in January.
10. You must list each item in your inventory log.

APPLICATION 6-3

Degrees of Comparison

Part A. Provide the comparative and superlative degree for each adjective.

Positive Degree	Comparative Degree	Superlative Degree
0. fine	finer	finest
1. appropriate	__________	__________
2. easy	__________	__________
3. good	__________	__________
4. talented	__________	__________
5. silly	__________	__________
6. mild	__________	__________
7. late	__________	__________
8. mature	__________	__________
9. heavy	__________	__________
10. many	__________	__________

Part B. Write the appropriate degree (positive, comparative, or superlative) of the adjective given in parentheses.

0. Interest rates are at their (low) lowest level this year.
1. My new chair is (comfortable) __________ than yours.
2. Of all the students in the class, Lucero is the (loud) __________.
3. Which of these two modems is the (fast) __________?
4. Ivan believes that 92 will be his (high) __________ grade.
5. This is the (thick) __________ blanket in the store.
6. The reception area is (clean) __________.
7. Maggie is (optimistic) __________ than Charles.
8. Of the four of us, Grace has the (few) __________ absences.
9. Min tries to be (helpful) __________ all the time.
10. Dan's temperature is (low) __________ today than yesterday.

Chapter 6 Review

Adjectives

Part A. Identify Adjectives

Underline all the adjectives (including articles, possessive nouns, and possessive pronouns) in the following paragraphs. Each correct answer is worth two points.

Stress is a common part of everyday life. Life changes, unpaid bills, and sick relatives are situations that may cause stress.

Stress is your body's reaction to different events or situations around you. Some stress is good because stress helps you to stay alert and to take action when necessary. Preparing for an important event or playing a vigorous game of tennis can produce good stress. If you experience long-term stress or have difficulty handling stressful situations, you may develop physical and emotional problems.

Generally, your personality and your reactions to day-to-day events will influence how you manage stress. These strategies will help you to cope effectively with stress:

- Recognize the problem and take control.
- When a situation is beyond your control, let go and move on to other activities.
- Set realistic goals, and learn to say no.
- Don't ignore your physical health.
- Learn to relax.

Part B. Form Comparisons

Write the appropriate degree (positive, comparative, or superlative) of the adjective given in parentheses. Each correct answer is worth four points.

1. My car was damaged by hail; the (bad) ____________________ damage occurred on the roof.
2. Lisa is the (good) ____________________ player on the basketball team.
3. The seats you purchased for this show are (good) ____________________ than the seats you purchased for last week's show.
4. Have you heard the saying "The grass is always (green) ____________________ on the other side of the fence"?
5. Of the twins, Georgia is the (athletic) ____________________ .
6. Ms. Creevy is the (practical) ____________________ person I know; each suggestion she makes seems (practical) ____________________ than her previous suggestion.
7. I cannot think of a (worthy) ____________________ opponent than the Blue Jays.
8. Of my four friends, Kang is not only the (old) ____________________ but also the (quiet) ____________________ .

Adverbs

CHAPTER 7

I can write better than anybody who can write faster, and I can write faster than anybody who can write better.

—A. J. Liebling
U.S. journalist, author, and columnist for the *New Yorker* (1904–1963)

Without adverbs (*better*, *faster*), this quotation has no meaning. Adverbs, when used purposefully, add meaning and punch to a message. When overused, however, adverbs dilute verbs and weaken the intended message. The advice from writing authorities is to *use adverbs sparingly*.

LEARNING OBJECTIVES

- Identify adverbs.
- Use the correct forms of adverbs.
- Use adverbs to make accurate comparisons.

DEFINITION OF ADVERBS

Adverbs modify verbs, adjectives, or other adverbs. Adverbs never modify nouns or pronouns.

Adverb Modifying a Verb

Mr. Chung *immediately* signed the check. (The adverb *immediately* modifies the verb *signed*.)

The cashier *precisely* counted the change. (The adverb *precisely* modifies the verb *counted*.)

Adverb Modifying an Adjective

Only an adverb can modify an adjective.

The candidate was *extremely* talkative. (The adverb *extremely* modifies the predicate adjective *talkative*.)

The music was *very* loud. (The adverb *very* modifies the predicate adjective *loud*.)

Adverb Modifying an Adverb

He will attend *quite* often. (The adverb *often* modifies the verb *will attend*; the adverb *quite* modifies the adverb *often*.)

The crowd moved *extremely* slowly. (The adverb *slowly* modifies the verb *moved*; the adverb *extremely* modifies the adverb *slowly*.)

USES OF ADVERBS

Adverbs limit or describe verbs, adjectives, and other adverbs by answering questions like *how*? *how often*? *when*? *where*? or *to what extent*?

How:	Chloe walked *quickly* to the boarding area. (Walked how? *Quickly.*)
How often:	Keiko *seldom* eats lunch. (Eats how often? *Seldom.*)
When:	Ava will arrive *soon*. (Will arrive when? *Soon.*)
Where:	Kristofer will meet you *there*. (Will meet where? *There.*)
To what extent:	I am *very* glad to see you. (Glad to what extent? *Very.*)

You have learned that a word can act as more than one part of speech, depending on how the word is used in a sentence. Sometimes words commonly used as nouns are also used as adverbs to answer the questions *when*? or *where*?

Tomorrow will come quickly. (*Tomorrow* is a noun and the subject of the sentence.)

Chen will leave *tomorrow*. (Leave *when*? *Tomorrow* is an adverb answering the question *when*?)

My *home* is Boston. (*Home* is a noun and the subject of the sentence.)

Julianne returned *home* to get her textbook. (Returned *where*? *Home* is an adverb answering the question *where*?)

[CHECKPOINT 7-1]

Identify Adverbs

Underline the adverb in each sentence. In the space provided, write which question—*how? how often? when? where?* or *to what extent?*—the adverb answers.

1. Shelly almost missed the bus. ____________
2. Jahira politely asked Bradford to make the telephone call. ____________
3. The waitstaff moved fast. ____________
4. The award for academic achievement is given annually. ____________
5. The frightened dog ran inside. ____________

ADVERB FORMS

Many adverbs end in *ly* and are formed by adding *ly* to an adjective. Sometimes the addition of *ly* results in a spelling change. If you are not sure how to spell an adverb, consult a dictionary.

Adjective	**Adverb**
basic	basically
beautiful	beautifully
easy	easily
greedy	greedily
simple	simply
smooth	smoothly
thoughtful	thoughtfully

Many other frequently used adverbs do not end in *ly*.

Adverbs Not Ending in *ly*

afterward	even	not	soon	what
again	forward	now	still	when
almost	here	often	then	where
always	indeed	rather	too	why
backward	late	seldom	up	
down	never	sometimes	very	

Some words may be used as either adjectives or adverbs. Examples include *early*, *daily*, *fast*, *low*, *monthly*, *only*, *weekly*, and *yearly*.

He consults with me *daily*. (*Daily* is an adverb that modifies the verb *consults* and answers the question *when*?)

Write the appointment in your *daily* calendar. (*Daily* is an adjective that modifies the noun *calendar* and answers the question *what kind*?)

Lovely, friendly, ugly, lonely, timely, costly, and elderly are adjectives, not adverbs.

Adverbs that answer the question when? *(including words such as* often, seldom, never, always, afterward, *and* late*) usually do not end in* ly.

Adverbs that answer the question where? *include words such as* everywhere, forward, backward, up, *and* down.

Complete Applications 7-1 and 7-2.

[CHECKPOINT 7-2]

Identify Adverbs and the Words They Modify

Underline the adverb(s) in each sentence. Circle the word or words modified by each adverb. Then write the part of speech (*verb*, *adjective*, or *adverb*) above each modified word.

1. That price is too high.
2. The first day was fairly easy.
3. My sister drives frustratingly slow.
4. The students are delightfully cheerful.
5. Tyler watched the movie intently.
6. Mr. Tai frequently plays golf on Saturday.

> *"I'm glad you like adverbs—I adore them; they are the only qualifications I really much respect."*
>
> **-Henry James, American writer (1843–1916)**

PLACEMENT OF ADVERBS

Adverbs that modify adjectives or other adverbs are placed immediately before the words they modify.

The children watched the *rapidly* melting snow. (The adverb *rapidly* modifies the adjective *melting*.)
My partner walked *too* briskly. (The adverb *too* modifies the adverb *briskly*.)

Most adverbs that modify verbs may be placed in a variety of positions within a sentence.

Nelson *enthusiastically* greeted everyone.
Enthusiastically, Nelson greeted everyone.
Nelson greeted everyone *enthusiastically*.

For a few modifiers such as *only* and *merely*, the position of the modifier can change the part of speech of the modifier and the meaning of a sentence. Place these modifiers as close as possible to the word you want to modify.

Only Carol made a recommendation. (No one else made a recommendation. *Only* acts as an adjective and modifies the noun *Carol*.)

Carol *only* made a recommendation (Carol made a recommendation; she did not insist upon an action. *Only* acts as an adverb and modifies the verb *made*.)

DEGREES OF COMPARISON

Adverbs, like adjectives, have three degrees of comparison: *positive*, *comparative*, and *superlative*.

Positive	**Comparative**	**Superlative**
soon	sooner	soonest
early	earlier	earliest
seriously	more seriously	most seriously

Positive Degree

The positive degree is the adverb itself. The *positive degree* is used to describe one action or to show that two actions are the same or equal.

Fred leaves work *early*. (describes one action)

Fred leaves work as *early* as Dell leaves. (shows equality of two actions)

Comparative Degree

The *comparative degree* compares one action with another action. The rules for forming the comparative and superlative degrees of adverbs are similar to those for adjectives.

To form the comparative degree of most adverbs ending in *ly*, add the word *more* or *less* immediately before the adverb.

Ray completed the tasks *more quickly* than Clay.

To form the comparative degree of other adverbs, add *r* or *er* to the positive form. If the adverb ends in *y*, change the *y* to *i* and add *er*.

Ben works *harder* than Fred.

Fred leaves work *earlier* than Ben does.

Superlative Degree

The *superlative degree* compares one action with two or more actions. To form the superlative degree of adverbs ending in *ly*, add the word *most* or *least* immediately before the adverb.

Of all his coworkers, Ray completed the tasks the *most quickly*.

To form the superlative degree of other adverbs, add *st* or *est* to the positive form. If the adverb ends in *y*, change the *y* to *i* and add *est*.

Of all the employees in his unit, Ben works the *hardest*.

Of all the staff members, Fred leaves work the *earliest*.

Sometimes the superlative degree is used for emphasis when no comparison is being made.

She responded *most harshly*.

Irregular Adverbs

A few adverbs are *irregular* because the spellings change completely from the comparative to the superlative forms. Some of these adverbs are identical in spelling to the adjective forms.

Positive	Comparative	Superlative
badly	worse	worst
far	farther/further	farthest/furthest
little	less	least
much	more	most
well	better	best

[Checkpoint 7-3]

Form Comparisons

Write the appropriate degree (positive, comparative, or superlative) of the adverb given in parentheses.

1. The supervisor decided that Caitlin proofreads as (careful) ____________________ as Dominic does.
2. Today's audience waited (patient) ____________________ than yesterday's audience.
3. Of the six teams in the tournament, the Hawks scored the (high) ____________________ .
4. Alan lives (far) ____________________ from school than anyone in his class.
5. Of all the students, Alan lives the (far) ____________________ from school.
6. Mr. Tai waited (anxious) ____________________ for his performance review.
7. Tyler's mother spoke (proud) ____________________ of his work.
8. Chynda's test scores were (good) ____________________ than Jake's test scores.

Complete Application 7-3.

DOUBLE NEGATIVES

Do not use **double negatives** (two negative words in the same sentence used to express one negative meaning). The second negative cancels the first, creating the opposite meaning from what you intended. In addition, negative adverbs such as *hardly*, *barely*, and *scarcely* cause confusion when they are used with other negative words such as *no*, *not*, *never*, and *none*.

Incorrect	**Correct**
Mr. Poe did not receive no money.	Mr. Poe did not receive any money.
Ty is not never going to help us again.	Ty is not going to help us again.
Ginny can't barely see the road signs.	Ginny barely can see the road signs.

Note: Most of the time, verb parts should be kept together.

[Checkpoint 7-4]

Eliminate Double Negatives

Revise each sentence to eliminate the double negative. Each sentence should have only one negative element.

1. I don't have no homework tonight.
2. I haven't never had to drive in Los Angeles.
3. Luisa doesn't have none of those books.
4. Mrs. Ehn did not receive no credit on her account.
5. The student hardly never gets the correct answer on the algebra quizzes.

ADVERB–ADJECTIVE CONFUSION

When you are confused about whether to use an adjective or an adverb as a modifier, ask yourself these two questions:

- ***What* part of speech does the modifier describe?**
  - If the answer is a verb, adjective, or adverb, use an adverb.
  - If the answer is a noun or pronoun, use an adjective.
- ***What* question does the modifier answer?**
  - If the modifier tells *how*, *how often*, *when*, *where*, or *to what extent*, use an adverb.
  - If the modifier tells *what kind*, *how many*, or *which one*, use an adjective.

Some adverbs and adjectives are commonly confused. They include *almost/most*, *badly/bad*, *well/good*, *really/real*, and *surely/sure*.

> *When you can substitute a form of the verb* to be *for a sense verb (*feel, look, smell, sound, taste*) or for the verbs* appear, grow, *and* seem, *an adjective must follow.*

Almost/Most

Almost is an adverb and means "nearly."

Dan has *almost* completed his degree. (*Almost* modifies the verb *has completed* and answers the question *to what extent*?)

Pamela *almost* convinced me that she was interested in the job. (*Almost* modifies the verb *convinced* and answers the question *to what extent*?)

> *Adverbs modify only verbs, adjectives, and other adverbs. Adjectives modify only nouns and pronouns.*

> *"Adverbs are crashers in the syntax house party. More often than not, they should be deleted when they sneak in the back door."*
>
> **-Constance Hale, American writer**
> ***Sin and Syntax: How to Craft Wickedly Effective Prose* (1999)**

Most is used as an adjective or as an indefinite pronoun; *most* means "the majority."

Most games are priced under $30. (*Most* is an adjective that modifies the noun *games* and answers the question *how many*?)

Most of the assignment is complete. (*Most* is an indefinite pronoun serving as the subject of this sentence.)

Badly/Bad

Badly is an adverb and means "in a bad way."

The dance troupe performed *badly*. (The adverb *badly* modifies the verb *performed* and answers the question *how*?)

Lars appeared *badly* frightened after the motorcycle accident. (The adverb *badly* modifies the predicate adjective *frightened* and answers the question *to what extent*?)

Bad is an adjective that is used after a linking verb or after verbs of the senses such as *feel*, *look*, *sound*, *taste*, and *smell*.

The *bad* weather kept us off the beach. (The adjective *bad* modifies the noun *weather* and answers the question *what kind*?)

Quyen feels *bad* (not *badly*) about the grade report. (The adjective *bad* is used with *feel*, a verb of the senses.)

Well/Good

Well can be used as either an adverb or an adjective. As an adverb, *well* answers the question *how*?

The dance troupe performed *well* during the rehearsal. (*Well* is an adverb that modifies the verb *performed*.)

The snowmobile trails in Ontonagon County are well groomed. (*Well* is an adverb that modifies the predicate adjective *groomed*.)

As an adjective, *well* usually means "in good health." *Well* is often used as an adjective after sense verbs like *looks*, *feels*, and *sounds*.

Neil feels *well*. (Neil is in good health.)
Neil looks *well*. (Neil looks as if he is in good health.)

Good, meaning "beneficial," is always an adjective and modifies a noun or a pronoun.

Erin did a good job. (*Good* modifies the noun *job* and answers the question *what kind*?)

Kate is a *good* candidate for the manager position. (*Good* modifies the noun *candidate* and answers the question *what kind*?)

Really/Real

Really is an adverb that adds emphasis to the meaning of the word it modifies.

Jane and Ann are *really* sad that they didn't win the award. (*Really* modifies the predicate adjective *sad* and tells how sad.)

Real is an adjective and means "genuine" or "true."

Karen wore *real* pearls at her wedding. (*Real* tells what kind—genuine—and modifies the noun *pearls*.)

Josef was the *real* winner. (*Real* tells which one—the true one—and modifies the noun *winner*.)

Do not use *real* to modify another adjective. If you must add emphasis, use *very* or *really*.

Melanie ate a *really* good lunch (not a *real* good lunch). (*Really* modifies the adjective *good* and tells how good.)

Anita was *very* happy (not *real* happy) about her grades. (*Very* modifies the adjective *happy* and tells how happy.)

Surely/Sure

Surely is an adverb that means "certainly" or "without a doubt."

Mrs. Neville, you *surely* can depend on those students. (*Surely* modifies the verb *can depend* and answers the question *how*?)

Sure is an adjective and means "confident," "convinced," "positive," or "reliable."

Virginia has a *sure* touch when she paints miniatures. (*Sure* means "confident," modifies the noun *touch*, and answers the question *what kind*?)

Do not use *sure* as an adverb; instead, use *surely* or *very*.

We were *surely* (not *sure*) welcomed at the meeting. (*Surely* modifies the verb *were welcomed*.)

We are *very* (not *sure*) excited about your participation. (*Very* modifies the predicate adjective *excited*.)

Avoid the incorrect expression *sure and*; instead, use *sure to*.

Be *sure to* (not be *sure and*) vote. (*Sure* means "certain.")

Workplace Connection

The trick is to know when to keep or to delete an adverb. Read through your message. Underline the adverbs, especially those that modify verbs. Can the adverb-verb combination be replaced with a strong verb? If so, make the replacement.

Avoid excessive use of very, *and do not use* very, very. *To make your sentences stronger, also avoid unnecessary adverbs such as* incredibly, really, awfully, *and* terribly.

Complete the Chapter 7 Web Exercise at **miller.swlearning.com**.

Complete Application 7-4.

Use Adverbs and Adjectives Correctly

Underline the correct word from the choices given in parentheses.

1. Ramona felt (bad // badly) about missing her appointment.
2. We may not finish, but we will (almost // most) be done by 4 p.m.
3. The acoustics in the room make the music sound (bad // badly).
4. The manager handled the situation (bad // badly).
5. My father was (sure // surely) excited about my grades.
6. Did you notice how (good // well) the supervisor handled the complaint?
7. This is a (real // very) good book.
8. (Be sure and // Be sure to) order the flowers by Monday.

Chapter Summary

- Use adverbs to limit or describe verbs, adjectives, or other adverbs.
- Choose the appropriate degree of comparison (positive, comparative, or superlative) for adverbs.
- Do not use double negatives, and do not combine negative adverbs with other negative words.
- Choose adverbs to modify verbs, adjectives, and other adverbs; choose adjectives to modify nouns and pronouns.

Complete the Chapter 7 Review.

iLrn Complete the Chapter 7 iLrn Activities at **miller.swlearning.com**.

APPLICATION 7-1

Identify Adverbs and Their Uses

Part A. Write which question—*how? how often? when? where?* or *to what extent?*—each underlined adverb answers.

0. Jeremy clearly explained the problem. how?
1. Weather forecasters often give an inaccurate prediction.
2. The four proposals created controversy locally.
3. Helena readily agreed to job share.
4. Min's family recently returned to China.
5. Alan frequently checks his e-mail messages.
6. Maj acted completely responsibly in reporting the event.
7. Sometimes Mr. Bandlow is too cautious.
8. You must deliver the flowers today.

Part B. Underline the adverb(s) in each sentence.

0. Crystal is perfectly satisfied.
1. Every product arrived safely.
2. Turn right at the corner.
3. Ada will work on her math later.
4. Finland has extremely long summer days.
5. Is July 1 too early to send our invitations?
6. The ridiculously low price attracted my attention.
7. Recovering from knee surgery, William walked especially slowly.
8. Do not move the desk there.
9. Ms. Mackey crossed the busy intersection very quickly.
10. The child threw the ball upward.

Application 7-2

Identify Adverbs and the Words They Modify

Underline the adverbs, and circle the words they modify. Then write the part of speech (*verb, adjective*, or *adverb*) of the modified words.

0. Marcus is behaving strangely. verb
1. My brother's performance indicates that he is especially talented. ______
2. Upon her return, my sister happily hugged me. ______
3. The wrist brace should fit snugly. ______
4. You should always listen to your conscience. ______
5. Listen to your voice mail daily. ______
6. The road was particularly muddy. ______
7. Rachel arrived early. ______
8. The men pushed the car backward. ______
9. The veterinarian worked diligently to save the dog. ______
10. Please sign the contract today. ______
11. Chandra's voice was barely audible. ______
12. The patient appears exceptionally pale. ______
13. The crowd left the stadium extremely quickly. ______
14. I seldom hear the person who lives upstairs. ______
15. Angel packed his suitcase hastily. ______
16. The basketball team will arrive soon. ______
17. Theresa very hurriedly read the manuscript. ______
18. Dr. Chang researches highly contagious diseases. ______
19. Our cat is very playful. ______
20. Jemma entered first. ______

APPLICATION 7-3

Form Degrees of Comparison

Part A. Provide the comparative and superlative degree for each adverb.

Positive Degree	Comparative Degree	Superlative Degree
0. quickly	more quickly	most quickly
1. swiftly	__________	__________
2. often	__________	__________
3. soon	__________	__________
4. smoothly	__________	__________
5. clearly	__________	__________
6. hard	__________	__________
7. neatly	__________	__________
8. nervously	__________	__________

Part B. Write the appropriate degree (positive, comparative, or superlative) of the adverb given in parentheses.

0. Martin can run (far) ____farther____ than Charles.
1. Addeco Express delivers packages (prompt) ____________ than any other delivery service.
2. At the football game, Ana cheered (loud) ____________ than Andrew.
3. Ramon walked the (far) ____________ of all the hikers on the trip.
4. Of all the sales representatives, Kevin presented his product the (assertive) ____________ .
5. Pack the glass paperweights (secure) ____________ this time than you packed them last time.
6. Tamiko spoke the (passionate) ____________ of all the people in the room.
7. The budget was cut (extensive) ____________ because funds were limited.
8. The customer became (extreme) ____________ upset when she couldn't find her debit card.
9. Calfax Corporation contributed the (little) ____________ of the five companies in our city.
10. Of all the students, Kayla was the (well) ____________ qualified.

APPLICATION 7-4

Use Adverbs Correctly

Part A. Revise each sentence to eliminate the double negative. Each sentence should have only one negative element.

0. Are you not never going to class?

   Are you ever going to class?

1. I don't have nothing to prepare for dinner.
2. Nick's loan application won't never get approved.
3. The basketball team couldn't hardly wait for the game to begin.
4. Maritza doesn't have no money.
5. Mr. Tobias has not given no assignments this week.
6. Buy a raffle ticket today because you may not never get another chance to win a big prize.
7. Ross and Kunio couldn't hardly finish the race.
8. Cheryl never doesn't need extra time to complete her assignments.

Part B. Underline the correct word from the choices given in parentheses.

0. Carmen played the cello (good // <u>well</u>) during the concert.
1. After a day of kayaking, my family is (real // really) tired.
2. Angela felt (bad // badly) after she scolded her dog.
3. By April, winter is (almost // most) over in the Midwest.
4. Did you do (good // well) on the test?
5. Roberto scored (bad // badly) on the college entrance exam.
6. Peter wanted to see the play (real // really) (bad // badly).
7. If our team performs (good // well) in the last round, we may win the competition.
8. Luckily, Tamarr did not have the flu this season; in fact, he remained (good // well) all winter.
9. Navarre and Ralph were (sure // very) quiet during the meeting.
10. You (sure // surely) can depend on me.

Chapter 7 Review

Adverbs

Part A. Identify Adverbs

Underline all adverbs in the following paragraphs. Each correct answer is worth two points.

We solve problems and make decisions daily. Some problems are very challenging, and a solution is not readily obvious. You can use problem-solving techniques to help you solve problems creatively. Brainstorm ideas, and rapidly record your thoughts. Carefully compare alternatives. Eliminate those solutions that you determine are absolutely unworkable, and consider those solutions that seem almost perfect. Decide which alternative is best.

Now analyze that alternative objectively. Ask yourself: Will my answer solve the problem satisfactorily? Sometimes you will discover that the solution you chose first was inadequate, and you may need to begin the process again.

Part B. Identify Adverbs and the Words They Modify

Underline the adverbs, and circle the words they modify. Then write the part of speech (*verb* or *adjective*) of the modified words. Each adverb, modified word (verb phrases are counted as one unit), and part of speech correctly identified is worth one point.

1. Profits this quarter are slightly lower than they were last quarter. ____________________
2. The shoes are attractively priced. ____________________
3. Can you cope effectively with changes on your job? ____________________
4. Liam enthusiastically read his report. ____________________
5. My office is best reached by bus. ____________________
6. I met Ms. Chamberlain once. ____________________
7. Do you always drink coffee in the morning? ____________________
8. The fans are still waiting for the game to begin. ____________________
9. Does he live close? ____________________
10. Is the font easily readable? ____________________

Part C. Use Adverbs Correctly

Underline adverb errors, and write the necessary corrections above each line. Each correct answer is worth two points.

Today's global market is rapid changing, so companies must stay abreast of technological developments. Employees oftener must learn new techniques, and they must learn the techniques quickly.

Don't never be afraid to consider a change. Approach change calm and logicaler. Show your employer that you can adapt successful to change and that you can perform productive. Update your skills continual so that you develop extreme marketable skills. Enthusiastic develop those skills soon rather than late. If you consistent follow this advice, you will significant increase your opportunities for advancement because your employer will sure see you as a leader.

Part D. Form Degrees of Comparison

Provide the comparative and superlative degree for each adverb. Each correct answer is worth one point.

Positive Degree	Comparative Degree	Superlative Degree
1. badly	__________	__________
2. fast	__________	__________
3. well	__________	__________
4. promptly	__________	__________
5. closely	__________	__________

Prepositions, Conjunctions, and Interjections

CHAPTER 8

Nouns and pronouns name persons, places, things, concepts, qualities, or events. Verbs express action or state of being; adjectives and adverbs add interest to what is being said. Interjections show feelings. Prepositions and conjunctions add clarity and coherence by connecting elements within a sentence or by connecting closely related sentences. Without prepositions and conjunctions, the following paragraph is difficult to understand:

____ you are looking ____ a job, considering a new job, ____ staying ____ your current employer, always have an updated resume ____ your files. Most employers want to see a resume, ____ be sure yours is readily available.

Notice the difference when prepositions and conjunctions are added:

Whether you are looking for a job, considering a new job, or staying with your current employer, always have an updated resume in your files. Most employers want to see a resume, so be sure yours is readily available.

Learning Objectives

- Recognize the parts of a prepositional phrase.
- Identify the types of conjunctions and explain their uses.
- Use prepositions, conjunctions, and conjunctive adverbs appropriately.
- Use interjections sparingly.

PREPOSITIONS

Prepositions are connectors; they connect a noun or pronoun (the **object of the preposition**) to some other part of a sentence. A preposition cannot stand by itself. The preposition, its object, and any modifiers of the object form a **prepositional phrase**.

	prep	modifier	noun (object)
He sat	*on*	*the*	*floor.*

A list of common prepositions follows:

Common Prepositions

about	behind	for	through
above	below	in	to
across	beside	into	toward
after	between	like	under
among	by	of	until
around	down	off	up
at	during	on	upon
before	except	over	with

The most commonly used prepositions are at, by, for, from, in, of, on, to, *and* with.

Review Chapter 3 for tips on how to form the objective case.

A sentence may contain more than one prepositional phrase, and a prepositional phrase may contain more than one object. When a pronoun is the object of the preposition, the pronoun must be in the objective case.

Luis went *to the movie with Karmeki*. (*Movie* is the object of the preposition *to* in the prepositional phrase *to the movie*. *Karmeki* is the object of the preposition *with* in the prepositional phrase *with Karmeki*.)

Please sit *beside Raul and me*. (*Raul* and *me* are the objects of the preposition *beside* in the prepositional phrase *beside Raul and me*. *Me* is an objective case pronoun.)

Some prepositions also serve as other parts of speech, such as adverbs, adjectives, and conjunctions. You can easily identify prepositions because they must have objects.

Tomas stayed *in his office*. (*Office* is the object of the preposition *in*.)

Tomas stayed *in*. (*In* is an adverb and answers the question *where*?)

A coat *like this one* costs $300. (*One* is the object of the preposition *like*.)

A *like* coat costs $300. (*Like*, meaning "similar," is an adjective and tells *which* coat.)

You may register *after dinner*. (*Dinner* is the object of the preposition *after*).

You may register *after Clara does*. (*After* is a subordinating conjunction that introduces a dependent clause.)

[Checkpoint 8-1]

Identify Prepositional Phrases and Their Parts

Underline the prepositional phrase(s) in each sentence. In the space above the sentence, identify prepositions as **P** and objects of prepositions as **OP**.

1. Kayla waited by the door, but after 20 minutes, she went into the theater.
2. I cannot apply for the job until February.
3. Straighten the items in the display case, and count the books on the shelf.
4. To whom did you give the directions?
5. The team walked through each building on the property except the Seifert Building.

Proper Use of Prepositions

Using prepositions properly may present some challenges. Study the following guidelines to help you make the right choices.

End-of-Sentence Prepositions. Avoid ending sentences with a preposition unless the sentence sounds awkward.

> He couldn't remember what he was looking *for*. (not *He couldn't remember for what he was looking*)

Do not end sentences with an unnecessary preposition.

> I am not sure where to find my brother. (not *brother at*)

One Preposition. Do not use two prepositions when one is enough. Also, avoid using *of* after *all* or *both* unless the following word is a pronoun or unless *of* is needed for clarity.

> I live near Highway J. (not *near to*)
> Julia talked to both teachers. (not *both of the*)
> Ms. Janko asked both *of* us to help her. (pronoun follows *of*)

Between You and Me (not *I*). Remember to use an objective case pronoun when a pronoun is the object of a preposition.

> This disagreement is *between you and me*. (not *you and I*)

Prepositional Phrases and Verbs. Generally, ignore a prepositional phrase when deciding whether to use a singular or a plural verb.

> A memo *about recent hiring issues* was sent yesterday. (The singular subject *memo* requires the singular verb *was sent*.)

When a prepositional phrase beginning with *of* follows certain indefinite pronouns (*all*, *any*, *none*, *some*, *more*, or *most*), the object of the phrase determines whether the pronoun is singular or plural (as you learned in Chapter 5).

> Most of Juan's teammates are from Baltimore. (Because the object of the *of* phrase, *teammates*, is plural, the indefinite pronoun *most* is plural. The plural verb *are* is required.)

Workplace Connection

To keep your messages "clutter-free," eliminate unnecessary prepositions.

"*This is the sort of pedantry up with which I will not put.*"

-Winston Churchill, British statesman and author (1874–1965)

Be sure to include necessary prepositions: a couple of days or that type of document.

[Checkpoint 8-2]

Use Prepositions Correctly

Rewrite the following sentences, deleting unnecessary prepositions and correcting preposition usage errors.

1. Deleting e-mail messages from off of a company network does not erase them permanently.
2. Think of all of the places around the world we have been to.
3. Between you and I, the Conway article needs major revision.

Complete the Chapter 8 Web Exercise at **miller.swlearning.com.**

Misused Words

Sometimes the wrong preposition is used, or a preposition is used incorrectly with other parts of speech. Review the following explanations, and consult a dictionary when you are unsure of your choice.

AGREE TO/AGREE WITH. *Agree to* means "to consent." *Agree with* means "to have the same opinion." You *agree to* a proposal; you *agree with* a person or an idea.

I *agree to* the terms of the employment contract. (proposal)
I *agree with* my coworker's suggestions. (person)

AMONG/BETWEEN. *Among* refers to more than two people or things; *between* refers to two people or things.

Aaron divided the candy *among* his three friends.
Aaron divided the candy *between* Charles and Jasmine.

BESIDE/BESIDES. *Beside* as a preposition means "next to" or "near." *Besides* as a preposition means "in addition to," "other than," or "except."

Will Evangeline sit *beside* you? (next to)
No one *besides* me wants to go to the dance. (other than or except)

COULD HAVE/WOULD HAVE/SHOULD HAVE. *Could*, *would*, and *should* are often combined with the preposition *of*. Pairing *of* with a verb is incorrect.

You *should have* made your calls this morning. (not *should of*)

Than *is not a preposition.* Than *is used for comparisons: Val is taller* than *I am.*

DIFFERENT FROM. *Different from* shows that one thing is unlike something else. *Different than* is incorrect.

The cruise to Alaska was *different from* any vacation I have taken.

IN/INTO. *In* means "location" or "position." *Into* means "motion" (from one place to another) or "change of condition."

The assistant inspected the equipment *in* the padded crate. (location)

We loaded the crate *into* the truck. (motion)

While reading the message, Unoji's curiosity quickly turned *into* concern. (change of condition)

To/Too. *To* begins either a prepositional phrase or an infinitive phrase (*to* plus a verb). *Too* is an adverb that means "also" or "more than enough."

I will deliver the package *to* your home. (*To your home* is a prepositional phrase.)

Arianna is going *to* the movies *too.* (*To the movies* is a prepositional phrase; *too* is an adverb meaning "also.")

I ate *too* much. (*Too* is an adverb meaning "more than enough.")

Chapter 9 discusses infinitive phrases.

Complete Application 8-1.

[Checkpoint 8-3]

Choose the Correct Word

Underline the correct words from those given in parentheses.

1. Sondra (could have // could of) earned an A in Japanese, but she did poorly on the final exam.

2. I (agreed to // agreed with) Rosa's assessment: The reimbursement contract is (to // too) complicated to enter (in // into) without further discussion.

3. NaJay was (to // too) tired to complain (to // too) the manager.

4. Investment booklets were distributed (among // between) the six participants so that they could decide whether these investment options were (different from // different than) the Bateman options.

5. Did you leave the camera (beside // besides) the phone?

CONJUNCTIONS

Like prepositions, **conjunctions** are also connectors: They connect words, phrases, or clauses within sentences.

A junction *is the point where two or more things join. A* conjunction *joins two or more sentence elements: words, phrases, or clauses.*

- A ***phrase*** is a group of related words that *does not* contain both a subject and a verb.
- A ***clause*** is a group of related words that *does* contain both a subject and its verb. A clause is either independent or dependent.
  - An ***independent clause*** (main clause) contains both a subject and a verb, expresses a complete thought, and can stand alone as a sentence.
  - A ***dependent clause*** contains both a subject and a verb, *does not* express a complete thought, and cannot stand alone as a sentence.

These different types of conjunctions connect **sentence elements** (words, phrases, or clauses):

- **Coordinating conjunctions** and **correlative conjunctions** join sentence elements that are grammatically equal.
- **Subordinating conjunctions** join unequal sentence elements.
- **Transitional expressions** (conjunctive adverbs and transitional phrases) connect one independent clause to another.

The acronym fan boys *(*for, and, nor, but, or, yet, so*) is one way to remember coordinating conjunctions.*

Coordinating Conjunctions

Coordinating conjunctions join equal sentence elements: words to words, phrases to phrases, or clauses to clauses. This means that the elements on each side of the conjunction must serve the same function and share the same construction.

Coordinating Conjunctions	Purpose
and	to add
but, yet	to show contrast
or	to show choice
nor	to exclude both choices
for	to indicate a reason
so	to show result or consequence

Akia, Lea, *and* Abbey plan to travel to Ireland next summer. (*And* joins the proper nouns *Akia*, *Lea*, and *Abbey*.)

Did you write to the owner *or* to the manager? (*Or* joins the prepositional phrases *to the owner* and *to the manager*.)

I was late for the luncheon, *yet* I arrived in time to hear the keynote speaker. (*Yet* joins the independent clauses *I was late for the luncheon* and *I arrived in time to hear the keynote speaker*.)

Review Chapter 5 for more information on subject-verb agreement.

When *or* or *nor* joins singular subjects, use a singular verb. When *or* or *nor* joins plural subjects, use a plural verb. When *or* or *nor* joins both a singular and a plural subject, use a verb that agrees with the subject placed nearest the verb. Typically, place the plural subject nearest the verb (as you learned in Chapter 5).

Correlative Conjunctions

Correlative conjunctions come in pairs and join equal sentence elements. Correlative conjunctions must be placed next to or as close as possible to the elements they connect.

Correlative Conjunctions	Purpose
both . . . and	to add
not only . . . but also	to add
either . . . or	to choose
neither . . . nor	to exclude both choices
whether . . . or	to indicate two options

When *either . . . or*, *neither . . . nor*, or *not only . . . but also* join singular subjects, use a singular verb. When they join plural subjects, use a plural verb. When they join both a singular and a plural subject, use a verb that agrees with the word nearest the subject (a plural subject next to the verb sounds better), as you learned in Chapter 5.

Neither Deanna *nor Jacob* has received a call from Raj (*Neither . . . nor* join singular subjects, *Deanna* and *Jacob*.)

Not only my uncles *but also* my aunts are included on the mailing list. (*Not only . . . but also* join the plural subjects, *uncles* and *aunts*.)

The correlative conjunctions *both . . . and* require a plural verb because they refer to both subjects in the sentence.

Both the paint *and* the wallpaper have been delivered. (The sentence subjects are *paint* and *wallpaper*.)

Complete Application 8-2.

[CHECKPOINT 8-4]

Provide Appropriate Coordinating or Correlative Conjunctions

From the lists of coordinating and correlative conjunctions on page 134, choose appropriate conjunctions for the spaces provided. A hint appears in parentheses at the end of each sentence.

1. ______________ the student fee ______________ the tuition are due March 1. (add)
2. Do you prefer a mezzanine seat ______________ an orchestra seat? (choice)
3. ______________ Friday tickets ______________ Saturday tickets are available. (exclude)
4. I appreciate your offer, ______________ I cannot accept the job. (contrast)

Subordinating Conjunctions

Subordinating conjunctions are unlike coordinating and correlative conjunctions because they join *unequal* sentence elements. Subordinating conjunctions join dependent clauses to independent clauses.

Common Subordinating Conjunctions and Their Purposes

Time	Cause or Reason	Comparison or Contrast
after	as	although
as soon as	because	as
before	if	as if
once	since	as though
until	so that	provided
when	that	than
while	unless	though

As shown in the following examples, adding a subordinating conjunction makes a clause dependent.

Independent	**Dependent**
snow covered the roads	*because* snow covered the roads
everyone has a copy of the file	*when* everyone has a copy of the file

A dependent clause must be joined to an independent clause to express a complete thought. Adding punctuation and capitalization makes the complete thought a sentence. In the following examples, the dependent clause is italicized, and the independent clause is underlined.

Because snow covered the roads, we had to delay our trip to Cheyenne.
We will begin the discussion *when everyone has a copy of the file.*

[CHECKPOINT 8-5]

Choose Appropriate Subordinating Conjunctions

Underline the appropriate subordinating conjunction from those given in parentheses.

1. (After // If) you leave by 7 a.m., you will miss the rush-hour traffic.
2. Register at the reception desk (as soon as // before) you arrive.
3. (Provided that // Unless) you buy your tickets early, you may have difficulty scheduling a convenient flight.
4. Teri acts (as though // though) she is the boss.
5. (Because // So that) we want good seats, we must buy our tickets early.

Consult a dictionary or thesaurus to confirm that the transitional expression you choose expresses the meaning that you intend.

Transitional Expressions

Transitional expressions include **conjunctive adverbs** (also called **linking adverbs**) that connect independent clauses **transitional phrases** (groups of words) that serve the same purpose. Transitional expressions help readers and listeners to move smoothly (*transition*) from one independent clause (complete thought) to the next. Conjunctive adverbs and transitional phrases are usually placed at the beginning of the second independent clause whether the clauses are in the same sentence or the clauses are two separate sentences.

Some of these expressions may serve as **parenthetical expressions** when they are placed *within* a clause.

Denzel swims four hours a day; *nonetheless*, he finds time to volunteer at an animal sanctuary. (The conjunctive adverb *nonetheless* joins the two independent clauses in this sentence.)

Denzel swims four hours a day. *Nonetheless*, he finds time to volunteer at an animal sanctuary. (The conjunctive adverb *Nonetheless* joins two separate but related sentences.)

Denzel swims four hours a day; he finds time, *nonetheless*, to volunteer at an animal sanctuary. (The parenthetical expression *nonetheless* is placed within the second clause of the sentence.)

Remember, transitional phrases have more than one word.

Common Transitional Expressions and Their Purposes

Addition	Contrast	Example	Result	Sequence
also	however	for example	as a result	first, second, third
besides	nevertheless	for instance	consequently	next, then, finally
in addition	nonetheless	in fact	therefore	afterwards
similarly	otherwise		thus	

Generally, do not follow a conjunctive adverb of one syllable with a comma.

Complete Applications 8-3 and 8-4.

[CHECKPOINT 8-6]

Choose Appropriate Conjunctive Adverbs or Transitional Phrases

Underline the appropriate conjunctive adverb or transitional phrase from those given in parentheses.

1. Gabriella volunteers at the local food pantry; (in addition // however), she volunteers at her son's high school.
2. Mohammad completed the tasks quickly; (as a result // for example), he impressed his supervisor.
3. (Also // First) Marcia and Olivia analyzed the problem; (then // thus) they developed a plan.
4. Please send your payment by May 1. (Nevertheless // Otherwise), we will turn over your account to a collection agency.
5. Sharifa's team has too many deadlines to meet today; (for example // consequently), three reports and a project estimate are due by 4 p.m.

INTERJECTIONS

Interjections express feelings but usually do not relate grammatically to other words in the sentence. Some examples of interjections are *oh*, *ouch*, and *wow*. Other words, such as *help*, may sometimes be used as

Chapters 10 and 11 provide more information about punctuation.

interjections. An exclamation point follows an interjection that expresses strong emotion, and a comma follows an interjection that expresses mild emotion.

Interjections are used sparingly and should be avoided in business messages. They appear most often in casual communication and advertising.

Wow! Toppings are "tops" at Kit's Custard Shop. (advertising)
Yes, we can make the arrangements for you. (casual communication)

Chapter Summary

- Use a preposition to connect a noun or pronoun to another part of the sentence.
- Recognize frequently misused prepositions, and use them correctly.
- Use coordinating conjunctions and correlative conjunctions to join grammatically equal sentence elements (words, phrases, and clauses).
- Use subordinating conjunctions to join dependent clauses to independent clauses.
- Use conjunctive adverbs and transitional phrases to help readers and listeners move smoothly from one related thought to another.
- Use interjections sparingly to express feelings, and avoid them in business messages.

iLrn

Complete the Chapter 8 Review.

Complete the Chapter 8 iLrn Activities at **miller.swlearning.com.**

Application 8-1

Prepositions

Part A. Underline the prepositional phrase(s) in each sentence. In the space above the sentence, identify prepositions as **P** and objects of prepositions as **OP**.

P OP OP

0. The discussion is between him and her.

1. You may purchase food before the class and during the morning and afternoon breaks.

2. He walked into the room with a frown on his face.

3. Before his presentation to the jury, Mr. Kelso reviewed the summary with his peers.

4. Mr. Espino looked for the folder behind the shelving unit and under the desk in his office.

5. The students, with their luggage, moved quickly toward the elevator.

Part B. Rewrite the following sentences, deleting unnecessary prepositions and correcting preposition usage errors.

0. The book fell off of the table. The book fell off the table.

1. I told my brother to meet me promptly at about 4 p.m. over at the Tiki Café, which has unusual furniture made out of bamboo.

2. Mr. Dakwar should of called earlier for directions; he doesn't know where the meeting is at.

3. Although my opinion was different than their opinion, I finally agreed that the material costs are too high and that we cannot divide the costs between the other three departments.

4. Table 12 is reserved for Murial, Mai, and I (seat Mr. Kantoki besides us); we would of had a better table if we had made our reservations earlier.

5. As the guide led us in the banquet hall, I noticed that most participants were into their seats.

APPLICATION 8-2

Coordinating and Correlative Conjunctions

Part A. Circle the coordinating and correlative conjunctions. Underline the sentence elements that are connected by the conjunctions.

0. Did you go to Chicago on Thursday (or) on Monday?
1. No one wanted to do the work, but everyone wanted to receive the credit.
2. My responsibilities include motivating and retraining employees.
3. Both Brenda and Nelson submitted an application.
4. The recipe calls for either bran or oatmeal.
5. Padma cannot decide whether to buy or to lease her next car.

Part B. Underline the correct coordinating or correlative conjunction from those given in parentheses.

0. Angel completed the state (and // but also) federal tax forms.
1. (Neither // Both) Anna (nor // and) Lea has driven a manual shift car.
2. That font is (not only // either) too small (but also // or) too light for clear fax transmission.
3. I do not like the title, (and // but) I do like the topic.
4. The Albas have viewed our house three times, (for // yet) we have not received an offer.
5. Josh could not register, (for // so) he had not paid his student fines.

Part C. From the lists of coordinating and correlative conjunctions on page 134, choose appropriate conjunctions for the spaces provided. A hint appears in parentheses at the end of each sentence.

0. Express your ideas clearly ______and______ confidently. (add)
1. The home features ______________ a theater system ______________ a spa. (add)
2. Christopher did not feel well, ______________ he went to the doctor. (result)
3. You may reach us ______________ by calling 1-800-555-0155 ______________ by e-mailing abcc@cat.com. (choice)
4. Rosalia bought ______________ refried beans ______________ cilantro. (add)
5. I recognized his face, ______________ I could not remember his name. (contrast)

Application 8-3

Subordinating Conjunctions and Transitional Expressions

Part A. Underline the subordinating conjunction (**SC**), conjunctive adverb (**CA**), or transitional phrase (**TP**) in each sentence. Identify the type of conjunction in the space provided. Refer to the lists of conjunctions on pages 135 and 137 if necessary.

0. As I told you, Neeva is not interested in the job. ___SC___
1. Because our profits increased, we increased our donations. ________
2. Although Mr. Sheng closed the Ohio branch, he opened a branch in Iowa. ________
3. Victor is a talented musician; for example, he plays the piano and the violin. ________
4. Make a decision quickly so that we can submit our proposal. ________
5. Finally, Mrs. Wilkes confirmed the seating. ________
6. Mr. Arellano changed his mind after he met with the managers. ________
7. They have been in session for hours; however, they have not made a decision. ________
8. Jack's absences affected department efficiency; consequently, he was fired. ________
9. The roads were icy; nonetheless, she kept driving. ________
10. We will leave as soon as the performance ends. ________

Part B. Read each sentence carefully to determine which subordinating conjunction (**SC**), conjunctive adverb (**CA**), or transitional phrase (**TP**) best fits the meaning of the sentence. Write your choice in the space provided. A hint is provided in parentheses. Refer to the lists of conjunctions on pages 135 and 137 if necessary.

0. ______If______ you need to contact Peter, call 555-0140. (SC, reason)
1. Clean the tile thoroughly; ________________ apply the sealer. (CA, sequence)
2. Drive carefully ________________ you don't get a speeding ticket. (SC, reason)
3. Victoria likes to run; ________________, she runs five days a week. (TP, example)
4. Nkose acted ________________ he didn't know me. (SC, comparison)
5. ________________ you are working in San Francisco, visit Nob Hill. (SC, time)
6. Our company offers attractive benefits; ________________, we match our employees' 401(k) contributions dollar for dollar. (TP, example)
7. Sherrie had not been trained on the software. ________________, she produced a professional-looking presentation in just a few hours. (CA, contrast)
8. ________________ you buy a cell phone, check the service prices carefully. (SC, time)

APPLICATION 8-4

Conjunctions

Part A. Coordinating and correlative conjunctions are missing from the following sentences. Use a caret (^) to show where conjunctions should be inserted. Then write the conjunctions in the space provided. Use the lists of conjunctions on page 134 if necessary.

0. You will find new shows ^ attractions at the theme park. ______and______
1. Miami's warm weather coastal location attract millions of visitors yearly. ____________
2. Miami is the home of the Miami Dolphins but also of the Orange Bowl. ____________
3. If neither football zoos interest you, you may prefer to visit the city's art galleries museums. ____________
4. You may also enjoy taking a walking tour eating lunch at one of the cafés scattered throughout the city. ____________
5. To move around in downtown Miami, many people either drive ride the monorail. ____________

Part B. Read each sentence carefully to determine which subordinating conjunction (**SC**), conjunctive adverb (**CA**), or transitional phrase (**TP**) best fits the meaning of the sentence. Write your choice in the space provided. A hint is provided in parentheses. Use the lists of conjunctions on pages 135 and 137 if necessary.

0. Please do not put through any calls ______unless______ they are urgent. (SC, reason)
1. ____________ identify the training objectives; ____________ identify the completion date for each objective. (CA, sequence)
2. Mac believed his sister's story ____________ she began laughing. (SC, time)
3. We have streamlined our shipping operations. ____________, shipments are occasionally delayed. (CA, contrast)
4. You must submit an online application by March 1. ____________, you may hand-deliver an application until March 5. (CA, contrast)
5. Carefully read the rental agreement ____________ you sign. (SC, time)
6. Charlene is a good player ____________ she had several injuries last season. (SC, contrast)
7. The tour price includes several extras; ____________, you receive two meals daily, transportation between airport and hotel, and three tours. (TP, example)
8. My cell-phone plan includes nationwide long-distance service. ____________, the plan provides free weekend and evening calls. (CA or TP, addition)

Chapter 8 Review

Prepositions, Conjunctions, and Interjections

Part A. Delete Unnecessary Prepositions

Cross out the unnecessary prepositions in the following sentences. Each correct answer is worth one point.

1. We jumped off of the riverbank.
2. Where did you go to?
3. The sculpture was made out of steel and copper.
4. Where did you put the report at?
5. The restaurant is located down under the Biscayne Bay Bridge.
6. Two sculptures stood outside of the building.
7. You can put those books anywhere you would like to.
8. Ms. Daremore lives over around the corner from Gerard's house.
9. Kerry climbed up a hill to reach the observatory.
10. The science museum is near to the railroad yard.

Part B. Identify Preposition Errors

Indicate whether prepositions are used correctly in the following sentences by writing **C** (correct) or **I** (incorrect). Each correct answer is worth one point.

1. Can you send someone besides Daryl or Lee? ________
2. The children cannot wait to get in the pool. ________
3. The choir is going too Vancouver in August. ________
4. Alberto's results were no different than yours. ________
5. I could have recommended you if I had known you were interested in the job. ________
6. Let's divide the payment between the four of us. ________
7. The delegates went into the meeting without a plan. ________
8. Sam would of sent the assignment earlier, but he forgot the fax number. ________
9. Both sides have agreed with the settlement. ________
10. Is anyone beside me concerned about the cost? ________

Part C. Choose the Correct Connector

Read each sentence carefully to determine which choice of those given in parentheses best fits the meaning of the sentence; then underline your choice. Each correct answer is worth four points.

1. Begin your job search by evaluating both your personal attributes (and // or) your professional skills.

2. You will find that your skills and characteristics are (different from // different than) those of your friends and classmates.

3. Use an assessment tool (so that // as soon as) you can learn more (about // of) yourself.

4. Many assessment tools are available, (and // so) compare them carefully (after // before) you make a choice.

5. You may choose either an online (or // and) a paper format.

6. If you (agree to // agree with) the assessment results, you may find the information helpful (after // while) you develop your job search strategy.

7. List not only job-specific skills (and // but also) your most positive characteristics (so that // that) you can easily see similarities (among // between) what you have to offer and what the company desires.

8. (Beside // besides) technical skills, emphasize transferable skills; (for example // consequently), mention your ability to organize or to negotiate.

9. As you look for jobs, consider transportation, child care, (and // but also) any other issue that may affect where you work.

10. By the time you begin the application process, you (should have // should of) gathered enough information to make a targeted job search.

11. You will find many places to look (for // about) jobs; (between you and I // between you and me), websites are my favorite sources.

12. Newspapers are not the best job sources, (but // for) they do provide keywords that you can use in your employment messages.

13. The information that you have gathered will enable you to move (in // into) the job market with confidence.

CHAPTER 9

Phrases, Clauses, and Sentences

Do you recognize these guides to daily living published in *Poor Richard's Almanack* (1732–1757)?

> Early . . . and early to rise makes a man healthy, wealthy, and wise.
> . . . to repent divine; to persist devilish.

These examples are not the words of wisdom Benjamin Franklin intended because they are incomplete and thus have little or no meaning. A prepositional phrase is missing from the first proverb; an independent clause is missing from the second proverb.

To relay the message that you intend, group related words into phrases and clauses and ultimately into complete thoughts. By the way, Mr. Franklin said:

> Early to bed and early to rise makes a man healthy, wealthy, and wise.
> To err is human; to repent divine; to persist devilish.

LEARNING OBJECTIVES

- Identify prepositional, infinitive, gerund, and participial phrases.
- Differentiate between independent and dependent clauses.
- Recognize nonessential and essential dependent clauses.
- Identify sentence structures and types.
- Write complete sentences in parallel form.

PHRASES

Phrases are groups of words that are related but *do not* contain both a subject and a verb and *do not* form a complete thought (as you learned in Chapter 8).

> in the garage
> to run the mile
> having eaten all the dessert

Sentences may contain prepositional phrases and verbal phrases (infinitive, gerund, and participial phrases).

Prepositional Phrases

In Chapter 8, you learned that a prepositional phrase begins with a preposition, ends with one or more nouns or pronouns (**objects** of the preposition), and includes any modifiers of the objects. Prepositional phrases act as adjectives or adverbs.

> Applicants *with customer service experience* are likely to be hired. (The prepositional phrase *with customer service experience* serves as an adjective and tells what kind of applicants are likely to be hired.)

> Emilia will go *to New York*. (The prepositional phrase *to New York* serves as an adverb and tells where Emilia will go.)

Verbals and Verbal Phrases

As you learned in Chapter 4, **verbals** are verb forms that are used as other parts of speech, *not* as verbs. Infinitives, gerunds, and participles are verbals. When verbals include words in addition to the verb form, they are called **verbal phrases**. In the examples that follow, the verbal is underlined, and the verbal phrase is italicized.

The decision *to sell this car* is not wise. (infinitive phrase)

Securing a job is my immediate goal. (gerund phrase)

The members *whispering loudly* annoyed the speaker. (participial phrase)

> *Do not confuse an* ***infinitive phrase*** *(to + verb + any nouns or pronouns + any modifiers) with a* ***prepositional phrase*** *that begins with to (to + any nouns or pronouns + any modifiers).*

INFINITIVES AND INFINITIVE PHRASES. As you learned in Chapter 4, **infinitives** consist of the word *to* combined with a verb form (*to* + verb). An **infinitive phrase** is an infinitive plus any objects (nouns or pronouns following the infinitive) and any modifiers of the objects. Infinitives and infinitive phrases are used most often as nouns and sometimes as adjectives and adverbs. In the following examples, the infinitive is underlined, and the infinitive phrase is italicized.

To organize a charity ball is time-consuming. (The infinitive phrase *to organize a charity ball* serves as a noun and is the subject of the sentence.)

Mazher wants *to return home*. (The infinitive phrase *to return home* serves as a noun and is the direct object of the verb *wants*.)

I may reach my goal *to run the Boston Marathon*. (*To run the Boston Marathon* serves as an adjective and tells which goal.)

Mr. deRoux is difficult *to please*. (*To please* serves as an adverb and tells how, or in what way, Mr. deRoux is difficult.)

> *Review verb tenses in Chapter 4.*

GERUNDS AND GERUND PHRASES. In Chapter 4, you also learned that **gerunds** are verb forms ending in *-ing*. A **gerund phrase** consists of a gerund, any modifiers, and any objects. Gerunds and gerund phrases are used as nouns. In the following examples, gerunds are underlined, and gerund phrases are italicized.

Climbing mountains is Denise's hobby. (The gerund phrase *climbing mountains* serves as a noun and is the subject of the sentence.)

Do you enjoy *teaching art classes*? (The gerund phrase *teaching art classes* serves as a noun and is the object of the verb *enjoy*.)

PARTICIPLES AND PARTICIPIAL PHRASES. **Participles** are verb forms that end in *ing*, *ed*, *en*, *d*, or *t*. In the chapter on verbs, you learned about two types of participles: **present** and **past.**

Present Participle	**Past Participle**
writing	written
walking	walked
bending	bent

A **participial phrase** is formed by a participle plus any modifiers and any objects. Participles and participial phrases are used as adjectives. In the following examples, participles are underlined, and participial phrases are italicized.

> *Prepared quickly*, the director's speech was humorous. (The participial phrase *prepared quickly* serves as an adjective and tells what kind of speech.)
>
> The agent *selling the most property* will receive a bonus. (The participial phrase *selling the most property* serves as an adjective and explains which agent.)

Complete Application 9-1.

[CHECKPOINT 9-1]

Identify Phrases

In Column 1, identify the italicized phrases as **PREP** (prepositional), **INF** (infinitive), **GER** (gerund), or **PART** (participial). In Column 2, indicate whether the phrase is used as a **N** (noun), an **ADJ** (adjective), or an **ADV** (adverb).

	Column 1	**Column 2**
1. Ms. deLuca's primary responsibility is *supervising three clerks.*	________	________
2. Do you remember any details *about the accident*?	________	________
3. *Released last month*, the CD is a favorite among teens.	________	________
4. *To wait any longer* is ridiculous.	________	________
5. The lamp was stored *in the attic.*	________	________
6. I dislike *balancing my checkbook.*	________	________
7. The customer wants *to place an order.*	________	________
8. *Selling the property immediately* is his recommendation.	________	________
9. Did you look *in the garage*?	________	________
10. The book *signed by Mark Twain* is on display.	________	________

Punctuating clauses is discussed in Chapters 10 and 11.

CLAUSES

As you learned in Chapter 8, **clauses** are groups of related words that contain *both* a subject and a verb. Clauses may be independent or dependent.

Independent Clauses

An **independent clause** meets these requirements:

- *Does* contain both a subject and a verb
- *Is* a complete thought
- *Can* stand alone as a sentence (when appropriately capitalized and punctuated)

WORKPLACE CONNECTION

Phrases and clauses that serve as modifiers should be placed as close as possible to the words they modify to ensure that sentences sound clear, logical, and professional.

The following groups of words are independent clauses because they meet all three requirements. When punctuated and capitalized appropriately, independent clauses become sentences.

Independent Clause	Sentence
several files are missing	Several files are missing.
you have a $75 balance	You have a $75 balance.

Dependent Clauses

A **dependent clause** has these characteristics:

- *Does* contain both a subject and a verb
- *Is not* a complete thought
- *Cannot* stand alone as a sentence

when Isabel plays the piano
if we sign by March 11

Dependent clauses "depend" on an independent clause to complete the thought. A subordinating conjunction beginning a clause makes the clause dependent. In the following examples, dependent clauses are italicized, and subordinating conjunctions are underlined.

Chapter 8 lists some subordinating conjunctions.

After she completed the training program, she was promoted.
I distributed 30 copies *before I noticed the error*.

Relative pronouns such as *who*, *whom*, *whose*, *which*, and *that* sometimes introduce dependent clauses. In the following examples, dependent clauses are italicized, and relative pronouns are underlined.

The proposal *that you believe will reduce the absentee rate* will be introduced at the May 1 board meeting.

Hannah, *whose mother is a college professor*, was awarded the Banff Scholarship.

Review pages 44–45 to refresh your understanding of relative pronouns.

[Checkpoint 9-2]

Identify Independent and Dependent Clauses

Identify the italicized clauses as **IC** (independent clause) or **DC** (dependent clause).

1. *When Carla receives her tax refund*, she plans to contribute to her IRA. __________
2. *Mr. Balnik*, the drivers' training instructor, *also works as a carpenter.* __________
3. Your account will have a zero balance *once you make this payment*. __________
4. The hotel will confirm your reservation *as soon as you send a deposit*. __________
5. *The prices are high*, so I did not order tickets. __________
6. Did you notice *that several pages are missing*? __________
7. As my sister scored the final point, *I watched proudly from the sidelines*. __________
8. *We dropped the price* so that the headsets will sell quickly. __________
9. *Until she moved to Houston*, Margot had never attended the opera. __________
10. James, *who has six nieces and nephews*, enjoys being a teacher. __________

Nonessential and Essential Clauses

Some dependent clauses are necessary to the meaning of a sentence, but others are not. **Nonessential clauses** (also called **nonrestrictive clauses**) are helpful but not necessary to the meaning of a sentence. Nonessential clauses are set off by commas. Notice that the information in the depen-dent clause in each of the following examples is helpful but not necessary to the meaning of the sentence.

The dress, *which is a designer original*, costs $3,000.
Mr. Birk, *who is the president of Stone Industries*, is the speaker.

Essential clauses (also called **restrictive clauses**) are necessary to the main meaning of a sentence. Essential clauses are *not* set off by commas. If the dependent clause in each of the following two examples were removed, the main meaning of the sentence would change.

The three students *who scored the highest* qualify for the award.
The bus company *that has the best safety record* is Doubleday.

To determine whether a clause is nonessential or essential, delete the clause from the sentence. If the sentence still conveys the intended meaning, the clause is nonessential *; if the meaning of the sentence changes, the clause is* essential.

Which *usually introduces nonessential clauses;* that *typically introduces essential clauses.*

Complete Applications 9-2 and 9-3.

[CHECKPOINT 9-3]

Identify Nonessential and Essential Clauses

Underline the dependent clauses in each sentence. Then identify each dependent clause as **NON** (nonessential) or **ESS** (essential). Commas that set off nonessential clauses have been removed.

1. The key that is hidden under the rock opens the back door. ________
2. Jenna whom you recommended was hired for the medical assistant position. ________
3. Houses that qualify as "historic treasures" may be eligible for preservation funds. ________
4. Thomas used to work in the Carroll Building which is slated for demolition. ________
5. Aaron whose grades were not good this semester is studying with a tutor. ________
6. Students who maintain a 3.7 grade point average may apply for the Brookfield Honor Scholarship. ________

"*You want to write a sentence as clean as a bone. That is the goal.*"

-James Baldwin, American writer (1924–1987)

SENTENCES

A **sentence** is a group of related words that contains a subject and a verb (predicate) and expresses a complete thought. A sentence begins with a capital letter and ends with a period, a question mark, or an exclamation point. Sentences are classified by *structure* (how they are constructed) and by *type* (how they express thoughts).

Sentence Structure

Sentences are *simple*, *compound*, *complex*, or *compound-complex*, depending on the type and number of clauses in the sentence.

SIMPLE SENTENCES. A **simple sentence** has one independent clause. That clause may have more than one subject or verb.

Hong Kong is a busy, crowded city. (one subject, *Hong Kong*; one predicate, *is*)

Brisbane and Sydney are cities in Australia. (two subjects, *Brisbane* and *Sydney*; one predicate, *are*)

COMPOUND SENTENCES. A **compound sentence** has two or more independent clauses. Usually, a coordinating conjunction (*for*, *and*, *nor*, *but*, *or*, *yet*, or *so*) joins the clauses. Independent clauses are underlined in the following examples.

<u>I paid for the tickets by credit card</u>, and <u>I received them yesterday</u>. (two independent clauses joined by *and*)

WORKPLACE CONNECTION

A knowledge of and a sensitivity to cultural factors will help you communicate more effectively with friends, coworkers, and customers.

I cannot attend the meeting this week, nor can I attend next week. (two independent clauses joined by *nor*)

> *Notice that a comma comes before the coordinating conjunction when the conjunction connects independent clauses.*

Complex Sentences

A **complex sentence** has one independent clause and one or more dependent clauses. In the following examples, independent clauses are underlined, and dependent clauses are italicized.

While Emma was at the concert, she saw four of her classmates. (one dependent clause; one independent clause)

Darnel, *who is a photographer*, displayed his work at the Riverside Arts Center, *which is a local gallery*. (one independent clause; two dependent clauses)

Compound-Complex Sentences.

A **compound-complex sentence** has two or more independent clauses and one or more dependent clauses. The following example shows the independent clauses underlined and the dependent clause italicized.

Merilee had lived in Jacksonville, and she had lived in Miami *before she moved to Baton Rouge*. (two independent clauses; one dependent clause)

[Checkpoint 9-4]

Identify Sentence Structure

Underline independent clauses and double-underline dependent clauses in each sentence. Then identify the sentence as **SIM** (simple), **COM** (compound), **CPX** (complex), or **CCX** (compound-complex).

1. Ming received six interview offers within two weeks. __________
2. John-Paul, who is a well-known photographer and who is also my neighbor, shows his work at the Abondazza Gallery. __________
3. Nanette, who works long hours as a firefighter, volunteers weekly. __________
4. Both my brother and I mailed you a postcard from Santiago. __________
5. Mai-Ling's house, which is more than 100 years old, is being renovated. __________
6. Mr. Parks sent the package last night, and he specified Sunday delivery. __________
7. I assembled a new birdhouse, and I hung a birdfeeder on the tree that is near the window. __________
8. Crystal waited nervously while the panel scored her test. __________
9. Michael's voice mail contained three messages that required immediate responses, but he was unable to reach the callers. __________
10. Apples, peaches, and kiwi are my favorite fruits; beans and cauliflower are my favorite vegetables. __________

Chapter 10 presents end-of-sentence punctuation, including punctuation for indirect questions and courteous requests.

Sentence Type

Sentences express ideas in a *declarative*, an *imperative*, an *exclamatory*, or an *interrogative* manner.

A **declarative sentence** simply makes a statement or expresses an opinion or a belief. A declarative sentence ends with a period.

Effective networking produces jobs.
First impressions do count.

An **imperative sentence** gives a command or makes a request. Usually, the subject of an imperative sentence is the pronoun *you*, even though the *you* does not appear. (This is often called "you understood.") An imperative sentence ends with a period.

Project a positive image.
Prepare for your job search by assessing your strengths.

An **exclamatory sentence** shows strong feeling. An exclamatory sentence ends with an exclamation point.

Stop the car!
You got the job!

An **interrogative sentence** asks a direct question. An interrogative sentence ends with a question mark.

Did the recruiter schedule an interview?
Has Sharon completed the online application?

Complete Application 9-4.

[CHECKPOINT 9-5]

Identify Sentence Type

Identify each sentence type as **DEC** (declarative), **IMP** (imperative), **EXC** (exclamatory), or **INT** (interrogative). End punctuation has been omitted.

1. Attach the birdhouse securely to the tree ________
2. Juana will attend the Art Institute of Chicago ________
3. Romi ordered office furniture from Benton's ________
4. Call the fire department now ________
5. Did anyone see Professor Yang ________
6. Hold the elevator ________
7. I think you should check the number before you fax the report ________
8. Has Courtney or Erik arrived ________

Parallelism

Parallelism means that a sentence is "balanced" because coordinating conjunctions or correlative conjunctions join grammatically *equal* sentence elements. In the following examples, joined elements are in italics; conjunctions are underlined.

- **Join elements that are grammatically the same.**

Not Parallel	Parallel
Joaquin *golfs*, *swims*, *and he enjoys jogging*. (*And* joins unequal elements: verbs to independent clause.)	Joaquin *golfs*, *swims*, *and jogs*. (*And* joins equal elements: verbs.)
To expand operations, we *must gain* employee support *and are seeking* community support. (*And* joins unequal verb tenses.)	To expand operations, we must gain *employee support and community support*. (*And* joins equal elements: nouns with their adjective modifiers.)
You can buy your supplies *in Waukesha or when you go to Merton*. (*Or* joins unequal elements: a prepositional phrase to a dependent clause.)	You can buy your supplies *in Waukesha or in Merton*. (*Or* joins equal elements: two prepositional phrases.)

- **Place correlative conjunctions next to the elements to be joined.**

Either *assign the Marsdon case to Victor* or *to Sara*. (*Either . . . or* join unequal elements: independent clause to prepositional phrase.)	Assign the Marsdon case to either *Victor* or *Sara*. (*Either . . . or* join equal elements: noun to noun.)

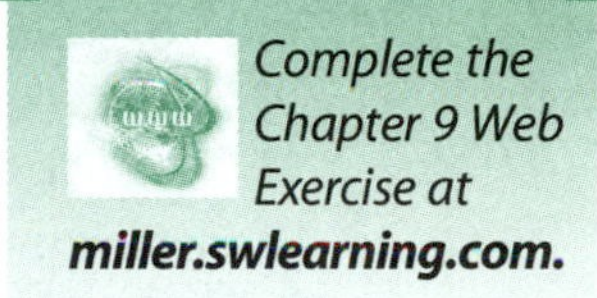
Complete the Chapter 9 Web Exercise at ***miller.swlearning.com.***

Complete Application 9-5.

[CHECKPOINT 9-6]

Write Parallel Sentences

Write **C** (correct) if the sentence is parallel. Otherwise, rewrite the sentence to be parallel.

1. Gloria drove on the icy highway and was having a difficult time controlling the car. ________
2. Parker received not only a scholarship but also was awarded a grant. ________
3. Neither my mother nor my father plays tennis. ________
4. I will vacation either in Gulf Shores or go to Pensacola. ________
5. The job responsibilities include arranging stock, watering plants, and pruning trees. ________

Chapter Summary

- Use prepositional phrases as adjectives or adverbs.
- Use infinitives and infinitive phrases primarily as nouns and sometimes as adjectives or adverbs.
- Use gerunds and gerund phrases as nouns.
- Use participles and participial phrases as adjectives.
- Identify independent clauses, which contain both a subject and a verb, state a complete thought, and can stand alone as a sentence.
- Identify dependent clauses, which contain both a subject and a verb, *do not* state a complete thought, and *cannot* stand alone as a sentence.
- Differentiate between nonessential clauses (which provide helpful but unnecessary information) and essential clauses (which provide information necessary to the meaning of the sentence).
- Identify simple sentences (one independent clause).
- Identify compound sentences (two or more independent clauses).
- Identify complex sentences (one independent clause and one or more dependent clauses).
- Identify compound-complex sentences (two or more independent clauses and one or more dependent clauses).
- Use declarative (statement), imperative (command), exclamatory (strong feeling), and interrogative (question) sentences appropriately.
- Make sentences parallel by joining grammatically equal sentence elements and by placing correlative conjunctions next to the elements to be joined.

Complete the Chapter 9 Review.

ILrn

Complete the Chapter 9 iLrn Activities at **miller.swlearning.com**.

Application 9-1

Phrases

Part A. Identify the italicized phrases as **PREP** (prepositional) or **INF** (infinitive).

0. Did you receive a recommendation *from Ms. Voravong*? PREP
1. Send your e-mail *to the service agent*. ________
2. Do you expect your candidate *to win the primary*? ________
3. Madame Boulanger prefers *to climb the stairs*. ________
4. *To reach a customer service representative* may take several minutes. ________
5. Freida hurried *to the call center*. ________
6. Would you like *to work overtime*? ________
7. The students want *to hear the musician*. ________
8. Did you give the key *to Jean and Ramon*? ________

Part B. In Column 1, identify the italicized phrases as **PREP** (prepositional), **INF** (infinitive), **GER** (gerund), or **PART** (participial). In Column 2, indicate whether the phrase is used as a **N** (noun), an **ADJ** (adjective), or an **ADV** (adverb).

	Column 1	Column 2
0. The boy *with the red shirt* asked for directions.	PREP	ADJ
1. The children raced *to the top*.	________	________
2. The menu, *written in Spanish*, was not easy to read.	________	________
3. Marivel and Chandra want *to write a novel*.	________	________
4. *Synchronized swimming* is my favorite exercise.	________	________
5. *Marco's skiing* has improved.	________	________
6. *Recently dented*, Grant's car is in the repair shop.	________	________
7. *Identifying animal tracks* is one of the assignments.	________	________
8. *During the winter*, Dale and Lilly Eng live in Georgia.	________	________
9. *Giving presentations* makes me nervous.	________	________
10. I may need *to enlist your help*.	________	________
11. The Smiths' offer, *submitted yesterday*, was accepted.	________	________
12. The student *with the most points* will receive a prize.	________	________

APPLICATION 9-2

Clauses

Part A. Identify the italicized clauses as **IC** (independent clause) or **DC** (dependent clause).

0. *Letters* written more than 100 years ago *are displayed in the library.* IC
1. Laisha must work late tonight *because we are behind schedule.* ________
2. *If you delay any longer,* you may miss the bus. ________
3. *Ellen will receive a 10 percent discount* if she enrolls today. ________
4. Orlando drew up the landscape plans, and *he made the plant purchases.* ________
5. I took three messages *while Paola was on the phone.* ________
6. *Do not make a final decision* until you read the contract carefully. ________
7. Ms. Cheevers recommended *that Kyle be hired.* ________
8. *You will not receive a certificate* if you do not complete the class. ________
9. *Rachel,* who graduated three years ago, *returned to speak to our class.* ________
10. Do you know *who received an A?* ________

Part B. Underline the independent clauses and double-underline the dependent clauses in each sentence. Then identify any dependent clause as **ESS** (essential) or **NON** (nonessential). Commas that set off nonessential clauses have been removed.

0. I hired Saren who previously worked here. NON
1. Beans and Bagels is a café that has inexpensive food. ________
2. I hire employees who demonstrate a positive attitude. ________
3. Martine whose father was an Argentine diplomat now lives in Egypt. ________
4. We need to hire someone who speaks fluent Hmong. ________
5. Yvonne Meas whose leadership ability is well-known recently wrote a book. ________
6. The report that completely explains the water problem is available online. ________
7. The employee who will be promoted next is Kenneth. ________
8. Psychology which wasn't my favorite course is popular among sophomores. ________
9. The Barlows who had been my neighbors for ten years moved to Florida. ________
10. The light fixture that has the antique glass shade needs a new electrical cord. ________

APPLICATION 9-3

Phrases and Clauses

Part A. Use the following abbreviations to identify each italicized group of words.

INF (infinitive phrase)
GER (gerund phrase)
PART (participial phrase)
PREP (prepositional phrase)
DC (dependent clause)
IC (independent clause)

0. Oliver tied the rope *to the truck hitch.* PREP
1. Virginia waited in line *for three hours.* ________
2. *When you complete the job,* you will get paid. ________
3. *To interview the president* would be an honor. ________
4. Martin, *whose letter was delivered today,* will be home soon. ________
5. The clerk, *carefully counting the customer's change,* smiled pleasantly. ________
6. *Hauling garbage* is Calendra's responsibility. ________
7. Because tickets sold quickly, *Dave Matthews added an extra performance.* ________
8. The dog, *at that particular moment,* decided to roll in the mud. ________
9. *Updating the telephone system* will decrease wait time. ________
10. Britt, *looking for the school,* stopped at an information center. ________

Part B. The following groups of words are either phrases or dependent clauses. Add an independent clause to each group of words to make a complete sentence. Apply appropriate punctuation and capitalization.

0. before you order supplies

   Before you order supplies, ask about shipping costs.

1. proposing a new recycling plan
2. because we received complaints
3. to investigate the complaint
4. having had the car repaired recently
5. speaking in a loud voice

Application 9-4

Sentence Structure and Type

Part A. Underline independent clauses and double-underline dependent clauses in each sentence. Then identify the sentence as **SIM** (simple), **COM** (compound), **CPX** (complex), or **CCX** (compound-complex).

0. While his brother ran the race, Nathan watched from the top of the hill. CPX
1. Rosa paid the fare once she boarded the train. ________
2. A coordinator will arrange transportation to and from the hospital, make appointments with each department, and reserve a room in a nearby hotel. ________
3. While he was at the airport, Mr. Fenton used wireless connections to make airline reservations for his next trip; he also booked hotels and purchased train tickets. ________
4. Golden Gate Park in San Francisco covers more than a thousand acres and is one of the largest city parks in the United States. ________
5. Read the contract carefully before you sign your name or before you make a deposit; also, call the Better Business Bureau to check for complaints. ________
6. Bettina and Roberto plan to buy a condominium, but they do not agree on the location. ________
7. Learn the difference between a phrase and a clause; then learn the difference between an independent and a dependent clause so that you will punctuate messages correctly. ________
8. The campus is within two miles of her home, so Professor Vincent rides her bicycle almost every day. ________

Part B. Identify each sentence type as **DEC** (declarative), **IMP** (imperative), **EXC** (exclamatory), or **INT** (interrogative). End punctuation has been omitted.

0. The shipment arrived this morning DEC
1. Visit our website ________
2. Did Lawrence send the bill ________
3. Janet's plans include a visit to the Field Museum of Natural History ________
4. Don't jump ________
5. Can you complete the report today ________
6. To reserve a seat, send $3 ________
7. Watch out ________
8. Why don't you ask Bailey ________

Application 9-5

Parallel Sentences

Write **C** (correct) if the sentence is parallel. Otherwise, rewrite the sentence to be parallel.

0. Mr. Hildalgo explained that both nursing and an engineer are good careers.

   Mr. Hildalgo explained that both nursing and engineering are good careers.

1. Ms. Bigus, our travel agent, suggested that we reserve either a room on the top floor (for a lake view) or on the third floor (for a garden view). ________

2. When hosting international visitors, learn some facts about the culture, dress conservatively, and you should avoid using slang in your conversations. ________

3. The responsibilities of the job include responding to customer inquiries, accessing information on coverage, recording policy changes, and to update client files. ________

4. Tamasha should talk to neither the defendant nor the defense attorney. ________

5. Do not apply for the managerial position unless you have not only strong writing skills but also exceptional speaking skills. ________

6. Will you lecture in both Seattle and Portland? ________

7. Our vacation plans include a visit to Everglades National Park and to stop at John Pennekamp Coral Reef State Park. ________

8. Maykemp's printer supplies are not only better but also less expensive than supplies sold by other companies. ________

9. Driving to Monterey or a drive to Carmel is a nice day trip. ________

10. College admissions officers examine your standardized test scores and what your grades were in class. ________

Phrases, Clauses, and Sentences

Part A. Identify Phrases

In Column 1, identify the italicized phrases as **PREP** (prepositional), **INF** (infinitive), **GER** (gerund), or **PART** (participial). In Column 2, indicate whether the phrase is used as a **N** (noun), an **ADJ** (adjective), or an **ADV** (adverb). Each correct answer is worth one point.

	Column 1	Column 2
1. *Valued at $150 to $250*, an assortment of baskets sold for $1,700 at the auction.	________	________
2. The auction, *earning $1.5 million*, was considered successful.	________	________
3. *Enthusiastic bidding* exceeded expectations.	________	________
4. Items *of historical significance* were donated to the American Historical Society.	________	________
5. A portrait of George Washington, *signed by the artist*, hangs in the library.	________	________
6. Mr. Velez does not want *to drive there*.	________	________
7. Jackie's interest is *teaching history*.	________	________
8. Kayla agreed *to meet later*.	________	________
9. The Treptows ate *at the Four Seasons Café*.	________	________
10. *Surveying the residents* is Kelly's responsibility.	________	________

Part B. Identify Sentence Elements

Use the following abbreviations to identify the elements of each sentence. End punctuation has been omitted. Each correct answer is worth one point.

Sentence Structure: **SIM** (simple), **COM** (compound), **CPX** (complex), or **CCX** (compound-complex)

Sentence Type: **DEC** (declarative), **IMP** (imperative), **INT** (interrogative), or **EXC** (exclamatory)

Italicized Element: **INF** (infinitive phrase), **GER** (gerund phrase), **PART** (participial phrase), **PREP** (prepositional phrase), **DC** (dependent clause), **IC** (independent clause)

1. *During the winter*, Angela went skiing in Vermont; in the spring, she went sailing off the coast of Mexico

   Sentence Structure: ________ Sentence Type: ________ Italicized Element: ________

2. *First published in 1772*, Poor Richard's Almanack contains witty, commonsense sayings

   Sentence Structure: ________ Sentence Type: ________ Italicized Element: ________

3. My assignment this week is *to call donors* ; next week, my assignment will be to call volunteers

   Sentence Structure: ________ Sentence Type: ________ Italicized Element: ________

4. The anatomy course, *which is offered only once a year,* fills quickly; therefore, you must register as soon as possible

   Sentence Structure: ________ Sentence Type: ________ Italicized Element: ________

5. *To receive a discount*, show your ID card at the door

   Sentence Structure: ________ Sentence Type: ________ Italicized Element: ________

6. Will you celebrate your birthday *on the 7th*

   Sentence Structure: ________ Sentence Type: ________ Italicized Element: ________

7. Will you participate in person, or *will you participate online*

   Sentence Structure: ________ Sentence Type: ________ Italicized Element: ________

8. *Maintaining these records* will be a challenge

   Sentence Structure: ________ Sentence Type: ________ Italicized Element: ________

9. *Having thoroughly researched salaries* is helpful when you must indicate a desired rate of pay

   Sentence Structure: ________ Sentence Type: ________ Italicized Element: ________

10. *Popular European cruise destinations are Ireland and Portugal*; other popular destinations include cities along the Mediterranean Sea

    Sentence Structure: ________ Sentence Type: ________ Italicized Element:________

11. After Masami has worked at Hines for six months, he is entitled *to a one-week vacation*; but I don't believe he plans to go anywhere

    Sentence Structure: ________ Sentence Type: ________ Italicized Element: ________

12. Do you receive a 10 percent discount *if you pay your bill online*

    Sentence Structure: ________ Sentence Type: ________ Italicized Element:________

13. Investors are concerned about the new policies *that the board of directors instituted* because stock prices dropped 5 percent

    Sentence Structure: ________ Sentence Type: ________ Italicized Element: ________

14. *Driven by competition*, the bank lowered mortgage rates

    Sentence Structure: ________ Sentence Type: ________ Italicized Element: ________

15. Avoid personalizing a child's clothing with the child's full name; also, avoid *adding other identifying details, such as birth date or school name*

    Sentence Structure: ________ Sentence Type: ________ Italicized Element: ________

Part C. Write Parallel Sentences

Rewrite each sentence to be parallel. Each parallel sentence is worth five points.

1. Ms. Parminter both reviewed the current organizational structure and the proposed structure.

2. You may register either for Botany I or Ecology 1.

3. The day is sunny and without clouds.

4. Ironwood Community College offers experienced instructors, well-equipped classrooms, online instruction, and parking is convenient.

5. Mr. Soga explained that he needs six new chairs and is asking for voice recognition software for three computers.

6. Dr. Kass examined the patient thoroughly and in an efficient manner.

7. Is Connie able to meet with the Toronto staff on Monday and Tuesday with the Ottawa staff?

Basic Punctuation

CHAPTER 10

Traffic laws help prevent accidents by setting rules to regulate the flow of traffic, and traffic signs give you the clues you need to complete your journeys safely. Punctuation marks are to writers what traffic signs are to motorists. The period, question mark, and exclamation point act as STOP signs to bring your readers to a halt. Other punctuation marks serve as YIELD signs by signaling your readers to slow down before reading further. Just as you obey traffic laws to travel safely, follow punctuation rules to communicate clearly.

LEARNING OBJECTIVES

- Choose appropriate end punctuation for sentences.
- Use periods correctly in sentences.
- Use commas correctly in sentences.

DEFINITION OF PUNCTUATION

Punctuation consists of a set of standard marks that show relationships among words, phrases, and clauses. Punctuation clarifies the meaning of writing and makes reading easier.

End punctuation indicates the end of a sentence and includes periods, question marks, and exclamation points. **Internal punctuation** indicates a pause or break within a sentence. Internal punctuation includes commas, semicolons, colons, apostrophes, hyphens, quotation marks, parentheses, and brackets.

PERIODS

Periods (.) act as end punctuation and, in some cases, as internal punctuation.

End Punctuation

The **period** is the punctuation mark used most often to end sentences. Use a period at the end of statements and commands.

Iris toured Spain last month. (statement)
Stop at all railroad crossings. (command)

Chapter 12 discusses abbreviations.

Consult a dictionary or other resource if you are not sure whether to use periods in an abbreviation.

Abbreviations

Use a period after initials and in many abbreviations.

Dr. Robin Bujnoski
Mrs. R. S. Mielczarski
Lt. Ken Murray
1100 Durant Ave.
7 a.m. to 9 p.m.

However, the trend is to eliminate periods in many lowercase abbreviations.

Do not drive faster than 35 mph on University Drive.
The engine turned 8,000 rpms during the race.

Workplace Connection

The U.S. Postal Service recommends using all capital letters and no punctuation in mailing addresses.

Do not include periods in two-letter state abbreviations that are used with ZIP Codes.

The address for Temino Corporation is 85 Shamrock Road, Omaha, NE 68114-5235.

As you learned in Chapter 1, acronyms are shortened forms of names or expressions typically made from the first letter of each word. Most acronyms consist of capital letters with no spaces and no periods.

NAFTA (North American Free Trade Agreement)
CBS (Columbia Broadcasting System)
MB (megabyte)
PIN (personal identification number)

Even amounts of money (whole dollars) do not include a decimal point ($50).

Do not use periods in abbreviated units of measure (oz, lb, in, ft).

Money and Decimal Fractions

Use a period (a decimal point) between dollars and cents expressed as figures and between whole numbers and decimal fractions.

Ramona paid $315.90 for the desk and chair.

The copper cylinder was 4.05 centimeters in length and 1.02 centimeters in diameter.

Sheldon ran from Fort Pickens to Navarre, a distance of 8.75 miles.

[CHECKPOINT 10-1]

Use Periods

In the space provided, write **C** if the item is punctuated correctly; otherwise, make appropriate corrections.

1. The program director's address is as follows:
   Mrs Ellen DeMarko ______
   W.Z.Y.O. TV ______
   3100 Mobile Highway ______
   Pensacola, FL. 32505-7015 ______
2. Theresa's last cell-phone bill totaled $89.25. ______
3. Dr. Janet Moore's flight will arrive at 10 am on Tuesday. ______
4. Please listen to the WCOA channel for the morning news ______
5. Patricia measured 2.5 liters of water for the experiment. ______
6. Dr Nancy Barnett earned her medical degree from Tulane University. ______
7. The speed limit on Highway 37 is 60 mph. ______
8. The postal abbreviation for Tennessee is TN. ______
9. We read three poems by TS Eliot. ______
10. Dr. Parr works with the CDC. ______

QUESTION MARKS

A **question mark (?)** serves as end punctuation after a direct question and after separate questions in series. Depending upon how you expect the receiver to respond, you may follow a courteous request with either a question mark or a period.

Complete Application 10-1.

Direct Questions/Indirect Questions

Use a question mark after a direct question but not after an indirect question.

Have you saved the latest version? (direct question)
Who won the soccer tournament? (direct question)

Mrs. Vincent asked me if I could travel with her. (indirect question)

Dr. Holman asked the students if they had completed the reviews. (indirect question)

Chapter 11 discusses the placement of punctuation marks in quotations.

Use a question mark after a direct question in quotation marks.

The director said, "Who will prepare the rehearsal schedule?"

"Who will attend the PBL Fall Rally?" asked the club sponsor.

Did you read the short story "Who Am I This Time?"

Series of Questions

Use a question mark after each question in a series of brief questions that come at the end of a sentence, that are dependent on the subject and verb of the sentence, and that require separate answers.

What are the arrangements? the date? the time? the location?

Does your trip include stops in Richmond? Washington? New York?

Courteous Requests

Courteous requests, suggestions, or commands worded as a polite question should end with a period if you think your reader will simply act on your request without replying. If you expect your reader to answer yes or no instead, use a question mark.

Will you please send me a copy. (or ?)
Roger, will you please close the door. (or ?)

WORKPLACE CONNECTION

The exclamation point is more often used in sales and advertising materials than in other business writing.

EXCLAMATION POINTS

An **exclamation point (!)** serves as end punctuation after interjections that express strong emotions or after strong commands. Also, use an exclamation point after exclamatory sentences.

Help! (strong emotion)

Stop! (strong command)

Jan announced very loudly, "I will not retire!" (exclamatory sentence)

[CHECKPOINT 10-2]

Use Question Marks and Exclamation Points

In the space provided, write **C** if the item is punctuated correctly; otherwise, make appropriate corrections.

1. The career counselor asked, "What are your hobbies." ______
2. Morgan screamed, "Watch for the falling rock." ______
3. Have you identified employment opportunities in Miami. ______
4. Wow. Look at the rainbow. ______
5. What did you say? hear? do? ______
6. "When can we drive to the mountains," asked Terry? ______

COMMAS

Complete Application 10-2.

The **comma (,)** provides punctuation for more circumstances than any other internal punctuation mark.

Series

Commas separate three or more elements in a series. To help readers distinguish between the last item and the preceding one, use a comma before the final item.

Laneissa bought shoes, dresses, and jewelry.

Alex's favorite meal includes soup and crackers, fish and chips, and dessert.

Note that "soup and crackers" and "fish and chips" are each one unit, not four separate units.

Introductory Remarks

Use commas after introductory words, phrases, or clauses.

Yes, Estella may attend the concert. (introductory word)

For the record, the program will be implemented in Dallas. (introductory phrase)

When you need assistance, please call 850-555-0100. (introductory clause)

[CHECKPOINT 10-3]

Use Commas in Series and After Introductory Remarks

In the space provided, write **C** if the item is punctuated correctly; otherwise, make appropriate corrections.

1. Tim's favorite vacation cities are San Diego, Denver and Boston. ______
2. When Julia traveled from Florida to Indiana she drove her new car. ______
3. The Price and Grant families arranged reunions in Chicago and Atlanta. ______
4. During the last decade, have you bought a house car or boat? ______
5. Nevertheless you may attend the conference by yourself on August 15. ______
6. Nadia bought a phone card, and a CD player. ______

"*When you have trouble getting the commas right, chances are you're trying to patch up a poorly structured sentence.*"

-Claire Kehrwald Cook as quoted in *Write Right!* Jan Venolia, author (1995)

Review page 134 for information on coordinating conjunctions.

Unnecessary Elements

Use commas to set off words, phrases, and clauses that are not necessary to the meaning of the sentence. In each of the following examples, the italicized words offer extra information that does not change the basic message.

The EPA, *however*, did not set new guidelines for wetland preservation. (unnecessary word)

Tien Li, *on the other hand*, has learned to speak seven languages. (unnecessary phrase)

Gretchen Werner, *who emigrated from Germany*, visited her mother in Munich. (unnecessary clause)

Independent Clauses

Use commas to separate independent clauses that are joined by a coordinating conjunction (*for*, *and*, *nor*, *but*, *or*, *yet*, and *so*).

James decided not to enroll in the radiology program, *for* the career field no longer interested him.

Quang graduated from Florida State University, *but* Kim graduated from the University of West Florida.

The Bill Bond Field in Hattiesburg was dimly lighted, *yet* the referees voted to continue the games.

[Checkpoint 10-4]

Use Commas for Unnecessary Elements and Independent Clauses

In the space provided, write **C** if the item is punctuated correctly; otherwise, make appropriate corrections.

1. John drove through Akron where he had lived for three years. ______
2. Anwar will shut down the computers before he leaves the classroom and Terri will lock the door when she goes. ______
3. Beccie Wiggins the nursing instructor demonstrated CPR. ______
4. Chih likes snow skiing, yet he went to Jamaica in December. ______
5. Did Curtis purchase new carpeting or did he select tile flooring? ______
6. The product, that sold the best, was our AT-1 digital camera. ______

States and Countries

Use commas to set off the names of states or countries that follow the names of cities.

> I took the train from Baltimore, Maryland, to Boston, Massachusetts.
>
> The convention will take place in Sydney, Australia.

Direct Quotations

Use commas to set off direct quotations.

> The professor said, "I plan to sit in the first row."
>
> "Although we have little time," Jean said, "we shall do our best work."
>
> "Please complete this report by 4 p.m. today," requested the supervisor.

Reversible adjectives are also known as coordinate adjectives.

Reversible Adjectives

Use commas to separate reversible adjectives. **Reversible adjectives** modify the same word and can switch places without changing the meaning of the sentence.

Peter creates expensive, colorful pottery. (*Expensive* and *colorful* both modify *pottery*. Reversing the modifiers does not change the meaning.)

The dark, angry clouds swirled over our heads. (*Dark* and *angry* both modify *clouds*. Reversing the modifiers does not change the meaning.)

However, omit a comma between modifiers that are not reversible.

Alice bought a bright yellow jacket. (*Bright* describes the intensity of the color. *Yellow* describes the color of the jacket. Switching the two modifiers would change the meaning.)

The day-month-year format used in military and international dates omits commas (1 January 2006).

Dates, Addresses, and Numbers

Use commas to separate the parts of dates and addresses. However, do not use a comma if the date has only two elements. Also, do not use commas between two-letter state abbreviations and ZIP Codes.

The club scheduled the European trip for June 2006. (two-element date)

Your appointment is on Monday, August 21, 2006, at 10 a.m. (three-element date)

Enter Anna's address, 213 Garden Avenue, Miami, FL 33140-3823, into the database. (two-letter state abbreviation and ZIP Code)

Use commas to separate the digits of numbers into groups of thousands.

The contract price for the house was $250,000.
The newspaper reported that 12,875 people attended the concert.

Commas are *not* used in numbers for these situations:

To express decimal parts of a number
To write invoice, model, or style numbers

The calculator showed a total of 72.57781.
Please locate a copy of Invoice 38561.
Matthew selected Model 7W2005 for the miniature car race.
After the fashion show, Amanda purchased Style 8946.

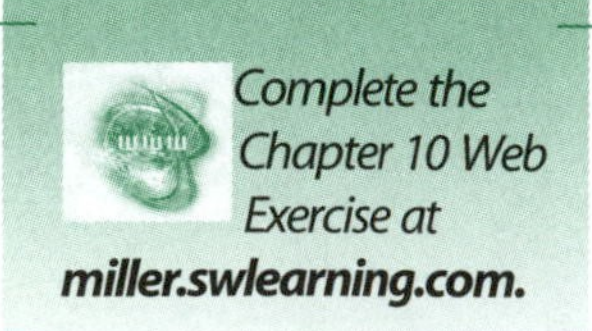
Complete the Chapter 10 Web Exercise at **miller.swlearning.com.**

If you are uncertain about the usage of commas with numbers, consult a comprehensive reference manual or follow the style of the source, such as a Social Security card or an insurance policy.

Complete Application 10-3.

[Checkpoint 10-5]

Use Commas for States and Countries; Direct Quotations; Reversible Adjectives; and Dates, Addresses, and Numbers

In the space provided, write **C** if the item is punctuated correctly; otherwise, make appropriate corrections.

1. After Esme completed the calculations, the display showed 91.7225. ______
2. Horace said, "Please meet me at 8:30 a.m. at the Judicial Center, 200 West Jackson Avenue, Knoxville, TN, 37902-1017." ______
3. Jill searched for a comfortable home costing under $100000. ______
4. "June 5 1955 was my wedding day" said Mrs. Miller. ______
5. Mark Twain grew up in Hannibal, Missouri. ______
6. Tourists thought the white sandy beaches on the Gulf Coast were the most beautiful beaches in the world. ______
7. Thomas ordered three Model 7J4499 tractors for his farm. ______
8. Tim said "Sending e-mail messages from the Internet Café in Juarez costs too much." ______
9. Michael and Lois paid $17350.95 for their new car. ______
10. Renee drives an ugly rusty jeep to work. ______
11. The webmaster said that he would update the site regularly. ______
12. We visited Oslo Norway and Copenhagen, Denmark. ______

Chapter Summary

- Select the appropriate end punctuation—periods, question marks, or exclamation points—to indicate complete sentences.
- Insert periods correctly to punctuate initials, abbreviations, addresses, amounts of money, and decimal fractions.
- Use question marks to punctuate direct questions, series of questions, and some courteous requests.
- Insert exclamation points after interjections that express strong emotions, after strong commands, and after exclamatory sentences.
- Use commas correctly to:
  - Separate two or more items in a series.
  - Indicate introductory remarks.
  - Set off unnecessary words, phrases, and clauses.
  - Separate independent clauses joined by a coordinating conjunction.
  - Set off the names of states or countries that follow the names of cities.
  - Set off direct quotations.
  - Separate reversible adjectives.
  - Separate the parts of dates, addresses, and numbers.

ILrn

Complete the Chapter 10 Review.

Complete the Chapter 10 iLrn Activities at **miller.swlearning.com.**

APPLICATION 10-1

Use Periods as Internal Punctuation

In the space provided, write **C** if the sentence is punctuated correctly; otherwise, make appropriate corrections.

0. F‸ Scott Fitzgerald was a famous author. ____________
1. Mr. Arnold wants the package delivered to 2139 Chickering Lane, Nashville, TN 37215-5401. ____________
2. Miriam has worked for G.T.E. for 20 years. ____________
3. Dr Abbott practices at Midtown Hospital in Des Moines. ____________
4. Mrs. Moore called you at 5 pm, but you did not answer. ____________
5. The lunch costs $27.00, including the gratuity. ____________
6. On a 4.0 scale, Lucy's grade point average was 2.96 for the term. ____________
7. Gary conducts research for NIH. ____________
8. R S Hansen owns the house at 215 Baker Avenue. ____________
9. His qualifying time at the Indianapolis 500 was 174 m.p.h.
10. Write the amount of your check in words and a fraction (*ten and 25/100*) and in numerals ($1025). ____________
11. Your preregistration cost is $35; on-site registration costs $50. ____________
12. Did you attend UCLA or USC? ____________
13. The Strawberry Cheesecake Company, Inc, makes delicious desserts. ____________
14. After passing the state board exams, Mr Harada is now Dr. Harada. ____________
15. Will the picture fit a frame that is 8.5 by 11 inches? ____________
16. Playing for the NBA was Nate's lifelong dream. ____________
17. The tiles were cut in rectangles that measured 5.5 by 8. inches. ____________
18. Cmd Ronald T. Harper will retire next year. ____________
19. Stacy toured the F.B.I. ____________
20. Is CA. the postal abbreviation for California? ____________

APPLICATION 10-2

Select Correct End Punctuation

Insert the correct end punctuation in the space provided.

0. Would you like to take swimming lessons this summer __?__
1. The phone bill arrived yesterday ______
2. I just won the $50 million lottery ______
3. What are the essential parts of your marketing plan ______
4. Grab the rope quickly ______
5. Did Sunita say that she is ready for lunch ______
6. Robert asked, "Have you finished developing the new formula ______"
7. Is the presentation software still available ______
8. The use of information technology has expanded rapidly in the last decade ______
9. Our vacation will begin July 1 ______
10. How many books can you place on the top shelf ______
11. When is your estimated completion date ______
12. A paper shredder should be used to destroy confidential documents ______
13. Hurrah ______ All items are marked 75 percent off the regular price.
14. Always follow directions when completing an employment application ______
15. Nina replied, "Why do you ask ______"
16. How much does the new software cost ______
17. Will you please wear your sunglasses at the beach ______ (expect the reader to act)
18. When will the "Continental Road Warrior" return from Oregon ______
19. I recommend that these students study more math and science ______
20. Will you please represent Celia at the conference ______ (expect a yes or no answer)

Application 10-3

Use Commas Correctly

In the space provided, write **C** if the sentence is punctuated correctly; otherwise, make appropriate corrections.

0. Oscar thinks that all airlines are equally safe. ______C______
1. We parked the car in the garage but Kerry forgot to close the door. ____________
2. On February 10, 1519 Hernán Cortez began his conquest of the Aztecs. ____________
3. Stella bought the blue candles and Ada bought the green ones. ____________
4. The sales representative told us that all the tickets had been sold. ____________
5. Likewise the stationery should be ordered tomorrow. ____________
6. The new math instructor Professor Sheng assigns too much homework. ____________
7. Fortunately Gloria found the missing puzzle piece. ____________
8. The conferences will be held in San Diego California; New Orleans Louisiana; and Philadelphia Pennsylvania. ____________
9. Have you ever served on a grand jury or a trial jury? ____________
10. Emma, on a buying spree, purchased an expensive new backpack. ____________
11. Fred walks the pets in the morning and Sarah walks them in the afternoon. ____________
12. We will either go to lunch or go to dinner with the clients. ____________
13. Printwork Corporation makes brochures for manufacturing plants but the artists also design posters for individuals. ____________
14. Send all reply cards to 18011 Rhodes Mill Road, Rockford, OH 45882-8709. ____________
15. Samuel analyzes the feedback and Gregory writes the final report. ____________
16. "Please answer the phone" requested Marvin. ____________
17. Josie claims that looking at ice cream makes her gain weight. ____________
18. Festival organizers expected 10,000 attendees, but 12000 participated during the weekend. ____________
19. The dessert menu featured apple pie and ice cream, five flavors of sherbet and carrot cake. ____________
20. The cold wet rocks were difficult to climb. ____________

Basic Punctuation

Insert periods, question marks, exclamation points, and commas wherever they are needed in the following paragraphs. Each correct punctuation mark is worth five points.

Scientists have debated whether the extinction of plants and animals threatens the normal functioning of ecosystems (communities of organisms and their environments) For years ecologists maintained that ecosystems work better when they have more rather than fewer species. In the 1970s a well-known respected ecologist named Robert May produced a study that seemed to show the opposite. Which view was correct

Several important studies support the hypothesis that diversity makes ecosystems more stable. One study was conducted by David Tilman a University of Michigan ecologist. For two decades, Dr Tilman tracked 342 plots seeded with different numbers of plant species at a nature preserve in Bethel Minnesota. He found that plots with more species were less affected by drought more resistant to insects and more productive.

The Biodepth project which examined about 500 test plots across Europe yielded similar results. Dr. Tilman remarked "[Biodepth] provides the strongest evidence yet that losing plant and animal species significantly decreases the ability of ecosystems to function"

The debate is far from over and other factors besides diversity play a role in ecosystem health. The results however have a direct impact on people. Ecosystems are amazing They clean the air and water. They yield foods, medicines and other useful materials. In addition ecosystems act as a buffer against climate change. Keeping ecosystems healthy is in everyone's best interests.

More Punctuation

CHAPTER 11

The notes I handle not better than many pianists. But the pauses between the notes—ah, that is where the art resides.

—Artur Schnabel
world-famous pianist
(1882–1951)

Experienced speakers emphasize important points with changes in volume, pitch, or timing. Speakers powerfully underscore points with skillfully placed pauses. Brief moments of silence allow listeners to reflect on what speakers have said.

Pauses give listeners time to understand what they have just heard. In written messages, internal punctuation marks serve the same purposes as volume, pitch, timing, and pauses do in spoken messages.

Learning Objectives

- Use semicolons correctly.
- Use colons where appropriate.
- Apply guidelines for using quotation marks.
- Insert apostrophes in correct locations.
- Use hyphens correctly.
- Use parentheses and brackets correctly.

SEMICOLONS

Semicolons (;) mark strong breaks between separate but closely related thoughts. Semicolons often divide main clauses; semicolons also may separate items in a series that include commas. Space once after a semicolon.

Main Clauses Without Conjunctions

Use a semicolon to join the main clauses of a compound sentence when a conjunction is not used to separate the clauses.

> The ZOOhop is scheduled for 9 a.m. to 4 p.m.; the event features large and small animals.
>
> Bob Miller's house is a colonial saltbox; Joe Walker's is a log cabin.
>
> Employers expect employees to communicate ideas, information, and messages in writing; good grammar skills help employees meet those expectations.

WORKPLACE CONNECTION

Competent workers in a high-performance workplace need speaking skills.

Independent Clauses with Transitional Expressions

Use a semicolon between independent clauses when transitional expressions such as *therefore*, *however*, and *moreover* introduce the second clause. Follow the transitional expression with a comma. You also may punctuate the second independent clause as a separate sentence.

Our flight was two hours late; *therefore*, we missed the connecting flight.

Lenora chose the "Improve Your Speaking Skills" seminar; *however*, Daleesha selected the "Increase Your Written Message Effectiveness" workshop.

The Environmental Resources Department planned to discuss wetlands conservation; *moreover*, they decided to continue the meeting until they reached an agreement.

List of Examples

Use a semicolon between a main clause and a list of examples introduced by such expressions as *for example*, *for instance*, and *e.g.* (abbreviation of *for example*).

The Elberta German sausage festival offers a variety of attractions; *for example*, continuous entertainment, food booths, and craft centers.

Word processing software offers helpful features for writing reports; *for example*, the footnotes, outline, and table of contents features.

When you prepare a report, answer specific questions; *e.g.*, who, what, when, where, why, and how.

A series of items can be words, phrases, or clauses.

Series

Use semicolons to separate a series of items when any item contains one or more commas.

The CEO at Indianola Healthcare announced the following appointments: Keats Gonzales, administrator; Merideth Summers, nursing director; and Juan Garcia, physical therapist.

The seminars are scheduled for Friday, October 13; Wednesday, October 18; and Tuesday, October 24.

As a gift to his mother, Zach promised to replace the broken wiper blades; to check the brakes, fluids, and radiator; and to wash the car.

[Checkpoint 11-1]

Use Semicolons Correctly

In the space provided, write **C** if the item is punctuated correctly; otherwise, make appropriate corrections.

1. During a presentation, use graphics to illustrate important points, keep the graphics uncluttered and easy to read. ______
2. People have become accustomed to viewing multicolored graphics. ______
3. Visual aids increase clarity therefore, use charts and other types of illustrations. ______
4. Try several approaches to determine which works best, for example, video clips, slide presentations, and flip charts. ______
5. The consultants for the "Improve Your Speaking Skills" seminar are Eugene Freeman, Texas, Ruth Kellerman, Colorado, and Pat Mason, Missouri. ______

COLONS

Colons (:) alert readers that additional important information will follow. Space once after a colon.

Lists, Examples, or Explanations

The information just before a colon makes a statement; the information after a colon presents related lists, examples, or explanations.

> Remember the six Cs of business writing: courtesy, clarity, conciseness, concreteness, correctness, and completeness. (list)
>
> The Sotos like to travel: Last March they went to Wales and London. (example)
>
> If you get stuck in the elevator, push the red button: Security will call for repairs (explanation)

Words like *the following*, *as follows*, *thus*, or *these* often signal that a colon will follow.

> You may choose one item from each of *the following* menu sections: Salads, Main Courses, and Desserts.
>
> The text before a colon is nearly always an independent clause.
>
> Please choose one item from each menu section: Salads, Main Courses, and Desserts.

When information that follows a colon can stand alone as a sentence, capitalize the first letter of the statement.

You may choose one item from Salads, Main Courses, and Desserts. (not *You may choose one item from: Salads, Main Courses, and Desserts*)

The only exception is when the information following the colon is formatted as a vertical list on separate lines.

You may choose one item from:
    Salads
    Main Courses
    Desserts

Business Letter Salutations

Use a colon after the salutation in a business letter when a comma is used after the complimentary close.

Dear Mrs. McPheron:
Sincerely yours,

Time Expressions

Place a colon between hours and minutes when writing the time in figures; however, omit the colon and zeroes in on-the-hour times.

Complete Application 11-1.

Your interview is scheduled for 8:30 a.m.
The meeting will begin at 9 a.m. and end at 5 p.m.

[CHECKPOINT 11-2]

Use Colons Correctly

In the space provided, write **C** if the item is punctuated correctly; otherwise, make appropriate corrections.

1. To create more effective presentations, consider three factors content, audience interaction, and choreography. ______
2. I will meet you at 4:00 p.m. to critique your speech. ______
3. Feedback will help you modify your vocal presentation in these areas pitch, timing, and volume. ______
4. You may select: ______
    CD or DVD format
    Closed or open captions
    Static or automated graphics
5. My favorite audiences included the following groups; student council members, service club representatives, and leadership awareness teams. ______

QUOTATION MARKS

Quotation marks (" / ") enclose a direct quotation (the words a person actually says or said). Do not use quotation marks unless you are quoting a person's exact words.

Jeff said, "We're leaving tomorrow."

Jeff said that we're leaving tomorrow.

Some Titles

Use quotation marks to enclose titles of articles and other parts of complete publications, short poems, song titles, television programs, and unpublished works.

Felix sang "Meet Me in St. Louis" at the opening of the NCAA basketball finals.

Did you read "Letters to the Editor" in the May 4 issue?

Unfamiliar Words and Unusual Usage

Use quotation marks to enclose words or phrases that may be unfamiliar to your readers or that are used in an unusual manner.

The camp director told Erik to bring the "sassy stick," the craft kit, and extra tent poles.

My "special prize" consisted of two pens and a refrigerator magnet.

Commas and Periods

Always place a comma or period inside a closing quotation mark.

David told me his mother's exact words were, "The closest I want to get to flying is riding an ostrich."

"I want to go home now," said Martha's mother when Martha visited her in the hospital.

Question Marks and Exclamation Points

Place a question mark or an exclamation point that belongs with a quotation inside the closing quotation mark.

Mrs. Hanson asked, "What food did you prepare for the party?"

The children shouted, "Let's go!"

When the entire sentence is a question or an exclamation, place the question mark or exclamation point outside the closing quotation mark.

Did Keiko say, "Put everything away before you leave for the weekend"?

All I can say is "I'm sorry"!

Semicolons and Colons

Always place a semicolon or colon outside a closing quotation mark.

Walter frequently said, "I have 600 acres of prime farm property for sale"; actually, the property contained 200 acres of wetlands that could not be cultivated.

I recall three points from the article "The Secrets of Communication": Write succinctly, use a positive tone, and practice active listening.

[CHECKPOINT 11-3]

Use Quotation Marks Correctly

In the space provided, write **C** if the item is punctuated correctly; otherwise, make appropriate corrections.

1. "Rain Man" claims his machine can make water from air. _______
2. In *Eight Habits of the Heart*, Clifton L. Taulbert stated, "True friendship can form bridges". _______
3. "How many guests are you expecting for the reception"? asked the catering director. _______
4. Robert Frost wrote the poem "The Road Not Taken". _______
5. Do you know how many chemicals will be placed on the toxic "Hot List?" _______
6. The trainer shouted, "Jump!" _______
7. Why did Carol Browner say, "People want a different kind of future?" _______
8. "Honest disagreement", said Mahatma Gandhi, "is often a good sign of progress." _______
9. Stop yelling, "Run faster!" _______
10. The manager said that three new parks are planned. _______

APOSTROPHES

The **apostrophe (')** shows *possession* (ownership), the location of missing letters, or the plural of letters and some other items. Insert no space before or after an apostrophe *within* a word. Also, insert no space before and one space after an apostrophe occurring at the *end* of a word.

As you learned in Chapter 2, use an of phrase to make inanimate objects possessive.

Singular and Plural Words

To show the possessive form of most singular nouns, add an *'s*. Add only an ' to most plural nouns. Add the possessive ending to the *last* word of a compound noun.

Singular	**Plural**
one student's computer	two students' computers
one baby's stroller	two babies' strollers
one brother-in-law's watch	two brothers-in-law's watches

When an item has several "owners," add *'s* to the final one to indicate joint or common possession. Add *'s* to each "owner" to show separate possession.

Bill, Michael, and Steve's project won first place. (joint)

The treasurer's and secretary's proposals received immediate approval. (separate)

Do not use apostrophes in possessive pronouns.

Is the painting *yours*?
Her sculptures were sold at the auction.
The elephant used *its* trunk to lift the logs.
Lot 17B is *ours*.

Review pages 25–28 to refresh your understanding of possessives.

Letters, Numbers, Symbols, and Abbreviations

Use an apostrophe to form the plural of letters, numbers, symbols, and abbreviations *only* if the apostrophe makes the plural clearer.

x's   i's   PDAs   A's   2s $s

Contractions

An apostrophe indicates the location of the missing letters in a **contraction** (a shortened form of one or more words).

Two Words	**Contraction**
will not	won't
have not	haven't
it is	it's
you are	you're

[CHECKPOINT 11-4]

Use Apostrophes Correctly

In the space provided, write **C** if the item is punctuated correctly; otherwise, make appropriate corrections.

1. According to the survey, Samuel, Ruth, Lourdes, and Arnold's project was ranked first. ______
2. Our neighbor's dog carries pine cones in it's mouth. ______
3. Joseph trimmed my mother-in-laws' trees. ______
4. Write x's in the empty blanks on the survey. ______
5. Three professor's parking places are reserved. ______
6. The tax assessor said, "Building 17J is your's." ______
7. Ximena claims that she only uses organic cosmetics'. ______
8. Is the wrecked car your's? ______

Complete Application 11-2.

You will learn about number usage in Chapter 12.

To review compound nouns, see pages 23–24. To review compound adjectives, see page 101.

Hyphens are used in phone numbers and sometimes in serial numbers.

HYPHENS

Hyphens (-) join two or more elements (numbers, letters, syllables, or words) into a single unit. In most cases, no space appears before or after the hyphen. However, one space occurs after a suspending hyphen (see page 185).

Numbers

Use a hyphen to join compound numbers from *twenty-one* to *ninety-nine* that are written out, two numbers that represent a range of numbers, and fractions that can be expressed easily in a few words.

Sixty-four delegates attended the opening session.

William Shakespeare (1564-1616) wrote 38 plays.

We found that *three-fourths* of customers favored the change.

Compound Words

Use hyphens to separate the words in some compound nouns and verbs and most compound adjectives. Check a dictionary if you are not sure whether to use a hyphen.

brother-in-law, trade-in, U-turn (compound nouns)

air-condition, dry-clean, fine-tune (compound verbs)

hard-hitting, high-level, one-sided (compound adjectives)

Suspending Hyphens

When two or more compound adjectives share the same last word, you can use a **suspending hyphen** after the first part of each compound adjective instead of repeating the last word.

Drake, Inc., offers both *long-term* and *short-term* payment plans.

Drake, Inc., offers both *long-* and *short-term* payment plans.

Word Division

Use a hyphen to indicate word division when a word must be divided between one line and the next. To determine correct word division, you may refer to a word division manual.

ex-traor-di-na-ry	ex-per-i-ment
tra-di-tion	knowl-edge

A ***dash (—)*** interrupts a thought and allows the writer to insert additional information. No space *appears before or after a dash.*

Complete the Chapter 11 Web Exercise at ***miller.swlearning.com.***

[CHECKPOINT 11-5]

Use Hyphens Correctly

In the space provided, write **C** if the item is punctuated correctly; otherwise, make appropriate corrections. Use a dictionary if necessary.

1. Ricardo completed the self evaluation form before meeting with his supervisor. ________
2. Two thirds of our students commute to school. ________
3. Indianola is the countyseat of Sunflower County. ________
4. Maria jokingly said, "Twenty three out of ten people prefer chocolate to vanilla ice cream." ________
5. The shutters go from the window ledge to the ceiling. ________
6. Print your resume on 8½ by 11-inch paper. ________
7. Elaine consulted an up to date manual. ________
8. Bill and Clark planned a two week vacation in Alaska. ________

Who says punctuation doesn't communicate?

PARENTHESES

Parentheses ( ) set off references, explanatory details, and other added information that is not necessary to the meaning of a sentence.

Subject-verb agreement (see Chapter 5) provides helpful information for both beginning and experienced writers.

Governor Miller (Arkansas) owns a construction firm in Fordyce.

Use parentheses to enclose identifying figures or letters in lists.

The directions read as follows: (1) pour the mix into a bowl, (2) add eggs and water, (3) beat for one minute, and (4) bake for 30 minutes at 350°F.

Parentheses also enclose figures following amounts that are spelled out.

Stanley paid the DeMaria Law Firm Nine Hundred Fifty Dollars and Seventy-Five Cents ($950.75).

> "*One has to dismount from an idea, and get into the saddle again, at every parenthesis.*"
>
> **-Oliver Wendell Holmes, Sr., American author and physician (1809–1894)**

BRACKETS

Brackets [ ] indicate remarks inserted into a direct quotation. Brackets mark language that is not part of the quotation.

The zoologist said, "South America's drylands [i.e., deserts, grassy plains, and scrub forests] support more mammalian species than rain forests do." (Bracketed information was added to clarify the term *drylands*.)

Brackets may also show that an error in a quotation was made by the person quoted; insert *sic* (meaning "this is the way it was" in the original quotation) within brackets immediately after the error.

Coach Sherrill said, "Our players have become a competitive team. There [*sic*] individual skills are highly developed." (*There* is incorrectly used. *Their* is the correct choice.)

Use brackets to enclose parenthetical material in text that is already enclosed in parentheses.

Governor Downing's memorandum (which suggested holding local forums before the final vote was taken [see the September 1 message to the legislature]) was not considered.

Complete Applications 11-3 and 11-4.

[CHECKPOINT 11-6]

Use Parentheses and Brackets Correctly

In the space provided, write **C** if the item is punctuated correctly; otherwise, make appropriate corrections.

1. During the home tour, you may visit these locations: (1) 1131 North Spring Street, (2) 3704 East Jackson Avenue, (3) 4400 Dakota Street, and (4) 1700 Bayou Boulevard. ________
2. The critic wrote, "The Renaissance Comedeans (*sic*) packed the house for the comedy night." ________
3. Our favorite breakfast [ham and eggs] awaited us every morning of the trip. ________
4. Works by Auguste Rodin (lithographs and bronze sculptures) will be presented in May at the Dothan Museum of Art. ________
5. Please review "Commonly Confused Verbs" [see Chapter 4] in your text. ________
6. The company will pay the consultant Six Thousand Dollars ($6,000). ________
7. Bill reported, "The new client (Ms. Fox) called yesterday." ________
8. The majority of respondents [86 percent] favored a light rail system. ________

Chapter Summary

- Use semicolons correctly to separate:
  - Main clauses that are not set apart by conjunctions
  - Independent clauses when transitional expressions introduce the second clause
  - A main clause and a list of examples
  - A series of items when any item contains one or more commas
- Use colons appropriately:
  - After statements followed by related lists, examples, or explanations
  - After a business letter salutation when a comma follows the complimentary close
  - Between hours and minutes when writing time in figures
- Observe the guidelines for the placement of quotation marks to enclose:
  - Direct quotations
  - Some titles
  - Unfamiliar words and words used in an unusual way
- Insert apostrophes in correct locations to indicate:
  - The possessive form of most singular and plural words
  - Plurals of certain letters, numbers, symbols, and abbreviations
  - Omitted letters in contractions
- Use hyphens correctly in these situations:
  - Compound numbers from *twenty-one* to *ninety-nine* that are written as words
  - Two numbers that represent a range of numbers
  - Fractions that can be expressed easily in a few words
  - Words in some compound nouns and verbs and most compound adjectives
  - Compound adjectives that share the same base (*long- and short-term*)
  - Words that must be divided from one line to the next
- Observe the correct usage of parentheses to set off:
  - References, explanatory details, and other added information within a sentence
  - Figures or letters in lists
  - Figures that follow spelled-out amounts of money
- Observe the correct usage of brackets to indicate:
  - Remarks inserted into a direct quotation
  - Errors in a quotation
  - Parenthetical material in text that is already enclosed in parentheses

Complete the Chapter 11 Review.

iLrn

Complete the Chapter 11 iLrn Activities at **miller.swlearning.com**.

APPLICATION 11-1

Semicolons and Colons

In the space provided, write **C** if the sentence is punctuated correctly; otherwise, make appropriate corrections.

0. Paul Revere lived from 1735 to 1818; Davy Crockett lived from 1786 to 1836. ___C___

1. Joji's bag contained the following items; one shirt, a bottle of shampoo, a towel, and a notebook. ______

2. Marcus and Mario must travel to Paris in October, however, they prefer to remain home that month. ______

3. The folded maps list street names: the atlases contain larger city maps. ______

4. The new air freshener works well, but the container is empty within five days. ______

5. The top three bowlers and their scores were Dennis Henson, 289, Ruby Nevins, 267, and Pat Schultz, 254. ______

6. Karen is going fishing on her vacation Sara is going camping. ______

7. Dr. Sean Carey will do his rounds at 7:30 a.m. the first two weeks in May and at 3:30 p.m. the last two weeks in May. ______

8. Prepare a highly marketable gift basket by adding these items; aromatherapy candles, organic fruit, and soap floaties. ______

9. Andres and Nestor have a common heritage, They were both born in Puerto Rico. ______

10. The children may choose one event, for example, bean bag toss, baseball throw, or relay race. ______

11. The guest performers are Luke McCoy, Florida, Patricia Buchanan, Texas, and Rachel Damingo, California. ______

12. Jake, who lives in Arizona, chose an unusual elective; underwater gardening. ______

Application 11-2

Quotation Marks and Apostrophes

In the space provided, write **C** if the sentence is punctuated correctly; otherwise, make appropriate corrections.

0. Can you understand what he's trying to say? C
1. Her favorite song is "Beyond the Sea". ______
2. "I'm going with you", said Clay. ______
3. They have dotted all their i's and crossed all their t's. ______
4. "Have you hiked the Inca Trail"? she asked. ______
5. He replied, Furthermore, when I was a boy, we walked at least three miles each day. ______
6. The house on the corner is their's. ______
7. Raydene hasnt called me since the incident at the birthday party. ______
8. Gary's "friend" took his cell phone and $50 from his wallet. ______
9. The teacher shouted, "We have a tornado warning"! ______
10. Mrs. Aponte's painting's are on display at the Fourth Street Gallery. ______
11. Mr. Ni asked, "Why did you take such a long break"? ______
12. Kurt Vonnegut wrote the short story *Who Am I This Time?* ______
13. Did you touch the bench that was marked "Wet Paint?" ______
14. The four students spreadsheets were perfect. ______
15. Toddlers often have difficulty pronouncing their rs. ______
16. Why did Nick say, "That report cannot be sent out tomorrow?" ______
17. Jeff's and Ruth's model won first place. ______
18. Marty's team held it's position after the break. ______
19. Williams' son graduated from Atlantic University. ______
20. After Hiram drove from Florida to Alaska, his family called him Road Warrior. ______

APPLICATION 11-3

Hyphens, Parentheses, and Brackets

In the space provided, write **C** if the sentence is punctuated correctly; otherwise, make appropriate corrections.

0. The fact that he had nine children was well-known. ___C___
1. Her exfiancé appeared as a contestant in a TV show. ______
2. The website said, "In most instances, *i* proceeds (*sic*) *e* except after *c*." ______
3. (Two articles (Smith, 2005; Kerns, 2006) call for more male teachers.) ______
4. We donated two thirds of the money we raised to Habitat for Humanity. ______
5. Stephanie's cell-phone number is 5550129. ______
6. The paddles with rubber grips (the ones without batteries) are easy to use. ______
7. Jeff flies super-sonic jets between Los Angeles and New York. ______
8. Before you paint, always do the following: 1 clean and dry the wood, 2 sand carefully, and 3 apply primer. ______
9. The answers to the quizzes see Instructor's Manual are separated by chapters. ______
10. Forty seven people escaped the fire without injury. ______
11. The technician fine tuned the settings on my computer. ______
12. Her self confidence was evident as she began to speak. ______
13. Because the holiday is on Monday, we will have a three day weekend. ______
14. Sonia is the mail-carrier in our neighborhood. ______
15. Corky is known for her happy go lucky attitude. ______
16. "The new marketing manager [Ms. Clayton] has created an entirely different campaign," stated Lucas. ______
17. Ms. Huff said, "Please remove the lamp-shades before you paint the room." ______
18. Rachel stated, "Check the latest references (i.e., electronic sites) at miller.swlearning.com." ______
19. Your medical bills that now total Three Thousand Six Hundred Dollars [$3,600] can be paid by electronic check. ______
20. In warmer weather, shade south- and west-facing windows. ______

APPLICATION 11-4

Punctuation Usage

In each pair, select the sentence that is correctly punctuated by writing a **C** in the space provided. Watch for correct usage of semicolons, colons, quotation marks, apostrophes, hyphens, parentheses, and brackets.

0. A. My favorite flowers include these: daisies, tulips, and roses. ___C___
   B. My favorite flowers include these; daisies, tulips, and roses. ______
1. A. Janet selected white chocolate, Elena chose dark chocolate. ______
   B. Janet selected white chocolate; Elena chose dark chocolate. ______
2. A. If you are caught in a riptide, do not panic: Swim parallel to the shore. ______
   B. If you are caught in a riptide, do not panic; Swim parallel to the shore. ______
3. A. He asked, "Did you discuss the environmental issues"? ______
   B. He asked, "Did you discuss the environmental issues?" ______
4. A. The traffic officer shouted, "Stop"! ______
   B. The traffic officer shouted, "Stop!" ______
5. A. Beverly sang "My Old Kentucky Home" during the convention in Lexington. ______
   B. Beverly sang *My Old Kentucky Home* during the convention in Lexington. ______
6. A. My mother-in-laws' home is in Boise, Idaho. ______
   B. My mother-in-law's home is in Boise, Idaho. ______
7. A. Is the new boat yours? ______
   B. Is the new boat your's? ______
8. A. Two senators cosponsored the legislation. ______
   B. Two senators co-sponsored the legislation. ______
9. A. Rinji displayed self confidence throughout the tennis match. ______
   B. Rinji displayed self-confidence throughout the tennis match. ______
10. A. Vince wrote, "Acrophobia (the fear of heights) effects [*sic*] many people." ______
    B. Vince wrote, "Acrophobia [the fear of heights] effects [*sic*] many people." ______
11. A. Did Marvin say, "Why are we meeting at 6:30 a.m."? ______
    B. Did Marvin say, "Why are we meeting at 6:30 a.m.?" ______
12. A. The new band members may choose from these instruments; flutes, clarinets, trumpets, or saxophones. ______
    B. The new band members may choose from these instruments: flutes, clarinets, trumpets, or saxophones. ______

Chapter 11 Review

More Punctuation

Insert or delete semicolons, colons, quotation marks, apostrophes, hyphens, parentheses, and brackets as appropriate in the following paragraphs. Each correct answer is worth four points.

Follow the B.E.S.T. plan as you prepare and deliver spoken presentations. B.E.S.T. stands for the following; (1) **B**e prepared, (2) **E**ncourage audience participation, (3) **S**how visuals, and (4) **T**ailor the presentation.

Be Prepared

Know the audience. Spend extra time determining who you're audience is; anticipate the type of message the audience expects. Abraham Lincoln (1809:1865) said that when he was preparing a speech, he spent two thirds of his time thinking about what the audience wanted to hear and one third thinking about what he wanted to say.

Audiences can detect a speakers' lack of preparation in less than a minute. "Practice until you thoroughly know your material", our communication teacher always reminded us. She makes presentations regularly in Orlando, Florida, Houston, Texas, and San Diego, California.

Encourage Audience Participation

Activities, relevant anecdotes, and audience directed questions keep listeners "tuned in". Establish two way communication by asking the right questions. Talk less, listen more.

When a participant makes a comment or asks a question, listen to the whole comment or question. Dont interrupt: never complete a sentence for another person. When someone in the audience asks a question, repeat the question so that everyone hears what was asked. Your audiences' questions will help you determine how successfully your presentation is progressing.

Show Visuals

Some speakers prefer to use slides with electronic projection equipment, others favor transparencies. Whiteboards, flip charts, and chalkboards are other choices. Elena Smythe usually includes graphs and charts made on her computer [see the attached article "Ten Tips for Effective Visuals"]. Your visuals should be simple enough that audiences can quickly understand them. Visuals also should be attractive and easy to see.

Tailor the Presentation

Tailoring begins during planning. Learn about your audience so that you prepare a presentation that will deliver your message and fit their needs. As you speak, make eye-contact with the audience as much as possible. When heads start bobbing and eyes begin looking glazed, you know your approach is not working. Scott Fordham said, "Do not overload your audience with information (i.e., put everything in one big bundle); the listeners may become confused."

Successful presenters do not lecture their audience, instead, they join their audience in discovering information and in reaching conclusions. With enough planning and rehearsing, your presentation will be received favorably by your audience.

You may conduct an electronic-search for additional information. Use these keywords; "speaking skills" and "effective presentations."

Capitalization and Numbers

CHAPTER 12

How quickly can you read the following paragraph? How much do you remember?

joshua tree national park comprises almost eight hundred thousand acres. the park includes five hundred one archeological sites, eighty-eight historic structures, and nineteen cultural landscapes. the first known inhabitants were members of the pinto culture. The park museum includes one hundred twenty-three thousand two hundred fifty-three items.

A paragraph without proper capitalization and correctly formatted numbers is difficult to read. You waste time determining where sentences begin and end and what ideas are important. You are also more likely to misinterpret incorrectly formatted numerical information.

Learning Objectives

- Capitalize words, abbreviations, and acronyms properly.
- Express numbers appropriately in figures and in words.

CAPITALIZATION

Capital letters alert you to the beginning of sentences. Capital letters also emphasize or attach importance to words; therefore, as you learned in Chapter 2, proper nouns are always capitalized.

Capitalization rules evolve through usage and custom, and the rules apply to many but not all words. Chapter 12 presents *basic* rules that govern typical situations. When you are unsure about capitalization, consult a comprehensive capitalization guide.

The Pronoun *I* and First Words

The first-person pronoun *I* is always capitalized. The first word of a sentence, an expression acting as a sentence, and an independent clause following a colon are capitalized to signal the beginning of a new thought.

Pronoun *I*. Always capitalize the pronoun *I*.

Marta and I worked at the concession stand.

First Words. Capitalize the first word of a sentence or an expression used as a sentence. As you learned in the last chapter, capitalize the first word of an independent clause that follows a colon.

The class ends at 8 p.m. (sentence)

Not now. (expression treated as a sentence)

Follow this policy: Do not accept returns that are not accompanied by a sales receipt. (independent clause after a colon)

WORKPLACE CONNECTION

Capitalize, space, and punctuate a person's name according to the person's preference.

Names, Titles, and Message Parts

The names and nicknames of people are always capitalized. Courtesy and professional titles that *precede* a person's name and titles used in certain parts of letters and envelopes are capitalized. Academic degrees and professional designations that *follow* a person's name are capitalized. In certain situations, family titles are capitalized.

If a nickname is used with a person's full name, the nickname is enclosed in quotation marks: Mike "Da Coach" Ditka.

NAMES OF PEOPLE. Capitalize each element of a person's name, including initials and abbreviations; also capitalize nicknames.

Richard J. Daley, Sr.	Richard J. Daley, Jr.
Babe Ruth	Janice Hixon-Schultz

Capitalize and space names that begin with prefixes, such as *d'*, *da*, *la*, *le*, *van*, and *von*, according to the person's preference. For names that begin with *O* plus an apostrophe, capitalize both the *O* and the letter following the apostrophe.

VanHoesen van Hoesen vanHosen O'Malley O'Rourke

For most professional titles, the preference is to spell out the title. The exception is Doctor, *which is usually abbreviated as* Dr.

COURTESY AND PROFESSIONAL TITLES. Capitalize courtesy titles such as *Mr.*, *Ms.*, *Miss*, and *Mrs.* Capitalize official titles (professional, academic, religious, organizational, and governmental) and their abbreviations that come *before* a person's name.

Mayor Hahn	Colonel Louis Betch (Col. Louis Betch)
Judge Nguyen	Doctor Sylvia Hyak (Dr. Sylvia Hyak)
Rabbi Greenberg	Professor Lee Siles (Prof. Lee Siles)

Do not capitalize a title within a sentence when the title follows a person's name, is used instead of a name, or is used as a general reference.

Nina Reinerio, *president* of the senior class, is my neighbor. (follows a name)

The *president* of the senior class is my neighbor. (replaces a name)

Nina Reinerio is *president* of the senior class. (makes a general reference)

However, *do* capitalize a title that represents a *high-ranking* official when the title follows or replaces the name of a specific person.

The President attended the funeral of Pope John Paul II. (*President* refers to President George W. Bush.)

Titles in Addresses, Signature Blocks, and Salutations.

Capitalize a title that immediately follows a person's name in the address block of a letter or an envelope. Capitalize the first word of the complimentary close of a letter, and capitalize a person's name in the signature block.

Address Block	**Complimentary Close/ Signature Block**
Ms. Elise Hue, Recruiter	Respectfully yours
Payroll Department	
Brannier, Inc.	
50 Delphi Road	
Memphis, TN 38128-0129	Dale Rhur
	Marketing Director

Capitalize the first word and all titles and nouns in the salutation of a letter.

Dear Parents and Supporters   Dear Mrs. Capelleti

Academic Degrees and Professional Designations.

Capitalize the abbreviations of academic degrees and professional designations that follow a person's name. *Do not* capitalize general references to degrees.

Stewart D'Abbra, OT   Danelle Hobson, B.A., M.A.

Some style manuals and dictionaries show academic and professional abbreviations without periods.

Family Titles.

Capitalize a family title, such as *father*, *mother*, *uncle*, or *aunt* when the title is used alone to refer to a specific person or when the title comes immediately before a person's name. *Do not* capitalize a family title when the reference to the title is general or when the title is preceded by a possessive noun, a pronoun, or an article (*a*, *an*, or *the*).

Did you drive Mom to the airport? (title used in place of a name)

Reena visited Aunt Meg. (title immediately precedes a name)

The Valdezes held a surprise birthday party for their dad. (title is preceded by a pronoun)

Religious References

Capitalize the names of specific religions and supreme beings. *Do not* capitalize a noun following a religious reference unless the noun is part of a proper name.

Protestant	God	Protestant church
Islam	Allah	Islamic mosque

Complete Application 12-1.

[Checkpoint 12-1]

Capitalize *I*, First Words, Names and Titles, and Religious References

Identify each capitalization error, and write the correction above the error.

1. carlos, a Registered Nurse, works with supervisor Terence O'malley.
2. has Ellie met mayor Patrick Lutz or Maria Cruz-hampton, a local Judge?
3. Mike drews, cpa, oversees 120 employees.
4. Glenda delivered superintendent Neisbaum's request to the committee.
5. the class will visit jewish and Buddhist Temples as well as muslim Mosques.
6. The Keynote Speakers for the ceremony are senators Jackson and Braun.
7. before making plans, i must check with dad.
8. distribute this message to all residents: after 11 p.m., you must use your pass code to enter the building.

In a title, do not *capitalize (a) conjunctions and prepositions of three or fewer letters, (b) articles, and (c) the word* to *in an infinitive* unless *these words begin or end a title or are capitalized by the person or organization that produced the work.*

The titles of artistic works (except songs) and of complete literary works are italicized when in print and underlined when handwritten.

Literary and Artistic Works

Most words in the titles of literary and artistic works are capitalized, but follow the preference of the person or organization that produced the work. Capitalize the word *the* only when *the* is part of the formal title.

Capitalize the first, last, and principal words in titles of **literary works**, such as books, magazines, newspapers, and reports, as well as subunits of these works, such as chapters and articles. Also capitalize the first, last, and principal words in titles of **artistic works**, such as sculptures, movies, paintings, and songs.

The Da Vinci Code (*The* is part of the book title.)
Chicago Tribune (newspaper)
"E-mail Emergencies" (chapter title)
Spider-Man (movie)
Two Cut Sunflowers (painting by Vincent van Gogh)
"Are You Lonesome Tonight?" (Elvis Presley song)

Geographic References

References to specific places, addresses, and directions are capitalized.

PLACES. Capitalize the names and abbreviations of specific places, including regions and natural features, because they are proper nouns. Capitalize *city* when the word is part of a legal name, and capitalize *state* when the word immediately follows the name of the state. Otherwise, capitalize words such as *city* and *state* in official documents only.

The Baileys will visit the Adirondack Mountains in northern New York State; then they will drive to New York City.

The state of Texas is home to the Alamo.

The U.S. Supreme Court case *San Remo Hotel et al. v. City and County of San Francisco* questions the constitutionality of a city ordinance.

ADDRESSES. Capitalize the names and abbreviations of specific streets and highways and both letters in state postal abbreviations.

100 Highway C
Milwaukee, WI 53210-1516

I-70 (Interstate 70)
W170 N12589 Windflower Dr.

DIRECTIONS. Capitalize directional terms when they are part of proper names and when they refer to specific regions. *Do not* capitalize general references to directions.

Darryl is from the South. (specific region)

Do you live in West Palm Beach? (city)

The apartment building is located at 625 East Wrightwood. (proper name)

Our family likes to fish in northern Minnesota. (general reference)

Organizations, Government Bodies, and Their Divisions

The names of organizations, government bodies, and their divisions should be capitalized. Words such as *university*, *hospital*, and *company* are not capitalized unless they are part of such a name. Follow the preference of the organization or government body in capitalizing.

Do not capitalize words such as pages(s), line(s), *and* size(s) *when they precede a number unless they are the first word in a sentence.*

Capitalize nicknames of specific locations and names of specific areas within a location, such as Windy City (nickname for Chicago) and SoHo *(area in New York City).*

Capitalize the common element used with two or more proper nouns used together, such as the Mississippi and Colorado Rivers.

Do not *capitalize general references to organizations, government bodies, or their divisions, such as* the committee meets Tuesdays, I work for the federal government, *or* I would like to work in payroll at a university.

The formal titles of laws, acts, and bills are also capitalized, such as the CAN-SPAM Act of 2003.

Organizations and Government Bodies. Capitalize the names of specific organizations, such as companies, universities, and associations. Also capitalize the names of specific government bodies.

St. Joseph's Medical Center	University of Wisconsin
Muscular Dystrophy Association	House of Representatives

Divisional Names. Capitalize the names of specific departments, committees, and agencies within organizations and government.

Department of Transportation	Assessment Committee
Central Intelligence Agency	

[Checkpoint 12-2]

Capitalize Literary and Artistic Titles, Geographic References, and Organizational and Government Names

Identify each capitalization error, and write the correction above the error.

1. John James Audubon was a naturalist, wildlife artist, and author; his book *the birds of America* (primarily birds of the south and the midwest) remains the standard against which the works of other bird artists are measured.

2. Audubon was born in Santo domingo (now haiti) in 1785 but spent much of his childhood with his stepmother in Nantes, france.

3. At 18, he was sent to america to the family-owned estate at mill grove, Pennsylvania (now part of the audubon wildlife sanctuary), where he drew birds and conducted the first known bird-banding experiment in north America.

4. When Audubon died, his widow tried to sell his original watercolors for *the birds of america* to the smithsonian institution. The smithsonian refused the offer, and his original artwork was sold in 1863 to the New York historical society.

Abbreviations and Acronyms

Abbreviations generally follow the capitalization of the words for which they stand. Remember that an *acronym* is a shortened form of a name or expression typically formed from the first letter of each word. Some acronyms are pronounced as a solid word; others, called *initialisms*, are pronounced letter by letter.

Some acronyms that have evolved into common usage are not capitalized. Examples include sitcom *(situation comedy) and* laser *(light amplification by stimulated emission of radiation).*

ABBREVIATIONS. Capitalize the first letter of an abbreviation that stands for a proper noun or is part of a specific name. Abbreviations are usually followed by a period.

Feb.	J. T. Jones	W. Va.
Gardee Mfg.	Solomon Bros.	Chan Ltd.

ACRONYMS. Capitalize all letters of most acronyms. Acronyms typically are not punctuated with periods.

IRS (pronounced *I-R-S*)	Internal Revenue Service
HIMA (pronounced *he-ma*)	Health Information Management Association

Product Names

Product names usually are developed to attract consumer attention, so they may have unusual spellings and capitalization. Many names are trademarked™ or registered® to ensure that no one else uses the name for commercial purposes. Capitalize product names according to the manufacturer's preference.

Vicks® VapoRub	9Lives®

Dates and Special Events

Dates and the names of special events are capitalized. The names of seasons are not capitalized.

DATES. Capitalize the names of days, months, and holidays.

Mr. Ting's vacation begins Friday, March 17.

To commemorate the signing of the Declaration of Independence on July 4, 1776, Independence Day is declared a national holiday in the United States.

Our children attend camps during the summer.

EVENTS. Capitalize the names of historic and religious events, including periods of time. Also capitalize the names of special events, such as sporting events and festivals.

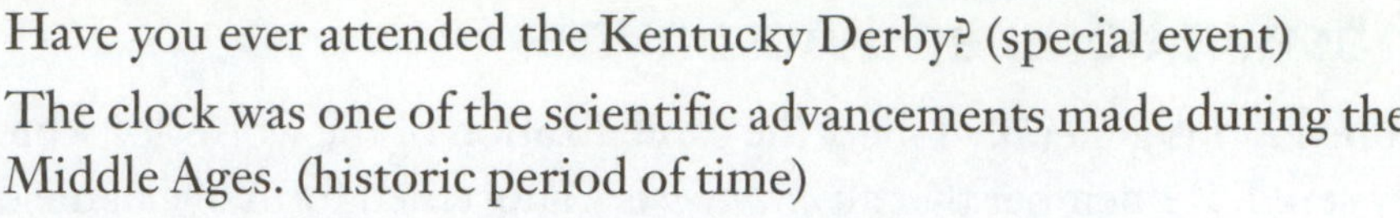

Have you ever attended the Kentucky Derby? (special event)

The clock was one of the scientific advancements made during the Middle Ages. (historic period of time)

Identification Numbers and Course Titles

Words combined with identification numbers, language course titles, and other specific course titles are capitalized.

Identification Numbers. Capitalize words that are combined with an identification number.

Please revise Bulletin 6721.
Keep Confirmation No. 2QRS321 in your files.

Complete the Chapter 12 Web Exercise at **miller.swlearning.com**.

Complete Application 12-2.

Course Titles. Capitalize specific course titles and titles that include a language or number in the name. *Do not* capitalize references to general areas of study.

All finance majors must complete Accounting IV, International Logistics, and Conversational Spanish. (General reference to *finance* is not capitalized; specific course titles are capitalized.)

[Checkpoint 12-3]

Capitalize Acronyms, Names of Special Events, Identification Numbers, Course Titles, and Other Specific Names

Identify each capitalization error, and write the correction above the error.

1. The war of the roses (1455–1487) was an internal war fought over the throne of England.
2. The occupational safety and health administration (osha) strives to ensure the safety and health of workers in the United States.
3. Read bulletin no. 12-445 before replacing the battery.
4. Some acronyms are the same, but they may refer to different organizations. For example, aha may refer to the American hospital association, the American heart association, or the American Historical association.
5. Stephen is enrolled in english Literature 202, global commerce, and microcomputers for business; he is also enrolled in a photography class.
6. Friday is the day that Muslims celebrate the sabbath.

NUMBERS

Numbers are written as figures, words, or a combination of figures and words, depending on the situation. Numbers from *one* to *ten* are generally written in words; numbers over *ten* are written as figures. Basic guidelines for presenting numerical information follow.

Cardinal numbers are 1, 2, 3 . . . *or* one, two, three. *Ordinal numbers are* 1st, 2nd, 3rd . . . *or* first, second, third.

Basic Number Format Guidelines

These basic number format guidelines cover typical situations. A comprehensive reference manual is a valuable source of information for those situations that require more detailed coverage.

NUMBERS *ONE* THROUGH *TEN*. In most cases, use words for numbers *one* through *ten* when the numbers are written in sentences.

> Four of us studied at the library.
> On its anniversary, the company raffled ten motorcycles.

NUMBERS ABOVE *TEN*. In most cases, use figures for numbers above *ten*.

> Does a case of eggs contain 12 cartons?
> The website lists 20 common interview mistakes.
> The staff addressed 1,250 donation request letters.

RELATED NUMBERS. When numbers in a sentence refer to similar items, use the same format for all the numbers. If the items are related but the numbers are above and below *ten*, format all the numbers as figures.

> United Parcel Service delivered three packages in Middleton, two in Allenton, and six in Madison. (related numbers under *ten*)
>
> The Chanticleer Inn served breakfast to 15 local businesspeople, lunch to a 75-member tour group, and dinner to 250 wedding guests. (related numbers over *ten*)
>
> Only 4 of the 62 applicants meet the job requirements. (related numbers above and below *ten*)

UNRELATED NUMBERS. When numbers in a sentence refer to unrelated items, follow the guideline appropriate for each number.

> Each of the three campuses ordered 500 reams of paper, 150 boxes of staples, 4 cases of CDs, and 1 gross of pens. (Related items represent numbers above and below *ten*, so they are written as figures. The number of campuses is unrelated and thus is written as a word.)

Numbers in the Millions. For easy reading, express numbers greater than a million as a figure-word combination when the number is a whole number or a whole number with a simple decimal.

All numbers of a million or higher in the same sentence must be expressed in the same format. If *all* the numbers in the sentence cannot be written as a figure-word combination, then *all* the numbers must be written in figures.

> Bectron Technology sold 3 million games in the first year and 3.5 million games in the second year. (All numbers can be written in a figure-word combination.)
>
> More than 2,500,000 acres suffered crop damage last year, compared to 1,575,000 acres the year before. (The number 1,575,000 *cannot* be written in a figure-word combination; therefore, both numbers must be written as figures.)

Numbers That Begin Sentences. When a number begins a sentence, write the number in words. If the number has more than two words, such as *one hundred twenty*, reword the sentence and place the number elsewhere.

> *Fifty* students received awards.
>
> *Seventy-five* people attended the book signing.
>
> The event was attended by 125 people. (not *one hundred twenty-five people attended the event*)

Complete Application 12-3.

[Checkpoint 12-4]

Format Numbers

Identify each number format error, and write the correction above the error.

1. The high school choir has 75 vocalists, the symphony orchestra has 93 members, and the high school jazz band has seven members.
2. 12 actors auditioned for 4 roles in the play.
3. Rate increase notices were mailed to more than one and a half million utility customers.
4. The survey indicates that only five of thirty flights arrived on time.
5. Of the 3 plans presented, 2 recommended eliminating at least fifty positions from each site.

Dates and Clock Times

In most instances, figures are used for days of the year, years, and clock times.

Complete Dates. When expressing a complete date, use words for the month and figures for the day and year. The sequence for most correspondence in the United States is month-day-year. The sequence for military and international correspondence is day-month-year (no comma separates the day from the month).

May 6, 2007 (Separate the day and year with a comma.)
6 May 2007 (*Do not* separate date parts with a comma.)

Partial Dates. When the month comes *before* the day, use words for the month and figures for the day. When the month comes *after* the day or is omitted, use ordinal words (*first*, *second*, *third*, and so on) or ordinal figures (*1st*, *2nd*, *3rd*, and so on).

Members will meet on January 12. (month before day)
Mr. Benik's vacation begins the first of August. (month after day)
Can you start the job on the 15th? (month omitted)

Clock Times. When you use *a.m.* or *p.m.*, use figures to express clock time. State on-the-hour time *without* a colon and minutes. When the time includes hours *and* minutes, use a colon to separate hours from minutes. When a sentence contains both on-the-hour times and hour-minutes times, format all the times as hour-minutes.

Beginning at 6 a.m., flights leave hourly for Houston. (on-the-hour)

Beginning at 6:30 a.m., flights leave every 55 minutes for Chicago (hour-minutes)

Flights to San Francisco leave at 8:30 a.m., 12:45 p.m., and 5:00 p.m. (all times formatted as hour-minutes)

Figures or words may express whole hours that precede the term *o'clock*. Words are usually used in formal situations. Figures are usually used in informal situations and for emphasis.

Do not use *a.m.* or *p.m.* with terms such as *o'clock* and *in the evening*. This wording is generally used in invitations and other formal correspondence.

six o'clock in the evening
not 6 p.m. in the evening

6 o'clock in the evening

Money

Figures are generally used to express money amounts, but sometimes a figure-word combination is best.

Workplace Connection

Business is conducted globally; therefore, use the international date format when writing to people outside the United States. To avoid confusion, *do not* use all numbers (05-06-2007 or 05/06/07) to represent dates.

The amount $2.5 million is read as two point five million dollars.

One Dollar or More. Use figures to express sums of money that are $1 or greater. Place a dollar sign ($) before the amount and a decimal point between the dollars and cents. If a sum is a whole dollar amount, omit the decimal and zeros.

A toner cartridge costs $68.50. (dollars and cents)
The heating bill was $450 last month. (whole amount)

Amounts Less Than One Dollar. Use figures and the word *cents* to express sums of money that are less than one dollar.

Computer CDs sell for 89 cents at the student bookstore.

Use figures and symbols to express related amounts of money of more than and less than one dollar that appear in the same sentence.

The pen costs $1.25; the notebook costs $.89.

Dollars in the Millions. For dollar amounts that are greater than one million, express the amounts as a figure-word combination when the number is a whole number or a whole number with a simple decimal fraction.

As with other numbers, all amounts of a million or higher in the same sentence must be expressed in the same format—either all as figure-word combinations or all as figures.

Sales increased $2.5 million in 2005 and $3.4 million in 2006. (All amounts can be written in a figure-word combination.)

The Dagget parcel sold for $2,785,000; the Hammond parcel sold for $2,100,000. (The amount $2,785,000 *cannot* be written in a figure-word combination; therefore, both must be written as figures.)

Percentages, Decimals, and Fractions

Always use figures with symbols or abbreviations: 8%; 9 ft. *This format is typically used for technical and reporting purposes.*

Most percentages, decimals, and fractions are expressed as figures.

Percentages. Use figures followed by the word *percent* to express percentages. When a percentage begins a sentence, write the number in words.

The best interest rate available is 9 percent.
Thirty percent of my clients invest in international funds.

Decimals. Express decimals in figures. When the number is less than *one*, insert a zero before the decimal point to avoid confusion.

Shelby finished the race in record time: 32.5 seconds.
This product contains 0.5 gram of saturated fat.

Mixed Numbers or Decimal Equivalents. Express mixed numbers (whole numbers and fractions) and decimals as figures.

Fractions	Decimal Equivalents
6 ½	6.5
10 ¾	10.75
33 ⅓	33.3

Half is an acceptable substitute for one-half. *Also, hyphenate the word* half *when used as a compound adjective (*half-hour break, half-dozen eggs*).*

Isolated Fractions. Use words to express common fractions that stand alone (unless the fraction is a technical measurement). Hyphenate fractions such as one-half, two-thirds, etc.

One-half of the membership is under age 35.
About two-thirds of the suites have business stations.

Complete Application 12-4.

[Checkpoint 12-5]

Format Dates, Clock Times, Money, Percentages, Decimals, and Fractions

Identify each number format error, and write the correction above the error.

1. The computer package is four hundred 99 dollars, and the software is one hundred thirty-five dollars.
2. You can order a fruit drink for 98 cents or a milk shake for $2 and 25 cents.
3. The rate of interest on an 18-month certificate of deposit is three and five-tenths percent.
4. The cost overruns are exceeding 1 1/2 million dollars.
5. Busses run every 1/2 hour beginning at 7:30 a.m.; the last bus leaves at 8:00 in the evening.
6. The survey indicates that fifty-five percent of residents did not vote in the last city election, which was held on November first.
7. The cleaning kit costs six dollars.
8. 40 percent of the class voted for Suzanne.

Chapter Summary

- Capitalize the pronoun *I*. Also capitalize the first word in a sentence, an expression used as a sentence, and an independent clause following a colon.
- Capitalize people's names, courtesy and professional titles that precede names, and some family titles. Also capitalize names and titles in addresses, signature blocks, and salutations.
- Capitalize the abbreviations of academic degrees and professional designations following a person's name.
- Capitalize specific religious references.
- Capitalize the first, last, and all important words in titles of literary and artistic works and their parts, such as chapters and articles.
- Capitalize the names of specific geographical locations and addresses.
- Capitalize directional terms that are part of proper names or that refer to specific regions.
- Capitalize the names of organizations, government bodies, and their divisions.
- Capitalize abbreviations when the terms they stand for are capitalized.
- Capitalize most acronyms.
- Capitalize product names according to the manufacturer's preference.
- Capitalize the names of days, months, and special events, as well as words combined with identification numbers and course titles.
- In most cases, write the numbers *one* through *ten* as words in sentences; write the numbers above *ten* in figures.
- Format related numbers in a sentence the same way; if the numbers are above and below *ten*, format the numbers as figures.
- Format unrelated numbers in a sentence according to the guidelines appropriate for each number.
- For numbers in the millions, express whole numbers or whole numbers with a simple decimal as figure-word combinations.
- Write numbers as words when they begin sentences, or reword the sentence.
- In most cases, use figures for days of the year, years, clock times, monetary amounts, percentages, decimals, and fractions.

Complete the Chapter 12 Review.

ILrn

Complete the Chapter 12 iLrn Activities at **miller.swlearning.com**.

APPLICATION 12-1

Capitalization

Identify each capitalization error, and write the correction above the error.

Dr. Kyle Trenton international

0. The article was submitted by dr. kyle trenton, an International travel guide.
1. Contact E. f. Saldana, jr., or Tisha Kreiss-hayes for more information.
2. One of our former graduates, captain Tina Washburn, will conduct a self-defense course.
3. Three students are interested in becoming an Emergency Medical Technician.
4. Did you call director Cruesas?
5. Jason Kaiser, the Union Treasurer, will retire next year.
6. My mother likes to listen to Frank "old blue eyes" Sinatra's music.
7. Our Professor, Lorenzo Tines, writes a travel column.
8. Every member of our family agrees: we must sell the property before December 1.
9. The recommendation from dr. Torres is that Maria Boyce, ph.D., be temporarily appointed to the committee.
10. Did your Brother graduate from college?
11. Did Lu Chang, who is Secretary-elect, qualify for the award?
12. Sean O'riley led the debate team to victory.
13. Ms. Pellagrino, Attorney, agreed to handle the club's legal matters.
14. William Bortsch, Mayor of Clinton, met officials of TexTron Corporation.
15. Did you know that grandmother Shiles was elected State Senator when she was 58?
16. Write a letter to the President of the company.
17. Sometimes Abraham Lincoln was referred to as honest abe.
18. Is your Aunt major Zweiffle or sergeant Zweiffle?
19. The Estate Planner talked with my Stepmother, Ruth Thames, about her will.
20. Textbooks often refer to hinduism as the world's oldest organized religion.

APPLICATION 12-2

Capitalization

Identify each capitalization error, and write the correction above the error.

S Harbor Drive

0. Cleo and Clayton Ung moved to their new condominium at 1258 s. Bay harbor drive.

1. On june 6, 1944, D-Day, Stella's great-uncle Edward participated in a major military invasion—the landing on omaha beach in normandy, france.

2. The Cass family lives one hour South of Portland, maine.

3. One of my favorite magazines is *midwest living*.

4. You will find great bargains at the mexican market at sixth and main streets.

5. The santa fe opera is housed in a unique outdoor theater.

6. The beatles were a popular british singing group.

7. Last month, the bayside players performed the musical *grease*.

8. The federal aviation administration is often referred to as the faa.

9. Two long-running plays on New York's broadway were *a chorus line* and *les miserables*.

10. If you drive about 50 miles North, you will find several small but luxurious Inns.

11. Has Mr. Yeng found the guide *france on a budget*?

12. Many americans were stationed in the philippines during world war II.

13. The National headquarters of the cdc (an agency of the department of health and human services) is in atlanta, georgia.

14. Most American Universities do not hold classes on labor day or on July 4, independence day.

15. The renaissance was a revival of cultural awareness and learning in Europe.

16. ViJay is fluent in both chinese and french.

17. Some of the countries of central america are costa rica, guatemala, panama, and honduras.

18. The American federation of labor and congress of industrial organizations is usually referred to as the afl-cio.

19. The article about the spanish-american war will appear in the march 12 issue of *historic chronicles*.

20. Vacation policies are clearly outlined in subsection 122-B on Page 144 of the handbook.

APPLICATION 12-3

Numbers Above and Below *Ten*

Identify each number format error, and write the correction above the error. If the sentence does not contain an error, write **C** in the space provided.

three
0. Samantha wrote 3 reports last night. ________
1. Lyle did not know that a gross contains one hundred forty-four items. ________
2. The students washed three motor homes, ten trucks, 12 SUVs, and 14 cars. ________
3. The 2 managers have combined experience of 18 years. ________
4. Did you want 10 top-bound or side-bound notebooks? ________
5. List five adjectives that describe you. ________
6. In 2000, natural gas consumption in the United States reached twenty-two point six trillion cubic feet. ________
7. Thirty-seven people contributed to the food pantry. ________
8. They propose opening one and a half million acres to gas exploration and production. ________
9. The committee expects 2 thousand five hundred people to attend the conference. ________
10. Thirty classic cars are entered in the parade; they represent 12 states. ________
11. 25 governors participated in the exercises. ________
12. We received seventeen calls requesting information about our Web services. ________
13. The visitor log showed that fourteen people signed in before noon. ________
14. Mayfair Mall has 24 retail stores, and they are adding twelve more next year. ________
15. John A. Kelley participated in the Boston Marathon sixty-one times. ________
16. I read the report four times and found twenty-three errors. ________
17. All one hundred two acres of the park are open to visitors. ________
18. One of my favorite websites provides quick access to ninety-nine different stores. ________
19. Airline tickets are usually cheaper if they are purchased 14 days in advance. ________
20. The two instructors accompanied twenty-nine students to the choral festival in Miami. ________

APPLICATION 12-4

Special Number Formats

Identify each number format error, and write the correction above the error. If the sentence does not contain an error, write **C** in the space provided.

18
0. The contract expires on July eighteen. ______

1. Do not spend more than $.79 for a pen. ______

2. The buyout price is $3 million 750,000. ______

3. Can we meet on the 12? ______

4. Oxygen makes up twenty-one percent of the earth's atmosphere. ______

5. I transferred 3/4 of my savings into a money market account. ______

6. Lucero's hours are nine in the morning to 3 p.m. ______

7. 12 percent is the lowest credit card rate that Cheryl found. ______

8. About half of the students have computers. ______

9. Almost twenty-five percent of my gross earnings are deducted for taxes. ______

10. All new employees begin on the first. ______

11. The house on Elmhurst Street is selling for $l.5 million, but the house on Elm Tree Court is selling for $975,000. ______

12. New Mexico became a state in nineteen twelve. ______

13. We experienced a record high temperature on May 15th. ______

14. Mr. Martinelli has appointments at 9 a.m., 9:30 a.m., 10 a.m., and 10:30 a.m. ______

15. The teachers received a three percent raise. ______

16. Our accountant, Ms. Rydel, expects $250 thousand in cost overruns. ______

17. Without the nationwide plan, the cost of out-of-area minutes is 25 cents a minute. ______

18. Patrick's bagel was 89 cents; his drink was $1.29. ______

19. About 1/3 of the survey questions focused on my purchases in the last 3 months. ______

20. The tuna salad lunch plate was $5.89 plus 35 cents tax. ______

Chapter 12 Review

Capitalization and Numbers

Part A. Correct Capitalization and Numbers

Identify each capitalization or number error, and write the correction above the error. Each correct answer is worth two points.

The Philosopher Aristotle, who was a student of plato and a Tutor to Alexander the great, studied and discussed human conduct—what enables people to act properly and live happily. Early greek Philosophers believed that knowledge was the key to making right and reasonable choices. In fact, Aristotle's belief in the power of knowledge is revealed in this quote: "the educated differ from the uneducated as much as the living from the dead." today, Society continues to struggle with standards of acceptable conduct, which are referred to as *Ethics*, derived from the greek word *ethos* (meaning "custom," "usage," or "character").

In recent years, Ethics debates have extended to online music swapping. Under the nineteen ninety-eight digital millennium Copyright Act, the recording industry association of America (Riaa) began aggressive pursuit of users who illegally distribute copyrighted music recordings for Internet downloading.

The Senior vice president of business and legal affairs for Riaa, which is the recording industry's main trade group, contended that within a 3-year period, the recording industry lost about 1/3 of its eighteen billion dollar annual U.S. market. He compared downloading and distributing digital music to robbing a bank: "it is theft, pure and simple."

Part B. Identify Sentences with Correct Capitalization and Number Format

In each pair, select the sentence that uses correct capitalization and number format by writing a **C** in the space provided. Each correct answer is worth five points.

1. A. The leaders of the Age of Enlightenment, a European philosophical and intellectual movement during the 18th century, believed that truth should be determined by reason and fact; the movement provided the framework for the American and French Revolutions. ______

   B. The leaders of the age of enlightenment, a European Philosophical and Intellectual Movement during the 18th century, believed that truth should be determined by reason and fact; the movement provided the framework for the American and French revolutions. ______

2. A. Hinduism appears to be the 3rd largest religion after Christianity and Islam, with more than 700,000,000 followers. ______

   B. Hinduism appears to be the third largest religion after Christianity and Islam, with more than 700 million followers. ______

3. A. After seven thousand four hundred eighty-five performances, *Cats* was the longest-running Broadway play when the musical closed in 2000. ______

   B. After 7,485 performances, *Cats* was the longest-running Broadway play when the musical closed in 2000. ______

4. A. The Equal Employment Opportunity Commission (EEOC) administers and enforces Title VII of the Civil Rights Act of 1964. ______

   B. The equal employment opportunity commission (EEOC) administers and enforces title VII of the Civil Rights act of 1964. ______

5. A. For more than 1 hundred years, the National Consumers League has advocated social and economic justice for consumers and workers in the United States and Abroad. ______

   B. For more than 100 years, the National Consumers League has advocated social and economic justice for consumers and workers in the United States and abroad. ______

6. A. The Greek Physician Hippocrates pledged the medical profession to the preservation of life and to the service of humanity. ______

   B. The Greek physician Hippocrates pledged the medical profession to the preservation of life and to the service of humanity. ______

7. A. In the early nineteen nineties, Metropolitan Life Insurance Company paid more than $90 million dollars to settle claims arising from deceptive sales tactics. ______

   B. In the early 1990s, Metropolitan Life Insurance Company paid more than $90 million to settle claims arising from deceptive sales tactics. ______

8. A. Some surveys indicate that fewer than 15 percent of fraud victims report fraud. ______

   B. Some surveys indicate that fewer than 15% percent of fraud victims report fraud. ______

9. A. The losses resulting from stolen works of art and priceless national treasures are approaching $8 billion a year. ______

   B. The losses resulting from stolen works of art and priceless national treasures are approaching eight billion dollars a year. ______

10. A. The FBI, 935 Pennsylvania Avenue, nw, Washington, DC, publishes the *FBI Law Enforcement bulletin*. ______

    B. The FBI, 935 Pennsylvania Avenue, NW, Washington, DC, publishes the *FBI Law Enforcement Bulletin*. ______

Appendix Frequently Confused/Misused Words

a lot	many; much
alot	not a word; do not use
accede	to agree; to give in
exceed	to be greater than
accept	to receive
except	other than
ad	an advertisement
add	to find the sum; to increase
advice	words of help
advise	to give advice or counsel
affect	to influence
effect	outcome or result; to bring about
agree to	to consent
agree with	to have the same opinion
almost	nearly; a little less than (*adv.*)
most	the majority; nearly all (*adj.* or *pron.*)
already	before the expected time
all ready	fully prepared
alternate	a substitute; to change repeatedly from one to another
alternative	a choice between or among things or actions
among	used with more than two people or things
between	used with two people or things
anyone	any person
any one	any one of many persons or things
anytime	no particular time (**not** preceded by *at*)
any time	no particular time (preceded by *at*); any amount of time
anyway	in any case
any way	by any manner
assure	to promise or guarantee
ensure	to make certain
insure	to protect life or property from loss

bad	of poor quality; morally wrong (*adj.*—use after linking or "sense" verbs)
badly	in a bad way (*adv.*)
beside	next to; near
besides	in addition to; other than; except
both	two items or people considered collectively
each	any number of items or people considered separately
bring	to carry to the speaker or the speaker's place
take	to carry away from the speaker or the speaker's place
can	able to do something
may	permission; possibility
capital	chief or main; a city that serves as the seat of government of a state or nation; an uppercase letter; a sum of money or wealth; a form of punishment
capitol	buildings used by a congress or state legislature
choose	to select
chose	past tense of *choose*
cite	to quote; to refer to
site	location
sight	something that is seen; the ability to see; to see
come	to move toward the speaker or the speaker's place
go	to move away from the speaker or the speaker's place
complement	something that completes another thing; to complete or go well with
compliment	a flattering comment; to praise
conscience	one's sense of right or wrong
conscious	fully aware
consul	a government official
council	an assembly for consultation or discussion
counsel	advice; an attorney; to give advice
could have should have would have	Use *have*, not *of*.
desert	arid, barren land; to abandon
dessert	the last course of a meal
different from	shows that one thing is unlike something else
different than	incorrect; do not use

eligible illegible	qualified; entitled difficult or impossible to read
everyday every day	routine; common each day
everyone every one	everybody each one
farther further	a greater distance to a greater extent; additional
fewer less	a smaller quantity or amount (used with plural nouns and with things that can be counted) a smaller amount or degree (cannot be counted)
fiscal physical	relating to financial matters pertaining to the body
formally formerly	in a formal manner previously
good well	skillful, admirable; having the right qualities (*adj.*) properly; with skill; in a kindly way (*adv.*); in good health (*adj.*)
in into	inside something (location) entering something; changing condition (movement)
irregardless regardless	not a word; do not use in spite of
its it's	possessive form of *it* contraction meaning "it is"
lead led	metallic element past tense of *lead*
lose loose	opposite of win not tight or not secure; free
passed past	moved beyond; ended; approved earlier; former
patience patient patients	calm; willingness to wait or tolerate difficulties willing to wait or tolerate difficulties persons receiving medical treatment
personal personnel	private workers; employees
precede proceed	to go before to advance

principal	main; chief; head of school; sum of money
principle	guide; rule
quiet	calm; without noise
quit	to stop; to halt
quite	almost completely; to a considerable degree
real	genuine or true (*adj.*)
really	truly or actually (*adv.*)
right	correct; true; privilege
rite	ceremony
write	to put characters on paper or another surface
somebody	a person
some body	a group composed of people
sometime	an undetermined or inexact time
some time	a period of time
sometimes	now and then
stationary	fixed; not moving
stationery	writing materials
sure	confident; convinced; positive; reliable (*adj.*)
surely	certainly; without a doubt (*adv.*)
than	as compared to
then	at that time
their	possessive pronoun
there	at that place
they're	contraction for *they are*
to	toward; for the purpose of
too	also; more than enough
two	the number *2*
weather	atmospheric conditions, such as rain
whether	indicates one of two possibilities or choices
who's	contraction of *who is* or *who has*
whose	shows ownership or possession

Checkpoint Solutions

CHAPTER 1

Checkpoint 1-1

Definitions and the inflected forms may vary.

	Correct Spelling	Part of Speech	Inflected Forms
1.	invade	*tr. v.*	vaded, -vading, -vades
	Definition: To enter by force in order to conquer.		
2.	ptomaine (*or* ptomain)	*n.*	
	Definition: Any of various nitrogenous materials, some poisonous, produced by the putrefaction and decomposition of protein.		
3.	mediocre	*adj.*	
	Definition: Of moderate to low quality; average.		
4.	acknowledgment	*n.*	
	Definition: The act of admitting or owning to something.		
5.	initiate	*tr. v.*	-ated, -ating, -ates
	Definition: To cause to begin.		
6.	grievous	*adj.*	
	Definition: Causing grief, anguish, or pain.		
7.	precipitate	*v.*	-tated, -tating, -tates
	Definition: To hurl downward; to fall.		
8.	pseudonym	*n.*	
	Definition: Fictitious name.		
9.	particularly	*adv.*	
	Definition: To a great degree; especially.		
10.	mnemonics	*n.*	
	Definition: System to improve or develop the memory.		

Checkpoint 1-2

Answers may vary.

1. promote (*v.*)
   Definition (1): To raise in rank.
   Synonyms: elevate, advance, upgrade, raise
   Antonym: demote

   Definition (2): To help bring about.
   Synonyms: cultivate, encourage, foster

   Definition (3): To seek increased importance by favorable publicity.
   Synonyms: boost, build up, enhance
   Antonyms: discredit, disparage

2. insipid (*adj.*)
   Definition (1): Lacking qualities necessary to be spirited.
   Synonyms: boring, colorless, dull, wishy-washy
   Antonym: exciting

   Definition (2): Lacking an appetizing flavor.
   Synonyms: flat, tasteless
   Antonym: spicy

3. huff (*n.*)
   Definition (1): Fit of anger or annoyance caused by an insult.
   Synonyms: offense, sulk

   Definition (2): Gasp (intake of breath).
   Synonyms: puff, pant, wheeze

4. hot (*adj.*)
   Definition (1): Marked by much heat.
   Synonyms: blistering, boiling, burning, fiery, scalding, torrid
   Antonyms: chilly, cold, frigid

   Definition (2): Being at a temperature higher than normal.
   Synonyms: febrile, feverish

   Definition (3): (slang) Particularly excellent.
   Synonym: marvelous

5. defeat (*v.*)
   Definition (1): To win a victory over someone or something.
   Synonyms: beat, conquer, triumph over

   Definition (2): To prevent accomplishment of a purpose.
   Synonym: frustrate

Checkpoint 1-3

know
Did you no that the word *ballot* (related to the English words *ball* and

balloon) is of Germanic origin? Small, individually marked or colored
used **for**
balls have been use over the centuries fore secret voting. For example,
or
jurors in ancient Athens voted to free ore to condemn a person using
accept
balls. Even today, some clubs except or reject candidates for

membership using white balls and black balls (thus the word *blackball*).

CHAPTER 2

Checkpoint 2-1

1. (Utah) is their favorite place to ski.
2. When the judge asked the question, (Aaron) answered.
3. Bungalows surround the (Lake of Seven Colors) in (Mexico).
4. (Elise) raised more money than (Lupe).
5. (TrimArt Inc.) shapes bushes into interesting sculptures.

Checkpoint 2-2

Answers will vary. Some additional collective nouns include *tribe*, *audience*, *bank*, *group*, *personnel*, *club*, *board*, *cabinet*, *agency*, and *congregation*.

Checkpoint 2-3

SUB **DO**
1. The *Kramms* repainted their *house*.

SUB **DO**
2. *Saran* ordered a *computer* yesterday.

SUB **DO**
3. *Amy* accepted her *award* with pride.

SUB **DO**
4. Two *employees* passed the *examination*.

SUB **DO**
5. The new shipping *containers* hold *vegetables*.

Checkpoint 2-4

1. songs
2. bunches
3. masses
4. drapes
5. careers
6. crutches
7. foxes
8. matches
9. crashes
10. tires

Checkpoint 2-5

1. patties
2. agencies
3. skies
4. birthdays
5. mysteries
6. McElys
7. valleys
8. flies
9. trays
10. McCraneys

Checkpoint 2-6

1. zoos
2. contraltos
3. lives
4. tomatoes
5. pianos
6. videos
7. logos
8. roofs
9. tariffs
10. heroes

Checkpoint 2-7

1. mice
2. cabooses
3. geese
4. clerks
5. bookshelves
6. teeth
7. runners-up
8. cities
9. accounts payable
10. printouts

Checkpoint 2-8

1. press's reaction
2. firefighter's uniform
3. hero's welcome
4. Ross's story
5. secretary-treasurer's report
6. coworker's illness
7. Christie Company's dividend
8. Tim and Kristen's computer
9. Isabel's and Rick's condo
10. CBS's schedule

Checkpoint 2-9

	Plural	Plural Possessive
1.	chefs	chefs' kitchens
2.	children	children's games
3.	vice presidents	vice presidents' offices
4.	brothers-in-law	brothers-in-law's homes
5.	nieces and nephews	nieces and nephews' camping gear
6.	authors	authors' names
7.	Lynches and Navarros	the Lynches' and the Navarros' pets
8.	Armies	Armies' gains
9.	teachers	teachers' degrees
10.	communities	communities' leaders

CHAPTER 3

Checkpoint 3-1

They
1. (Vianne and Carrie) should arrive within an hour.

she
2. David and (Miss Rocher) opened a new shop across the street.

them
3. The club recommended a new style of hiking boots for (Craig and Joanne).

me
4. "The furniture was divided between Radji and (myself)," said Tanya.

him **us**
5. The letter from (Sam) says nothing about (you and me).

him
6. The manager complimented Chris and (Larry).

he
7. When I asked for Roberto, he answered, "This is (Roberto)."

him
8. Bradley's mother sent money to (Bradley).

Checkpoint 3-2

1. Please take (you're/your) seats before the presentation begins.
2. (Their/They're) home page is excellent; (their/they're) scheduled to update the site next week.

3. The patent is (our's/ours).
4. The choice is (mine/mine's) to make.
5. The bird lost (it's/its) tail feathers during the tropical storm.

Checkpoint 3-3

1. Gerald, please do not place yourself in danger by exceeding the speed limit.
2. The Turners taught themselves how to ski.
3. Tarah herself signed the documents.
4. You yourself said that the vote was surprising.
5. We must lower the bid, or we will find ourselves without a contract.
6. I myself will never encounter that kind of issue.
7. Must we wait for approval, or may we proceed with the changes ourselves?
8. The Kleins themselves offered a sizable reward.

Checkpoint 3-4

1. (Who's/Whose) briefcase was left in the foyer?
2. Elena is on the committee (which/that) drafted the retirement plan.
3. The computer, (that/which) was assembled in Canada, is mine.
4. For (who/whom) was the report prepared?
5. (Which/What) is better—the first suggestion or the second?

Checkpoint 3-5

1. Is anyone available to help us?
2. Someone needs to explain (that) to the audience.
3. Some of the font styles do not transmit clearly; (those) should be changed.
4. Neither of your proposals is appropriate because both have disadvantages.
5. I noticed that everybody has chosen something from the catalog.

Checkpoint 3-6

1. Neither (Heather) nor (Lisa) has received her check.
2. The (employees) requested new computers, but they are not likely to have their requests approved.
3. (Abelardo) takes good care of his ghost costume.
4. The (company) has closed its doors after 30 years in business.

5. (Several) agreed to have their cell-phone numbers published.
6. (Few) of the beach residents have returned to their property.
7. (Mrs. Delgado), as well as the others, thinks that her visa will be approved.
8. (Both) have their reports ready.
9. (Larry) and (Karen) donated to their favorite charity.
10. (Everyone) wants his or her grades today.

CHAPTER 4

Checkpoint 4-1

trims	**A**	provides	**A**	am	**L**
very		printer		see	**A**
observed	**A**	was	**L**	sad	
is	**L**	walks	**A**	rapidly	
wallet		speak	**A**	draw	**A**

Checkpoint 4-2

1. Colonel Hernandez (had) called for an appointment.
2. (Will) you attend the seminar?
3. Quong (should) (have) selected an alternate category.
4. You (may) play the second round with us.
5. The production manager (has) recommended more efficient techniques.

Checkpoint 4-3

1. Andres writes positive statements. **present**
2. Sarah will copy the report. **future**
3. My assistant completed the repairs. **past**
4. The tourists climbed the hill. **past**
5. I shall speak with Gladys and Kevin. **future**

Checkpoint 4-4

1. Virginia has exported the fragile items. **present perfect**
2. Ester will have planted the trees by March 10. **future perfect**

3. Ocean Blue Contractors had installed the pipes before the flood. **past perfect**
4. He has tested the sample many times. **present perfect**
5. Sonia had called before every visit. **past perfect**

Checkpoint 4-5

1. I (saw/seen) you yesterday in the bookstore.
2. Dave had never (swam/swum) in Lake Dawson.
3. Jacob has (did/done) all the baking for the reception.
4. Kelly (knew/knowed) all the answers.
5. Who has (drank/drunk) all the tea?
6. You (was/were) given two assignments.
7. Jed has (went/gone) to Columbia to visit friends.
8. Charles has (began/begun) dance lessons at Gulf Point.
9. They could not have (built/build) to code.
10. Rosa has (drawn/drawed) quilt patterns for the craft show.

Checkpoint 4-6

1. The workers will (lay/lie) the carpet when the shipment arrives.
2. She (set/sat) at the back of the auditorium.
3. Evelyn, please (sat/set) the vase on the second shelf.
4. The official flag has been (risen/raised).
5. Justin (sat/set) there yesterday.
6. Martha has (lain/laid) down for a few hours.
7. Aaron (rose/raised) the blinds before sunrise.

Checkpoint 4-7

1. You (have) created a lovely bracelet. **A**
2. Marjorie (had) proofread and edited the copy by 11:30 a.m. **A**
3. The report (was) bound by Kimberly. **P**
4. The text (was) published by the new company. **P**
5. The anesthesiologist (had) (been) certified by the board. **P**
6. Luis and Gina (have) leased an air compressor. **A**
7. The site (has) listed cruises to Alaska and Mexico. **A**
8. Sympathy notes (were) mailed to the family members by Jessica. **P**

9. Raymond (has) contracted for telecommunication service from Arco. **A**
10. The stadium (was) cleaned by the SGA members. **P**

CHAPTER 5

Checkpoint 5-1

1. You (play/plays) with the city jazz band.
2. The doctor (work/works) in the clinic at 110 Langley Avenue.
3. The pants (wrinkle/wrinkles) when you sit.
4. We (perform/performs) in the 3 p.m. matinee.
5. I (approve/approves) your recommendation.

Checkpoint 5-2

1. You (has/have) many opportunities to advance in that career field.
2. Ramon (has/have) completed the aptitude tests.
3. (Has/Have) they made any career plans?
4. She (has/have) changed careers three times.
5. I (has/have) recommended the career DVD to my students.

Checkpoint 5-3

1. I (am/is) on time for the rehearsal.
2. (Was/Were) you present for the award ceremony?
3. If Hugh (was/were) musically gifted, he would compete in the talent show.
4. They (is/are) in favor of the waste management plan.
5. The nursing program director (was/were) absent from the meeting.

Checkpoint 5-4

1. Either a cello or a bass (play/plays) in the bass clef.
2. Either the trumpets or the flugelhorns (carries/carry) the lead brass line.
3. Neither the conductor nor the violinists (is/are) familiar with the concerto.

4. Not only the audience but also the musicians (applaud/applauds) the guest performer.
5. The violin or the flutes (is/are) out of tune.

Checkpoint 5-5

1. (Wolves), when they run in a pack, (attack/attacks) larger animals.
2. (Water) from the treatment plants (spill/spills) into the bay.
3. (Tires) in a landfill (do/does) not stay buried.
4. The air quality (index), as well as the ozone level, (is/are) important.
5. (Oxygen) for people with bronchitis (come/comes) in two-liter containers.

Checkpoint 5-6

1. (Most) of the students (use/uses) backpacks with wheels.
2. A (few) of the oranges (is/are) ready to be picked.
3. (Everybody) (buy/buys) snacks in the Oregon Grill.
4. (All) of the cherry pie (was/were) eaten at the banquet.
5. (None) of my prescriptions (has/have) been filled.

Checkpoint 5-7

1. The young crew (is/are) on its third mission.
2. The Harris family (travel/travels) to Washington each year.
3. After each performance, the audience (score/scores) the contestants on separate ballots.
4. The Coastal Waters Council (select/selects) grant winners.
5. The squadron (was/were) putting on camouflage suits.

CHAPTER 6

Checkpoint 6-1

1. A two-tiered platter of Italian pastries was at the center of the table, which was covered with a lace tablecloth.

2. Jerry Ramirez is a well-known author of mystery books.
3. Jai saw a clever comedy act at a historic theater.
4. The mysterious stranger disappeared into the deep, dark tunnel.
5. At a recent festival, Ralph purchased colorful fans, Chinese tea, and fortune cookies.

Checkpoint 6-2

1. a; an
2. a; an
3. an
4. an
5. These members are meeting to discuss both proposals.
6. Jonathan Cullen will receive an honorable discharge in three months.
7. Most of the letters have many errors.
8. Mario's sisters cleaned oil from the feathers of several birds.
9. Those posters were designed by our art class.
10. All the applicants should be seated either in my office or in William's office.

Checkpoint 6-3

Positive Degree	Comparative Degree	Superlative Degree
1. busy	busier	busiest
2. cheap	cheaper	cheapest
3. high	higher	highest
4. stunning	more stunning	most stunning
5. incredible	more incredible	most incredible

Checkpoint 6-4

Most/least means that either *most* or *least* is acceptable.

1. Her claim is the most/least outrageous claim that I have ever heard.
2. Your cake is better than the cake that I bought at the bakery.
3. Of all the offices in the building, Anna's office is the most/least relaxing.
4. Which of the three sofas is the best choice for my apartment?
5. Evan bought the most/least expensive camera in the store.

6. This salsa is spicier than the salsa that I make.
7. My dog is smarter than my neighbor's dog; in fact, my dog is the smartest dog on the block.
8. Jackson was hungrier than Miriam.
9. My husband is the youngest of four children.
10. I feel better today than I did yesterday.

CHAPTER 7

Checkpoint 7-1

1. Shelly almost missed the bus.	**to what extent?**
2. Jahira politely asked Bradford to make the telephone call.	**how?**
3. The waitstaff moved fast.	**how?**
4. The award for academic achievement is given annually.	**when? (or how often?)**
5. The frightened dog ran inside.	**where?**

Checkpoint 7-2

1. That price is too (high). — **adjective**
2. The first day was fairly (easy). — **adjective**
3. My sister (drives) frustratingly (slow). — **verb**, **adverb**
   (The adverb *slowly* modifies the verb *drives*; the adverb *frustratingly* modifies the adverb *slow*.)
4. The students are delightfully (cheerful). — **adjective**
5. Tyler (watched) the movie intently. — **verb**
6. Mr. Tai frequently (plays) golf on Saturday. — **verb**

Checkpoint 7-3

More/less means that either *more* or *less* is acceptable. *Most/least* means that either *most* or *least* is acceptable.

1. The supervisor decided that Caitlin proofreads as carefully as Dominic does.
2. Today's audience waited more/less patiently than yesterday's audience.
3. Of the six teams in the tournament, the Hawks scored the highest.
4. Alan lives farther from school than anyone in his class.
5. Of all the students, Alan lives the farthest from school.
6. Mr. Tai waited anxiously for his performance review.
7. Tyler's mother spoke proudly of his work.
8. Chynda's test scores were better than Jane's test scores.

Checkpoint 7-4

Revisions may vary.

1. I don't have no homework tonight.
   I don't have any homework tonight.
2. I haven't never had to drive in Los Angeles.
   I haven't ever had to drive in Los Angeles.
3. Luisa doesn't have none of those books.
   Luisa doesn't have any of those books.
4. Mrs. Ehn did not receive no credit on her account.
   Mrs. Ehn did not receive credit on her account.
5. The student hardly never gets the correct answer on the algebra quizzes.
   The student hardly ever gets the correct answer on the algebra quizzes.

Checkpoint 7-5

1. Ramona felt (bad // badly) about missing her appointment.
2. We may not finish, but we will (almost // most) be done by 4 p.m.
3. The acoustics in the room make the music sound (bad // badly).
4. The manager handled the situation (bad // badly).
5. My father was (sure // surely) excited about my grades.
6. Did you notice how (good // well) the supervisor handled the complaint?
7. This is a (real // very) good book.
8. (Be sure and // Be sure to) order the flowers by Monday.

CHAPTER 8

Checkpoint 8-1

1. **P OP P OP P** Kayla waited by the door, but after 20 minutes, she went into the **OP** theater.
2. **P OP P OP** I cannot apply for the job until February.
3. **P OP P** Straighten the items in the display case, and count the books on the **OP** shelf.
4. **P OP** To whom did you give the directions?
5. **P OP P OP P** The team walked through each building on the property except the **OP** Seifert Building.

Checkpoint 8-2

1. Deleting e-mail messages from a company network does not erase them permanently. (Delete *off of*.)
2. Think of all the places around the world we have been. (Delete *of* and *to*.)
3. Between you and me, the Conway article needs major revision. (Change *I* to *me*.)

Checkpoint 8-3

1. Sondra (could have // could of) earned an A in Japanese, but she did poorly on the final exam.
2. I (agreed to // agreed with) Rosa's assessment: The reimbursement contract is (to // too) complicated to enter (in // into) without further discussion.
3. NaJay was (to // too) tired to complain (to // too) the manager.
4. Investment booklets were distributed (among // between) the six participants so that they could decide whether these investment options were (different from // different than) the Bateman options.
5. Did you leave the camera (beside // besides) the phone?

Checkpoint 8-4

1. Both the student fee and the tuition are due March 1.
2. Do you prefer a mezzanine seat or an orchestra seat?
3. Neither Friday tickets nor Saturday tickets are available.
4. I appreciate your offer, but I cannot accept the job. (OR *yet*)

Checkpoint 8-5

1. (After // If) you leave by 7 a.m., you will miss the rush-hour traffic.
2. Register at the reception desk (as soon as // before) you arrive.
3. (Provided that // Unless) you buy your tickets early, you may have difficulty scheduling a convenient flight.
4. Teri acts (as though // though) she is the boss.
5. (Because // So that) we want a good seat, we must buy our tickets early.

Checkpoint 8-6

1. Gabriella volunteers at the local food pantry; (in addition // however), she volunteers at her son's high school.
2. Mohammad completed the tasks quickly; (as a result // for example), he impressed his supervisor.
3. (Also // First) Marcia and Olivia analyzed the problem; (then // thus) they developed a plan.
4. Please send your payment by May 1. (Nevertheless // Otherwise), we will turn over your account to a collection agency.
5. Sharifa's team has too many deadlines to meet today; (for example // consequently), three reports and a project estimate are due by 4 p.m.

CHAPTER 9

Checkpoint 9-1

1.	Ms. deLuca's primary responsibility is *supervising three clerks.*	GER	N
2.	Do you remember any details *about the accident*?	PREP	ADJ
3.	*Released last month*, the CD is a favorite among teens.	PART	ADJ
4.	*To wait any longer* is ridiculous.	INF	N
5.	The lamp was stored *in the attic.*	PREP	ADV
6.	I dislike *balancing my checkbook.*	GER	N

7. The customer wants *to place an order.* INF N
8. *Selling the property immediately* is his recommendation. GER N
9. Did you look *in the garage*? PREP ADV
10. The book *signed by Mark Twain* is on display. PART ADJ

Checkpoint 9-2

1. *When Carla receives her tax refund*, she plans to contribute to her IRA. DC
2. *Mr. Balnik*, the drivers' training instructor, *also works as a carpenter.* IC
3. Your account will have a zero balance *once you make this payment.* DC
4. The hotel will confirm your reservation *as soon as you send a deposit.* DC
5. *The prices are high*, so I did not order tickets. IC
6. Did you notice *that several pages are missing*? DC
7. As my sister scored the final point, *I watched proudly from the sidelines.* IC
8. *We dropped the price* so that the headsets will sell quickly. IC
9. *Until she moved to Houston*, Margot had never attended the opera. DC
10. James, *who has six nieces and nephews*, enjoys being a teacher. DC

Checkpoint 9-3

1. The key that is hidden under the rock opens the back door. ESS
2. Jenna whom you recommended was hired for the medical assistant position. NON
3. Houses that qualify as "historic treasures" may be eligible for preservation funds. ESS
4. Thomas used to work in the Carroll Building which is slated for demolition. NON
5. Aaron whose grades were not good this semester is studying with a tutor. NON
6. Students who maintain a 3.7 grade point average may apply for the Brookfield Honor Scholarship. ESS

Checkpoint 9-4

1. Ming received six interview offers within two weeks. SIM
2. John-Paul, who is a well-known photographer and who is also my neighbor, shows his work at the Abondazza Gallery. CPX

3. Nanette, who works long hours as a firefighter, volunteers weekly. CPX
4. Both my brother and I mailed you a postcard from Santiago. SIM
5. Mai-Ling's house, which is more than 100 years old, is being renovated. CPX
6. Mr. Parks sent the package last night, and he specified Sunday delivery. COM
7. I assembled a new birdhouse, and I hung a birdfeeder on the tree that is near the window. CCX
8. Crystal waited nervously while the panel scored her test. CPX
9. Michael's voice mail contained three messages that required immediate responses, but he was unable to reach the callers. CCX
10. Apples, peaches, and kiwi are my favorite fruits; beans and cauliflower are my favorite vegetables. COM

Checkpoint 9-5

1. Attach the birdhouse securely to the tree	IMP
2. Juana will attend the Art Institute of Chicago	DEC
3. Romi ordered office furniture from Benton's	DEC
4. Call the fire department now	EXC or IMP
5. Did anyone see Professor Yang	INT
6. Hold the elevator	EXC or IMP
7. I think you should check the number before you fax the report	DEC
8. Has Courtney or Erik arrived	INT

Checkpoint 9-6

Answers may vary; sample solutions are provided.

1. Gloria drove on the icy highway and had a difficult time controlling the car.
2. Parker received not only a scholarship but also a grant.
3. C
4. I will vacation either in Gulf Shores or in Pensacola.
5. C

CHAPTER 10

Checkpoint 10-1

1. The program director's address is as follows:
   Mrs. Ellen DeMarko
   WZYO TV
   3100 Mobile Highway — C
   Pensacola, FL 32505-7015
2. Theresa's last cell-phone bill totaled $89.25. — C
3. Dr. Janet Moore's flight will arrive at 10 a.m. on Tuesday.
4. Please listen to the WCOA channel for the morning news.
5. Patricia measured 2.5 liters of water for the experiment. — C
6. Dr. Nancy Barnett earned her medical degree from Tulane University.
7. The speed limit on Highway 37 is 60 mph. — C
8. The postal abbreviation for Tennessee is TN. — C
9. We read three poems by T. S. Eliot.
10. Dr. Parr works with the CDC. — C

Checkpoint 10-2

1. The career counselor asked, "What are your hobbies?"
2. Morgan screamed, "Watch for the falling rock!"
3. Have you identified employment opportunities in Miami?
4. Wow! Look at the rainbow.
5. What did you say? hear? do? — C
6. "When can we drive to the mountains? asked Terry.

Checkpoint 10-3

1. Tim's favorite vacation cities are San Diego, Denver, and Boston.
2. When Julia traveled from Florida to Indiana, she drove her new car.
3. The Price and Grant families arranged reunions in Chicago and Atlanta. — C
4. During the last decade, have you bought a house, car, or boat?

5. Nevertheless, you may attend the conference by yourself on August 15. ______
6. Nadia bought a phone card_and a CD player. ______

Checkpoint 10-4

1. John drove through Akron, where he had lived for three years. ______
2. Anwar will shut down the computers before he leaves the classroom, and Terri will lock the door when she goes. ______
3. Beccie Wiggins, the nursing instructor, demonstrated CPR. ______
4. Chih likes snow skiing, yet he went to Jamaica in December. C
5. Did Curtis purchase new carpeting, or did he select tile flooring? ______
6. The product_that sold the best_was our AT-1 digital camera. ______

Checkpoint 10-5

1. After Esme completed the calculations, the display showed 91.7225. C
2. Horace said, "Please meet me at 8:30 a.m. at the Judicial Center, 200 West Jackson Avenue, Knoxville, TN_37902-1017." ______
3. Jill searched for a comfortable home costing under $100,000. ______
4. "June 5,1955, was my wedding day," said Mrs. Miller. ______
5. Mark Twain grew up in Hannibal, Missouri. C
6. Tourists thought the white, sandy beaches on the Gulf Coast were the most beautiful beaches in the world. ______
7. Thomas ordered three Model 7J4499 tractors for his farm. C
8. Tim said, "Sending e-mail messages from the Internet Café in Juarez costs too much." ______
9. Michael and Lois paid $17,350.95 for their new car. ______
10. Renee drives an ugly, rusty jeep to work. ______
11. The webmaster said that he would update the site regularly. C
12. We visited Oslo, Norway, and Copenhagen, Denmark. ______

CHAPTER 11

Checkpoint 11-1

1. During a presentation, use graphics to illustrate important points; keep the graphics uncluttered and easy to read. ______
2. People have become accustomed to viewing multicolored graphics. C
3. Visual aids increase clarity; therefore, use charts and other types of illustrations. ______
4. Try several approaches to determine which works best; for example, video clips, slide presentations, and flip charts. ______
5. The consultants for the "Improve Your Speaking Skills" seminar are Eugene Freeman, Texas; Ruth Kellerman, Colorado; and Pat Mason, Missouri. ______

Checkpoint 11-2

1. To create more effective presentations, consider three factors: content, audience interaction, and choreography. ______
2. I will meet you at 4 p.m. to critique your speech. ______
3. Feedback will help you modify your vocal presentation in these areas: pitch, timing, and volume. ______
4. You may select: C

   CD or DVD format

   Closed or open captions

   Static or automated graphics
5. My favorite audiences included the following groups: student council members, service club representatives, and leadership awareness teams. ______

Checkpoint 11-3

1. "Rain Man" claims his machine can make water from air. C
2. In *Eight Habits of the Heart*, Clifton L. Taulbert stated, "True friendship can form bridges." ______
3. "How many guests are you expecting for the reception?" asked the catering director. ______
4. Robert Frost wrote the poem "The Road Not Taken." ______

5. Do you know how many chemicals will be placed on the toxic "Hot List"? | ______
6. The trainer shouted, "Jump!" | C
7. Why did Carol Browner say, "People want a different kind of future"? | ______
8. "Honest disagreement," said Mahatma Gandhi, "is often a good sign of progress." | ______
9. Stop yelling, "Run faster"! | ______
10. The manager said that three new parks are planned. | C

Checkpoint 11-4

1. According to the survey, Samuel, Ruth, Lourdes, and Arnold's project was ranked first. | C
2. Our neighbor's dog carries pine cones in its mouth. | ______
3. Joseph trimmed my mother-in-law's trees. | ______
4. Write x's in the empty blanks on the survey. | C
5. Three professors' parking places are reserved. | ______
6. The tax assessor said, "Building 17J is yours." | ______
7. Ximena claims that she uses only organic cosmetics. | ______
8. Is the wrecked car yours? | ______

Checkpoint 11-5

1. Ricardo completed the self-evaluation form before meeting with his supervisor. | ______
2. Two-thirds of our students commute to school. | ______
3. Indianola is the county seat of Sunflower County. | ______
4. Maria jokingly said, "Twenty-three out of ten people prefer chocolate to vanilla ice cream." | ______
5. The shutters go from the window ledge to the ceiling. | C
6. Print your resume on 8½- by 11-inch paper. | ______
7. Elaine consulted an up-to-date manual. | ______
8. Bill and Clark planned a two-week vacation in Alaska. | ______

Checkpoint 11-6

1. During the home tour, you may visit these locations: (1) 1131 North Spring Street, (2) 3700 East Jackson Avenue, (3) 4400 Dakota Street, and (4) 1700 Bayou Boulevard. C
2. The critic wrote, "The Renaissance Comedeans [sic] packed the house for the comedy night." ____
3. Our favorite breakfast (ham and eggs) awaited us every morning of the trip. ____
4. Works by August Rodin (lithographs and bronze sculptures) will be presented in May at the Dothan Museum of Art. C
5. Please review "Commonly Confused Verbs" (see Chapter 4) in your text. ____
6. The company will pay the consultant Six Thousand Dollars ($6,000). C
7. Bill reported, "The new client [Ms. Fox] called yesterday." ____
8. The majority of respondents (86 percent) favored a light rail system. ____

CHAPTER 12

Checkpoint 12-1

The corrected words are underlined.

1. <u>Carlos</u>, a <u>registered</u> <u>nurse</u>, works with <u>Supervisor</u> Terence O'<u>Malley</u>.
2. <u>Has</u> Ellie met <u>Mayor</u> Patrick Lutz or Maria Cruz-<u>Hampton</u>, a local <u>judge</u>?
3. Mike <u>Drews</u>, CPA, oversees 120 employees.
4. Glenda delivered <u>Superintendent</u> Neisbaum's request to the committee.
5. <u>The</u> class will visit <u>Jewish</u> and Buddhist <u>temples</u> as well as <u>Muslim</u> <u>mosques</u>.
6. The <u>keynote</u> <u>speakers</u> for the ceremony are <u>Senators</u> Jackson and Braun.
7. <u>Before</u> making plans, I must check with <u>Dad</u>.
8. <u>Distribute</u> this message to all residents: <u>After</u> 11 p.m., you must use your pass code to enter the building.

Checkpoint 12-2

The corrected words are underlined.

1. John James Audubon was a naturalist, wildlife artist, and author; his book *The Birds of America* (primarily birds of the South and the Midwest) remains the standard against which the works of other bird artists are measured.
2. Audubon was born in Santo Domingo (now Haiti) in 1785 but spent much of his childhood with his stepmother in Nantes, France.
3. At 18, he was sent to America to the family-owned estate at Mill Grove, Pennsylvania (now part of the Audubon Wildlife Sanctuary), where he drew birds and conducted the first known bird-banding experiment in North America.
4. When Audubon died, his widow tried to sell his original watercolors for *The Birds of America* to the Smithsonian Institution. The Smithsonian refused the offer, and his original artwork was sold in 1863 to the New York Historical Society.

Checkpoint 12-3

The corrected words are underlined.

1. The War of the Roses (1455-1487) was an internal war fought over the throne of England.
2. The Occupational Safety and Health Administration (OSHA) strives to ensure the safety and health of workers in the United States.
3. Read Bulletin No. 12-445 before replacing the battery.
4. Some acronyms are the same, but they may refer to different organizations. For example, AHA may refer to the American Hospital Association, the American Heart Association, or the American Historical Association.
5. Stephen is enrolled in English Literature 202, Global Commerce, and Microcomputers for Business; he is also enrolled in a photography class.
6. Friday is the day that Muslims celebrate the Sabbath.

Checkpoint 12-4

The corrected words are underlined.

1. The high school choir has 75 vocalists, the symphony orchestra has 93 members, and the high school jazz band has 7 members.

2. Twelve actors auditioned for four roles in the play.
3. Rate increase notices were mailed to more than 1.5 million utility customers.
4. The survey indicates that only 5 of 30 flights arrived on time.
5. Of the three plans presented, two recommended eliminating at least 50 positions from each site.

Checkpoint 12-5

The corrected words are underlined.

1. The computer package is $499, and the software is $135.
2. You can order a fruit drink for $.98 or a milk shake for $2.25.
3. The rate of interest on an 18-month certificate of deposit is 3.5 percent.
4. The cost overruns are exceeding $1.5 million.
5. Busses run every half hour beginning at 7:30 a.m.; the last bus leaves at 8:00 p.m.
6. The survey indicates that 55 percent of residents did not vote in the last city election, which was held on November 1.
7. The cleaning kit costs $6.
8. Forty percent of the class voted for Suzanne.

INDEX